MAPS

Welcome to Santa Fe

Santa Fe brims with reminders of four centuries of Spanish and Mexican rule, and of the Pueblo cultures that have been here for hundreds of years more. With a vibrant diversity seen in its food, art, and shopping scenes, Santa Fe remains a magical place for visitors looking for that Southwestern flair. This book was produced in the middle of the COVID-19 pandemic. As you plan your upcoming travels to Santa Fe, please confirm that places are still open and let us know when we need to make updates by writing to us at editors@fodors.com.

TOP REASONS TO GO

★ **Food:** From enchiladas to blue corn pancakes, Santa Fe is an exceptional dining town with a diverse culinary history.

★ **Art:** See why Georgia O'Keeffe was so inspired here or check out the modern-day galleries lining Canyon Road.

★ **Markets:** From weekly farmers' markets to the yearly Indian Market, the city delivers with its local goods.

★ **Outdoor Adventures:** Hike the incredible, and surprisingly lush, mountains that rise out of Santa Fe, raft the Rio Grande, snowboard, snowshoe, or try mountain biking.

Contents

EXPERIENCE
SANTA FE

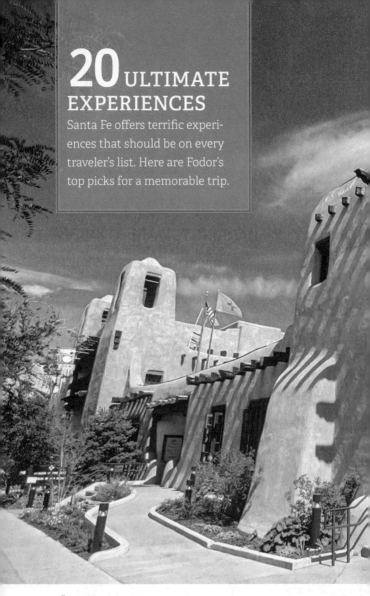

20 ULTIMATE EXPERIENCES

Santa Fe offers terrific experiences that should be on every traveler's list. Here are Fodor's top picks for a memorable trip.

1 Museums

Learn about local and regional art and culture at the excellent institutions on Santa Fe's Museum Hill, including the Museum of Indian Arts and Culture. *(Ch. 4)*

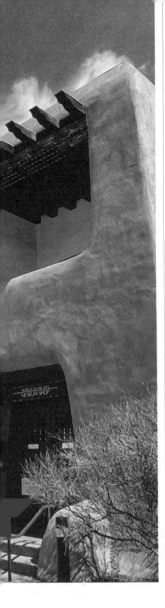

2 Dining

A rising national culinary destination, the city has superb restaurants that offer both traditional and contemporary New Mexican fare as well as more eclectic global cuisine. *(Ch. 3–6)*

3 Railyard District

A popular indoor–outdoor farmers' market, a fun urban park, and hip restaurants, galleries, and indie shops keep things bustling in this redeveloped historic neighborhood. *(Ch. 5)*

4 Albuquerque Balloon Festival

More than 500 hot air balloons ascend over the Rio Grande Valley during this colorful October gathering, the largest ballooning festival in the world. *(Ch. 8)*

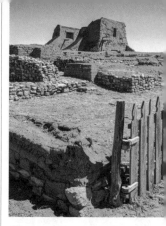

5 Santa Fe Trail

This nearly 900-mile, 19th-century trade route crosses the Sangre de Cristo Mountains from historic Pecos National Historical Park into the heart of downtown Santa Fe. *(Ch. 7)*

6 The Turquoise Trail

A scenic alternative route to Interstate 25, this 70-mile road starts in Santa Fe and plunges through offbeat villages like Madrid and the dramatic highlands of Sandia Crest. *(Ch. 7)*

7 Canyon Road

Winding about 3 miles from downtown Santa Fe, this narrow road is lined with colorfully preserved adobe houses, many of which now contain highly regarded art galleries. *(Ch. 4)*

8 Intimate Inns

Unwind in a Southwestern-style abode or one of the city's intimate inns and bed-and-breakfasts, many featuring original artwork and handcrafted furnishings. *(Ch. 3–6)*

9 Meow Wolf

Spend a few hours wandering through this madly imaginative and completely immersive 22,000-square-foot collaborative art installation. *(Ch. 6)*

10 Bandelier National Monument

Climb inside cliff dwellings and ceremonial kivas of ancestral Puebloans within this 33,000-acre natural wonder. *(Ch. 7)*

11 Markets

Annual market weekends like the Santa Fe Indian Market offer some of the best opportunities for shopping and art collecting in New Mexico. *(Ch. 1)*

12 The High Road to Taos

For a scenic adventure, drive between Taos and Santa Fe via this breathtaking alpine route through quaint Spanish-colonial villages and past sweeping vistas. *(Ch. 7)*

13 Santa Fe Plaza

Soak up the energy and take in the culture of the city's lively and historic central plaza, which is lined with stellar museums and colorful shops and restaurants. *(Ch. 3)*

14 Georgia O'Keeffe

Connect with the work of this iconic American Modernist artist, who drew inspiration from the area's landscape, at the exceptional Georgia O'Keeffe Museum downtown and her house in Abiquiú. *(Ch. 3, 7)*

15 Rafting on the Rio Grande

From peaceful floats to rollicking rafting trips, the nation's fourth-longest river is one of the region's top destinations for outdoor recreation. *(Ch. 7, 8, 9)*

16 Santa Fe Opera

Simply stunning, this internationally acclaimed opera's indoor–outdoor amphitheater is carved into a hillside and presents five works during its annual eight-week summer season. *(Ch. 6)*

17 Galleries

Gallery hopping is a prime activity in Santa Fe, especially during First Friday Night Art Walks. The city's more than 300 galleries tempt with ceramics, paintings, photography, and sculptures. *(Ch. 3–6)*

18 Taos Pueblo

Continuously occupied for roughly 1,000 years, this rambling, carefully preserved adobe-walled pueblo looks much as it has for centuries. Fascinating guided tours are offered. *(Ch. 9)*

19 Native American Culture

Santa Fe celebrates Native culture at historic monuments and museums throughout the city, including Native American dances and jewelry-making demonstrations in Milner Plaza. *(Ch. 3–7)*

20 Kasha Katuwe Tent Rocks National Monument

Known for bizarre sandstone rock formations that look like stacked tepees, this dramatic box canyon and lofty promontory is a memorable hiking getaway about 40 miles southwest of Santa Fe. *(Ch. 7)*

WHAT'S WHERE

1 The Plaza and Downtown Santa Fe. The heart of historic Santa Fe is the Plaza. The Old Santa Fe Trail is a historic section of the city that joins the Plaza from north of Museum Hill after passing the state capitol and some of the area's oldest neighborhoods.

2 East Side with Canyon Road and Museum Hill. Taking in some of the city's prettiest and most historic streets, the East Side is bisected by charming Canyon Road, which is lined with galleries, shops, and restaurants housed in adobe compounds. To the south, Museum Hill is home to four excellent museums and the Santa Fe Botanical Garden.

3 The Railyard District. A model for urban green space, this colorful district just southwest of Downtown contains a vibrant farmers' market, hip restaurants, shops, art galleries, and the SITE Santa Fe contemporary art museum.

4 Greater Santa Fe. West of the city center are several historic, mostly residential neighborhoods with a few notable restaurants and shops on Guadalupe Street. North, a scenic expanse of the Sangre de Cristo foothills is home to the Santa Fe Opera House and some high-profile resorts. South, you'll find the more modern and suburban parts of the city, along with the city's hottest arts attraction, Meow Wolf.

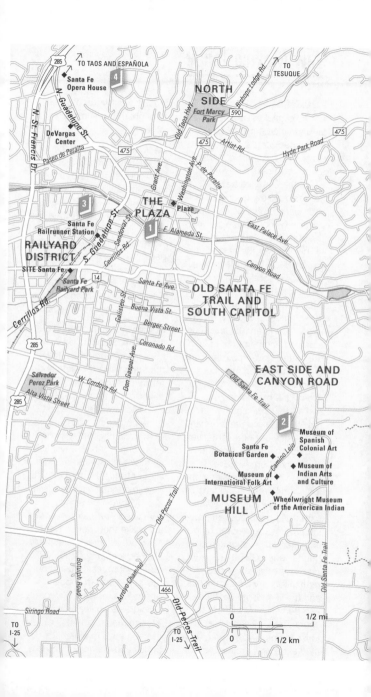

New Mexico Today

POLITICS

As the capital of New Mexico (and the oldest capital city in the United States), Santa Fe plays an outsized role in the state's political scene and when the state legislature is in session, Downtown hums with elected officials and other political workers. Ideologically, the state has moved steadily to the left over the past couple of decades—New Mexico has voted Democrat in every U.S. Presidential election since 1988 with the exception of 2004, when George W. Bush edged John Kerry by less than a percentage point. As of 2020, the state's governor, both senators, and all three members of congress are Democrats, and Team Blue maintains 26 to 16 and 47 to 23 advantages in the New Mexico State Senate and House of Representatives, respectively. Moreover, the state's northern Rio Grande corridor hews especially to the left, with Santa Fe and Taos (and to only a slightly lesser extent, Albuquerque) embracing progressive elected officials and agendas, including racial, gender, and LGBTQ equality, gun control, reproductive rights, conservation initiatives, and the like. Santa Fe, Taos, and Bernalillo (Albuquerque) counties are all sanctuary jurisdictions, and all three areas held extremely well-attended Black Lives Matter protests throughout the summer of 2020.

IMMIGRATION AND DEMOGRAPHICS

New Mexico is one of the most ethnically diverse states in the nation—as of the last census, nearly 50% of the population identifies as Hispanic (of any race), by far the highest percentage of any U.S. state. Just under 15% of residents identify as Native American; New Mexico trails only Alaska and Oklahoma in this regard.

At the very southern end of New Mexico, about a five-hour drive south of Santa Fe, the state has a desolate and relatively short (about 180 miles long) international border with Mexico. There are just three border crossings, none of them connected to large cities or major highways, and so they generally do not see a lot of traffic. However, many who immigrate via the busier nearby border crossings in Texas and Arizona do eventually make their way to New Mexico, which as of 2018 had claimed just under 200,000 foreign-born residents (about 9% of the state's population). About 72% of New Mexico's immigrants originally hail from Mexico, and roughly 40% of the state's foreign-born population are naturalized U.S.

citizens. Immigrants play a vital role in the state's economy and cultural fabric, making up about 12% of the workforce. The state also has nearly 6,000 active DACA recipients.

New Mexico also claims the highest number of U.S. residents who identify as Hispano, meaning they're descended from the Spanish settlers who inhabited this land when it was part of the Spanish Empire (1598–1821) and then Mexico (1821–48). Often identifying as being of both European and indigenous American heritage, Hispanos in New Mexico can often trace their roots in the state back 10 or 12 generations, and rank among many of the state's leading political, civic, and business movers and shakers. Anglos, on the other hand, are New Mexico's relative latecomers, having only begun to settle here in significant numbers during the second half of the 19th century.

ART ON THE EDGE
In contrast with its more traditional artistic past, increasing numbers of galleries in the area now specialize in abstract, contemporary, and often international works. One of the first major forces in the city's artistic evolution, the acclaimed SITE Santa Fe museum, opened in 1995 and underwent a dramatic redesign and expansion in 2017. The surrounding Railyard District has seen an emergence of provocative, modern galleries in recent decades, as have Downtown and Canyon Road. But the biggest artistic development in Santa Fe has been the opening and growing popularity of a permanent multimillion-dollar art complex by Santa Fe's edgy Meow Wolf collective, which has plans to open additional locations in both Las Vegas and Denver in the next couple of years.

HOTEL HAPPENINGS
It's been a busy time for the region's hotel industry, although the pandemic has led to delays for some properties that had planned openings or revamps in 2020. With a highly anticipated launch of spring 2021, the historic and storied Bishop's Lodge Resort has undergone an ambitious renovation and expansion following its acquisition by the posh Auberge Resorts group. The vaunted Ojo Caliente Mineral Springs spa resort has added stylish midcentury trailers to its selection of distinctive accommodations, and in summer 2020, Sunrise Springs spa resort reopened as Ojo Santa Fe, an elegant and supremely relaxing sister to the original resort located 50 miles north.

What to Eat and Drink in Santa Fe

CHOCOLATE
Archaeologists have traced the consumption of chocolate in this part of the world to AD 900 Chacoan culture. These days, you'll find a bounty of artisan chocolatiers in Santa Fe.

CHILES
New Mexico's famous hot chiles are featured in many traditional New Mexican dishes, from tamales to cheeseburgers, served either with green or red chiles (or "Christmas" for both).

POSOLE
What might look to the uninitiated like popcorn soup is actually a sublime marriage of hominy, lime, pork, garlic, and spices. It's a regional staple of Mexico that's become a huge hit in New Mexico.

CRAFT BEER
The beer scenes in Santa Fe, Taos, and especially Albuquerque—which has more beer producers per capita than even Portland, Oregon—are impressive and innovative. Breweries like Bosque Brewing earn raves, and awards, for their distinctive creations.

SOPAIPILLAS
Puffy, deep-fried bread that's similar to Navajo fry bread (which is native to Arizona and western New Mexico), sopaipillas are served either as a dessert drizzled with honey or as a savory dish stuffed with pinto beans or meat and smothered with chile sauce.

ENCHILADAS
Between burritos, tacos, tostadas, chiles rellenos, and New Mexico's many other comfort-food standards, enchiladas are perhaps the most celebrated here.

Posole

BLUE CORN PANCAKES

The Southwest's Puebloan and Hopi tribes popularized the cultivation of blue-corn meal, which these days appears on New Mexico menus in just about anything flour-based, from enchiladas to corn chips. But blue corn's slightly sweet personality makes it especially delicious in breakfast foods, namely pancakes but also waffles.

COFFEE

A distinct regional take on this beverage is New Mexico Piñon Coffee, a company begun in the late '90s that infuses its beans with natural piñon flavoring during the roasting process, giving the coffee a nutty, slightly sweet quality—it's sold in most grocery stores around the state.

FRITO PIE

Said to be originally from Texas— although some New Mexicans claim it comes from Santa Fe—the Frito pie is also extremely popular in New Mexican diners and short-order restaurants. This savory, humble casserole consists of Fritos corn chips layered with chile, cheese, green onions, and pinto beans.

MARGARITAS

Originally invented just over the border in either Tijuana or Ciudad Juárez, depending on which origin story you believe, these sweet-and-sour cocktails consisting of tequila, lime juice, and either Triple Sec or Cointreau have been a mainstay of north-ern New Mexico bar culture for decades.

What to Buy in Santa Fe

WEAVINGS AND TEXTILES
Hand-woven goods rank among the region's most prized shopping finds, including price-less antique Navajo rugs and Spanish-colonial blankets.

TURQUOISE JEWELRY
Dazzling, hand-crafted turquoise jewelry has been a symbol of Santa Fe and nearby pueblos for generations. Note that authentic Southwest-mined turquoise is increasingly hard to find. If you're seeking top-quality turquoise jewelry crafted by local Native American artists, stick with a reputable gallery or the certified vendors working in front of the Palace of the Governors.

ART AND CRAFTS FROM ANNUAL MARKETS
Santa Fe's legendary summer exhibi-tions—including the International Folk Art Market n July—are great opportunities to find hand-woven and hand-crafted items, and to meet the talented makers.

COWBOY BOOTS AND HATS
O'Farrell Hat Company has produced custom cowboy hats for over three decades while colorful, bespoke cowboy boots fashioned from alligator, ostrich, and other precious skins are another favorite local good.

PUEBLO POTTERY
From the Navajo Nation to the state's many pueblos, native artisans in New Mexico have a centuries-old tradi-tion of producing intricate pottery with striking, complex designs and in a breathtaking range of colors and styles that are often specific to a particu-lar tribe.

Pueblo Pottery

FETISHES

These small and often fanciful stone carvings for which New Mexico's Zuni tribe is famous are said to bring out the characteristics of whomever possesses them.

FOLK FURNITURE

The often brightly hued, hand-carved furniture you see all around Santa Fe—from massive dining tables to smaller *equipale* (pigskin) chairs and punched-tin lamps and frames—make terrific additions to any home.

LOCAL ARTWORK

Santa Fe boasts one of the world's most impressive art scenes, with more than 300 galleries, from international showcases like the 44,000-square-foot Gerald Peters Gallery to other renowned spaces like Peyton Wright, Nedra Matteucci, LewAllen, and Monroe Gallery. Although traditional artwork, such as regional landscape paintings, proliferates here, the city also supports an edgy contemporary arts scene.

LOCAL SALSAS AND ROASTED CHILES

Looking to bring New Mexico's inimitable green- and red-chile salsas home with you? Several companies sell flavorful sauces by the jar along with bags of flash-frozen roasted chiles. Powdered chiles, strings of dried chiles (*ristras*), and chile-inflected candies, honey, jams, and other gourmet items are also popular.

Best Outdoor Adventures in North-Central New Mexico

ASPEN VISTA TRAIL

This winding alpine hike takes in breathtaking fall foliage scenery, but also makes for an enjoyable trek in spring and summer, too. In winter, it's a popular spot for snowshoeing.

VALLES CALDERA NATIONAL PRESERVE

A spectacular expanse anchored by one of the world's largest volcanic calderas, this 100,000-acre preserve in the Jémez Mountains is popular for hiking, skiing, and mountain biking.

KASHA-KATUWE TENT ROCKS NATIONAL MONUMENT

This stunning geological wonder is named for its bizarre rock formations, which look like tepees rising over a narrow box canyon. The hike here is relatively short and only moderately challenging.

THE DALE BALL TRAIL NETWORK

This 24-mile complex of hiking and mountain-biking trails winds through the eastern foothills of Santa Fe and is easily accessed from several areas, including Hyde Park and the end of Canyon Road.

TAOS SKI VALLEY

One of the West's preeminent ski areas, this dramatic valley famed for its vertiginous slopes and sunny conditions draws serious skiers and snowboarders from late November through early April.

WHEELER PEAK

One of the more strenuous hiking challenges in the area, the 8-mile round-trip trek to New Mexico's highest point (elevation 13,161 feet) rewards visitors with stunning views in all directions.

Experience Santa Fe BEST OUTDOOR ADVENTURES IN NORTH-CENTRAL NEW MEXICO

Taos Ski Valley

RIO GRANDE NATURE CENTER STATE PARK

A 270-acre urban oasis just north of downtown Albuquerque, this peaceful park contains the country's largest forest of cottonwood trees.

RIO GRANDE DEL NORTE NATIONAL MONUMENT

The signature feature of this 242,555-acre national monument is its stunning stretch of the Rio Grande. It's best viewed from the Rio Grande Gorge Bridge, which soars 650 feet above the river.

RANDALL DAVEY AUDUBON CENTER

This 135-acre nature center offers a couple of fairly short but wonderfully scenic trails for observing wildlife, especially local and migrating birds, of which more than 200 have been spotted.

PETROGLYPH NATIONAL MONUMENT

The several trails through this expanse of extinct volcanoes on Albuquerque's west side pass by hundreds of well-preserved petroglyphs that date from as far back as 3,000 years ago.

BANDELIER NATIONAL MONUMENT

More than 70 miles of trails traverse this remarkable 33,000-acre wilderness near Los Alamos, the most popular of which wind past wooden ladders that lead into centuries-old cliff dwellings.

What to Read and Watch

BLESS ME, ULTIMA BY RUDOLFO ANAYA

Written in 1972 and widely considered one of the most important and impressive works of Chicano literature, this coming-of-age novel set in a small, largely Hispano New Mexican community shortly after World War II is based partly on the writer's early life in the town of Santa Rosa. Anaya, who passed away in 2020, continued to write about New Mexico throughout his life. A 2013 movie adaptation was filmed around Albuquerque and Santa Fe.

BREAKING BAD AND BETTER CALL SAUL

High school teacher–turned–meth-dealing antihero Walter White might just be New Mexico's most infamous resident, fictional or otherwise (with apologies to Billy the Kid). *Breaking Bad* and its similarly acclaimed prequel *Better Call Saul* were both set and filmed in Albuquerque, where an entire cottage industry of tours that visit the shows' noted locations has sprung up in recent years.

CITY SLICKERS

This classic 1991 Billy Crystal comedy about friends in New York City who confront their respective midlife crises by embarking on a two-week cattle drive through New Mexico and Colorado packs plenty of laughs and shows off the stunning landscapes of Abiquiú, the Nambé and Santa Clara pueblos, and Santa Fe.

DANCE HALL OF THE DEAD BY TONY HILLERMAN

One of the state's most treasured fiction writers, the late Albuquerquean Tony Hillerman set 18 detective novels on and around the Native American reservations of the Four Corners region of New Mexico and Arizona. It's hard to pick a favorite among his many gripping page turners, but *Dance Hall of the Dead*—which won a coveted Edgar Award in 1974—is one of the best.

DEATH COMES FOR THE ARCHBISHOP BY WILLA CATHER

The great American novelist Willa Cather—who spent time with D. H. Lawrence, Witter Bynner, and other notables of New Mexico's early-20-century literary and arts scene—penned this tale of the attempts by Catholic Archbishop Jean-Baptiste Lamy to establish a diocese in Santa Fe. Although it's a fictionalized account, it does touch on a number of real events and actual characters who played an important role in northern New Mexico history during the late 19th century.

EASY RIDER
With key scenes in Santa Fe, Taos, and Las Vegas, this ode to road-tripping, bikers, and counterculture brought international fame to Peter Fonda, Dennis Hopper, and Jack Nicholson, and also the mesmerizing scenery of New Mexico.

GODLESS
Netflix's 1880s-period Western consists of just seven episodes, but earned critical acclaim for its gripping portrayal of an outlaw on the run and the proprietress of a ranch who takes him in. Like another stellar TV Western, *Longmire*, the show was filmed entirely in and around Santa Fe, but *Godless* stands out for having also been set in a New Mexico mining town, the fictional community of La Belle.

MANHATTAN
Although it never scored high ratings, this TV drama about the lives of scientists and their families living in Los Alamos during the Manhattan Project earned great reviews and is still easy to find through streaming services. It was filmed around Santa Fe and Los Alamos, and it offers an interesting glimpse of the intrigue and personal complexities that surrounded Los Alamos National Lab and its community during World War II.

THE MILAGRO BEANFIELD WAR BY JOHN NICHOLS
This humorous, poignant 1970s novel about a small-town New Mexico farmer taking on soulless government bureaucracy and deep-pocketed developers in order to save his humble beanfield was adapted into an entertaining movie in 1988. Directed by Robert Redford, the film was shot primarily in the beautiful village of Truchas, located along the High Road to Taos.

THE MYTH OF SANTA FE BY CHRIS WILSON
This rich and thorough study explains how and why Santa Fe came to look as it does today. The legacy of the city's earliest Native American and then Spanish settlers is explored, as are the conscious efforts by enterprising business owners in the early 20th century to turn the city into a bona fide international tourist destination.

PUEBLO NATIONS: EIGHT CENTURIES OF PUEBLO INDIAN HISTORY BY JOE S. SANDO
One of the most definitive and engrossing histories of New Mexico's 19 Indian Pueblos was written by the late Joe S. Sando, who was born—and later served as an elder—on Jémez Pueblo.

TRUE GRIT

Countless Westerns have been filmed in north-central New Mexico, including *All the Pretty Horses, A Million Ways to Die in the West,* and the remakes of *3:10 to Yuma* and *The Magnificent Seven,* but this Coen Brothers revisionist adaptation of the John Wayne classic stands out for the way it captures the breathtaking landscape around Santa Fe. The Coen Brothers are fans of shooting in the Land of Enchantment, having also filmed parts of *No Country for Old Men* and *The Ballad of Buster Scruggs* here.

TRAVEL SMART

Updated by
Andrew Collins

★ **CAPITAL:**
Santa Fe

⚠ **EMERGENCIES:**
911

🕐 **TIME:**
2 hours behind New
York

👥 **POPULATION:**
84,612

🚗 **DRIVING:**
On the right side of
the road

🌐 **WEB
RESOURCES:**
www.newmexico.org
www.santafe.org

💬 **LANGUAGE:**
English

⚡ **ELECTRICITY:**
120–240 v/60 cycles;
plugs have two or
three rectangular
prongs

$ **CURRENCY:**
U.S. Dollar

☎ **AREA CODE:**
505

Know Before You Go

As one of the American Southwest's most popular destinations, Santa Fe and the surrounding region have dozens of notable attractions and can even be a little overwhelming for a first-time visitor. Here are some key tips to help you navigate your trip, whether it's your first time visiting or your twentieth.

WHEN TO GO
Santa Fe has four distinct seasons, and the sun shines brightly during all of them (about 300 days a year). In June through August temperatures typically hit the high 80s to low 90s during the day and the low to mid-50s at night, with afternoon rain showers often cooling the air. These sudden rain showers can come unexpectedly and quickly drench you so pay attention to weather forecasts and have an umbrella and jacket with you, even if it looks sunny in the morning or early afternoon. September and October bring beautiful weather and a marked reduction in crowds.

Temperatures—and prices—drop significantly after Halloween. December through March is ski season, but even nonskiers can appreciate this quieter time when the air smells of piñon burning in fireplaces, and the mountains and even the Plaza at times can be draped in powdery snow. Spring comes late at this elevation. March and April are blustery, with warmer weather finally arriving in May and June.

HOURS OF OPERATION
Although hours differ little in New Mexico from other parts of the United States, some businesses do keep shorter hours here than in more densely populated parts of the country. Within the state, businesses in Santa Fe, Albuquerque, and Taos tend to keep later hours than in rural areas, where it's always a good idea to confirm that a business or attraction is open before you make a special trip.

Most major museums and attractions are open daily or six days a week (with Monday or Tuesday being the most likely day of closing). Hours are often shorter on Saturday and especially Sunday, and a handful of museums in the region stay open late one night a week, usually Friday. In Santa Fe and Albuquerque—and to a lesser extent in Taos—you can find some convenience stores and drugstores open 24 hours, and quite a few supermarkets open until 10 or 11 at night. Bars and nightclubs stay open until 1 or 2 am.

PACKING

Typical of the Southwest and southern Rockies, temperatures can vary considerably in north-central New Mexico from sunup to sundown. Generally, you should pack for warm days and chilly nights from late spring through early fall, and for genuinely cold days and freezing nights in winter if you're headed to Taos and Santa Fe (Albuquerque runs about 6 to 12 degrees warmer). Any time of year you should pack at least a few warm outfits and a jacket or sweater (along with gloves and a hat from September through April); in winter pack very warm clothes—coats, parkas, and whatever else your body's thermostat and your ultimate destination dictate. And bring comfortable shoes; you're likely to be doing a lot of walking.

Bring skin moisturizer; even people who rarely need this elsewhere in the country can suffer from dry and itchy skin in New Mexico. Sunscreen is a necessity. And bring sunglasses to protect your eyes from the glare of lakes or ski slopes, not to mention the brightness present everywhere. The high altitude (around 7,000–7,200 feet in Santa Fe and Taos and 5,300 feet in Albuquerque) can cause headaches and dizziness for some, especially if you're unaccustomed to these conditions, so at a minimum drink at least half your body weight in ounces in water each day (150-pound person equals 75 ounces). When planning even a short day trip, especially if there's hiking or exercise involved, always pack 1 or 2 liters of water per person—it's very easy to become dehydrated in New Mexico.

VISITOR ETIQUETTE

The Albuquerque–Santa Fe–Taos corridor contains a number of smaller, sometimes quite insular, indigenous or predominantly Hispanic villages. Tread lightly and behave respectfully as you travel in these areas, and never take pictures of locals or enter private property without first receiving permission. Many members of the state's 23 indigenous communities—usually called pueblos—refer to themselves as Indians more commonly than Native Americans, but the best practice is to refer to persons who reside in a particular community by their tribal name. Many pueblos welcome visitors and have museums, galleries, hiking trails, and other attractions, and some are open for guided tours or allow outsiders to attend feast days and other events. It's best to check tribal office websites or call ahead to be sure a community is welcoming visitors on the day you plan to visit. Photography, sketching, and video recording is typically not allowed at pueblos; occasionally permission is granted in exchange for a fee (if in doubt, always ask first).

Getting Here and Around

A car is the best way to take in Santa Fe and the surrounding region. City buses and taxis are available in Santa Fe, Albuquerque, and Taos, as are Lyft and Uber, but buses are not very convenient for visitors, and the costs of taxis and ride-sharing services can quickly exceed that of a rental car, especially if you're staying outside the city centers. You can get around Santa Fe's Plaza area as well as some Taos and Albuquerque neighborhoods on foot, but a car is essential for roaming farther afield and visiting many of north-central New Mexico's most prominent attractions and scenic byways.

Air

Most visitors to the area fly into Albuquerque, home of the region's main airport, but Santa Fe also has a charmingly small and handily located airport with daily nonstop service to a few key hubs. From Albuquerque, ground transportation is available to both Santa Fe (65 miles away) and Taos (130 miles), although most visitors rent a car.

Albuquerque's airport is served by all major U.S. airlines and has direct flights from most major West Coast and Midwest cities and a few cities on the East Coast (JFK in New York

City on JetBlue, Atlanta on Delta, and Baltimore-Washington on Southwest). Santa Fe Regional Airport has direct flights on American Airlines from Dallas and Phoenix and United Airlines from Denver. Flights into Santa Fe tend to cost a bit more than those to Albuquerque, but the convenience can be well worth the extra expense. If you're venturing north from Santa Fe up to Taos, you might also consider flying into Denver, which is an hour or two farther than Albuquerque (the drive is stunning) but offers a huge selection of direct domestic and international flights.

Flying time between Albuquerque and Dallas is 1 hour and 45 minutes; Los Angeles, 2 hours; Chicago, 2 hours and 45 minutes; New York, 4 to 4½ hours (direct, which is available only on JetBlue; factor in another hour if connecting).

GROUND TRANSPORTATION

From the terminal at Albuquerque's airport, Groome Transportation provides scheduled van service to hotels, bed-and-breakfasts, and several other locations around Santa Fe; the cost per person is $36 each way. RoadRunneR offers private rides from both the Albuquerque and Santa Fe airports to locations throughout Santa

Fe and the surrounding area (including Albuquerque, Los Alamos, and Española)—for a price, you can charter a shuttle to just about any town in the state. The Taos Rides shuttle service provides scheduled van service from Albuquerque and Santa Fe to Taos, and Santa Fe and Taos to Taos Ski Valley; fares range from $100 to $135 round-trip.

Bus

The city's bus system, Santa Fe Trails, covers 10 major routes through town and is useful for getting from the Plaza to some of the outlying attractions. Route M is most useful for visitors, as it runs from Downtown to the museums on Old Santa Fe Trail south of town, and Route 2 is handy if you're staying at one of the motels out on Cerrillos Road and need to get into town (if time is a factor for your visit, a car is a much more practical way to get around). Individual rides cost $1, and a daily pass costs $2. Buses run from early morning to mide-vening about every 30 minutes on weekdays, every hour on weekends.

There's no intercity bus service to Santa Fe, but you can get to Albuquerque from a number of cities throughout the South-west and Rocky Mountain regions, and then catch a Rail Runner commuter train from Albuquerque's bus station to Santa Fe. This strategy really only makes sense if you're unable or unwilling to drive or fly; bus travel in this part of the world is relatively economical but quite time-consuming.

Car

A car is a basic necessity in New Mexico, as even the few cities are challenging to get around solely using public transportation. Distances are considerable, but you can make excellent time on long stretches of interstate and other four-lane highways with speed limits of up to 75 mph. If you wander off major thor-oughfares, slow down. Speed limits here generally are only 55 mph, and for good reason. Many such roadways have no shoulders; on many twisting and turning mountain roads speed limits dip to 25 mph. For the most part, the scenery on rural highways makes the drive a form of sightseeing in itself.

Interstate 25 runs north from the state line at El Paso through Albuquerque and Santa Fe, then angles north-east into Colorado and up to Denver. Interstate 40 crosses the state from Arizona to Texas, intersecting with Interstate 25

Getting Here and Around

in Albuquerque, from which it's an hour's drive to Santa Fe. Although it's a long journey from big cities like Los Angeles, Dallas, and Chicago, plenty of visitors drive considerable distances to visit Santa Fe, which makes a great stop on a multiday road trip around the Four Corners region, or across the Southwest.

U.S. and state highways connect Santa Fe, Albuquerque, and Taos with a number of key towns elsewhere in New Mexico and in neighboring states. Many of these highways, including large stretches of U.S. 285 and U.S. 550, have four lanes and high speed limits. You can make nearly as good time on these roads as you can on interstates. Throughout the region, you're likely to encounter some unpaved surface streets. Santa Fe has a higher percentage of dirt roads than any other state capital in the nation.

Morning and evening rush-hour traffic is light in Santa Fe. It can get a bit heavy in Albuquerque. Keep in mind that there are only a couple of main routes from Santa Fe to Albuquerque, so if you encounter an accident or some other obstacle, you can expect significant delays. It's a big reason to leave early and give yourself extra time when driving to Albuquerque to catch a plane.

Parking is plentiful and either free or inexpensive in Santa Fe, Albuquerque, and Taos. During the busy summer weekends, however, parking in Santa Fe's most popular neighborhoods—the Plaza, Canyon Road, and the Railyard District—can be a bit more challenging. There are pay lots both Downtown and in the Railyard District.

Here are some common distances and approximate travel times between Santa Fe and several popular destinations, assuming no lengthy stops and averaging the 65 to 75 mph speed limits: Albuquerque is 65 miles and about an hour; Taos is 70 miles and 90 minutes; Denver is 400 miles and 6 hours; Phoenix is 480 miles and 7 to 8 hours; Las Vegas is 630 miles and 9 to 10 hours; Dallas is 650 miles and 10 to 11 hours, and Los Angeles is 850 miles and 12 to 14 hours.

GASOLINE

Once you leave Santa Fe or other larger communities in the region, there's a lot of high, dry, lonesome country in New Mexico—it's possible to go 50 or 60 miles in some of the less-populated areas between gas stations. For a safe trip, keep your gas tank full. Self-service gas stations are the norm in New Mexico. The cost of unleaded gas in New Mexico is close to the U.S. average, but it's usually a bit higher in small out-of-the-way communities, and significantly cheaper on some Indian reservations—on the drive between Santa Fe and Albuquerque, the gas stations just off Interstate 25 at Santo Domingo Pueblo (Exit 259), San Felipe Pueblo (Exit 252), and Sandia Pueblo (Exit 234) all have very low-priced gas.

RENTAL CARS

All the major car-rental agencies are represented at Albuquerque's airport, and several of them have branches at Santa Fe airport (Avis and Hertz) or in Downtown Santa Fe (Avis, Budget, Enterprise, Hertz).

Rates at the airports in Albuquerque and Santa Fe can vary greatly depending on the season (the highest rates are usually in summer) but typically begin at around $35 a day and $200 a week for an economy car with unlimited mileage.

If you want to explore the backcountry, consider renting an SUV, which will cost you about $45 to $60 per day and $240 to $400 per week, depending on the size of the SUV and the time of year. You can save money by renting at a nonairport

location, as you then are able to avoid the hefty (roughly) 10% in extra taxes charged at airports.

ROAD CONDITIONS

Arroyos (dry washes or gullies) are bridged on major roads, but lesser roads often dip down through them. These can be a hazard during the rainy season, late June to early September. Even if it looks shallow, don't try to cross an arroyo filled with water. Wait a little while, and it will drain off almost as quickly as it filled. If you stall in a flooded arroyo, get out of the car and onto high ground if possible. In the backcountry, never drive (or walk) in a dry arroyo bed if the sky is dark anywhere in the vicinity. A sudden thunderstorm 15 miles away can send a raging flash flood down a wash in a matter of minutes.

Unless they are well graded and graveled, avoid unpaved roads in New Mexico when they are wet. The soil contains a lot of caliche, or clay, which gets slick when mixed with water. During winter storms roads may be shut down entirely; check with the State Highway Department for road conditions.

At certain times in fall, winter, and spring, New Mexico winds can be vicious for large

Getting Here and Around

vehicles like RVs. Driving conditions can be particularly treacherous in passages through foothills or mountains where wind gusts and ice are concentrated.

New Mexico has a high incidence of drunk driving and uninsured motorists. Factor in the state's high speed limits, many winding and steep roads, and eye-popping scenery, and you can see how important it is to drive as alertly and defensively as possible.

Taxi

Santa Fe has no taxi company, but the city is well served by Lyft and Uber, which are also widely available in Taos and Albuquerque.

🚆 Train

Amtrak's *Southwest Chief,* from Chicago to Los Angeles via Kansas City, stops in Las Vegas, Lamy (near Santa Fe), and Albuquerque.

The state's commuter train line, the *New Mexico Rail Runner Express,* runs from Santa Fe south through Bernalillo and into the city of Albuquerque, continuing south through Los Lunas to the suburb of Belén, covering a distance of about 100 miles and stopping at 15 stations. The Rail Runner offers a very inexpensive and scenic alternative to getting to and from the Albuquerque airport to Santa Fe (shuttle buses run from the airport to the *Rail Runner* stop in Downtown Albuquerque).

The *New Mexico Rail Runner Express* runs numerous times on weekdays from early morning until late evening, and less often on weekends. Tickets cost $2 to $10 one way, depending on the distance traveled; day passes are available (and will save you money on round-trip journeys).

Essentials

Lodging

Although New Mexico itself has relatively affordable hotel prices, tourist-driven Santa Fe (and to a slightly lesser extent Taos) can be fairly pricey, especially during high season from spring through fall, with rates particularly high during major Santa Fe festivals (such as the Indian and Spanish markets). Generally, you'll pay the most at hotels within walking distance of the Plaza and those located in some of the more scenic and mountainous areas north and east of the city; B&Bs usually cost a bit less, and you can find some especially reasonable deals on Airbnb, which has extensive listings throughout the region.

The least expensive Santa Fe accommodations are south and west of town, particularly along drab and traffic-clogged Cerrillos Road, on the south side of town. The best of these, from roughly most to least expensive, are the DoubleTree, Holiday Inn Express, Hyatt Place, Fairfield Inn & Suites, Hampton Inn, Best Western Plus, Comfort Inn, and Econolodge. Rates in Albuquerque, just an hour away, can be half as expensive (sometimes even less), except during busy festivals, particularly the Balloon Fiesta in early October. In Taos and the smaller towns

near Santa Fe, expect to pay somewhere between what you would in Albuquerque and Santa Fe.

Prices are for a standard double room in high season, excluding 12%–13% tax.

WHAT IT COSTS in U.S. Dollars			
$	$$	$$$	$$$$
HOTELS			
under $110	$110–$200	$201–$300	over $300

Dining

Dining out is a major pastime in Santa Fe as well as in Taos, Albuquerque, and even many of the small towns throughout the region. Although Santa Fe in particular has a reputation for upscale dining at restaurants with several high-profile chefs where dinner for two can easily set you back more than $200, the region also offers plenty of low-key, affordable spots, from mom-and-pop taquerias and diners to hip coffeehouses and gastropubs.

Waits for tables are common during the busy summer season, so it's a good idea to call ahead even when reservations aren't accepted, if only to get a sense of the waiting time. Reservations for dinner at the better restaurants are a must in summer and on weekends

Essentials

the rest of the year. In cities like Santa Fe and Albuquerque, you'll find at least a few restaurants that serve food (sometimes from a bar menu) late, until 10 or 11, and sometimes a bit later on weekends. In smaller communities, including Taos, many kitchens stop serving around 8 pm. It's smart to call first and confirm closing hours if you're looking forward to a leisurely or late dinner.

The region's top eateries have increasingly embraced a farm-to-table approach to cuisine, sourcing more and more from local farms and ranches, while also frequently incorporating Latin American, Mediterranean, and East Asian influences. Yet plenty of traditional, old-school restaurants still serve authentic New Mexican fare, which combines both indigenous and Hispanic traditions and is quite distinct from other Americanized as well as regional Mexican cooking. Most longtime residents like their chile sauces and salsas with some fire—throughout the state, chile is sometimes celebrated for its ability to set off smoke alarms. Most restaurants offer a choice of red or green chile with one type typically being milder than the other (ask your server, as this can vary considerably). If you want both kinds with your meal, when your server asks you if you'd like "red or

green," reply "Christmas." If you're not used to spicy foods, you may find even the house salsa served with chips to be hotter than back home so proceed with caution or ask for chile sauces on the side. Excellent barbecue and steaks also thrive throughout northern New Mexico, with other specialties being local game (especially elk and bison) and trout.

Santa Fe's culinary reputation continues to grow not just in terms of restaurants but also in businesses that produce or sell specialty foods and beverages, from fine chocolates and local honeys and jams to increasingly acclaimed New Mexico wines, beers, and spirits (which you'll find on many local menus). To find many of these products in one place, don't miss the Santa Fe Farmers' Market, one of the best in the Southwest.

Prices in the restaurant reviews are the average cost of a main course at dinner or, if dinner is not served, at lunch.

WHAT IT COSTS in U.S. Dollars			
$	$$	$$$	$$$$
RESTAURANTS			
under $15	$15–$22	$23–$30	over $30

🍸 Nightlife

Culturally endowed though it is, Santa Fe has a pretty mellow nightlife scene. The city does have a decent, and steadily improving, crop of bars, many specializing in craft beers and artisan cocktails, but evening carousing tends to wind down early, and this is not a destination for clubbing and dancing. When popular acts do occasionally come to town, the whole community shows up and dances like there's no tomorrow. Taos is even quieter in terms of nightlife but does have a few notable spots, while Albuquerque has emerged in recent years as one of the top craft-beer cities in the country and also has a handful of scene-y cocktail bars.

🎭 Performing Arts

Few small cities in America can claim an arts scene as thriving as Santa Fe's—with opera, symphony, and theater in splendid abundance. The music acts here tend to be high caliber, but rather sporadic. A wonderful eight-week series of music on the Plaza bandstand runs through the summer with performances four nights a week. Gallery openings, poetry readings, plays, and dance concerts take place year-round, not to mention the city's famed opera and chamber-music festivals. Check the arts and entertainment listings in Santa Fe's daily newspaper, the *New Mexican* (⊕ *www. santafenewmexican.com*), particularly on Friday, when the arts and entertainment section, "Pasatiempo," is included, or check the weekly *Santa Fe Reporter* (⊕ *www.sfreporter. com*) for shows and events. As you might suspect, activities peak in the summer.

🛍 Shopping

Santa Fe has been a trading post for eons. Nearly a thousand years ago the great pueblos of the Chacoan civilizations were strategically located between the buffalo-hunting tribes of the Great Plains and the Indians of Mexico. Native Americans in New Mexico traded turquoise and other valuables with Indians from Mexico for metals, shells, parrots, and other exotic items. After the arrival of the Spanish and the West's subsequent development, Santa Fe became the place to exchange silver from Mexico and natural resources from New Mexico for manufactured goods, whiskey, and greenbacks from the United States. The construction

Essentials

of the railroad in 1880 brought Santa Fe access to all kinds of manufactured goods.

The trading legacy remains, but now Downtown Santa Fe caters increasingly to those looking for handmade furniture and crafts, and bespoke apparel and accessories. Sure, a few chains have moved in and a handful of fairly tatty souvenir shops still proliferate, but shopping in Santa Fe consists mostly of high-quality, one-of-a-kind independent stores. Canyon Road, packed with internationally acclaimed galleries, is the perfect place to browse for art and collectibles. The Downtown blocks around the Plaza have unusual gift and curio shops, as well as clothiers and shoe stores that range from theatrical to conventional. You'll find quite a few art galleries here, too. The hip, revitalized Railyard District (sometimes referred to as the Guadalupe District), less touristy than the Plaza, is on Downtown's southwest perimeter and includes a wide-ranging mix of hipster boutiques, gift shops, and avant-garde contemporary art galleries—it's arguably the most eclectic of Santa Fe's shopping areas.

 ## Activities

When it comes to outdoor adventure, Santa Fe—along with Taos and Albuquerque—are four-season destinations. Low humidity and, thanks to the high elevation, year-round cool temperatures make north-central New Mexico a mecca for hiking, biking, wildlife viewing, rafting, and golfing from late spring through autumn. During the winter months, snow sports dominate in the mountains above the city and at renowned ski areas like Taos and Angel Fire, which are both within day-tripping distance (although better suited to overnight excursions).

Santa Fe National Forest lies right in the city's backyard and includes the Dome Wilderness (more than 5,000 acres in the volcanically formed Jémez Mountains) and the Pecos Wilderness (about 225,000 acres of high mountains, forests, and meadows at the southern end of the Rocky Mountains chain). The 12,500-foot Sangre de Cristo Mountains (the name translates as "Blood of Christ," for the red glow they radiate at sunset) fringe the city's east side. To the south and west, several less formidable mountain ranges punctuate the sweeping high desert. From the Plaza in the center of the city, you're within a

10-minute drive of truly rugged and breathtakingly beautiful wilderness.

Health

A new novel coronavirus brought all travel to a virtual standstill in the first half of 2020. Although the illness is mild in most people, some experience severe and even life-threatening complications. Once travel started up again, albeit slowly and cautiously, travelers were asked to be particularly careful about hygiene and to avoid any unnecessary travel, especially if they are sick.

Older adults, especially those over 65, have a greater chance of having severe complications from COVID-19. The same is true for people with weaker immune systems or those living with some types of medical conditions, including diabetes, asthma, heart disease, cancer, HIV/AIDS, kidney disease, and liver disease. Starting two weeks before a trip, anyone planning to travel should be on the lookout for some of the following symptoms: cough, fever, chills, trouble breathing, muscle pain, sore throat, new loss of smell or taste. If you experience any of these symptoms, you should not travel at all.

And to protect yourself during travel, do your best to avoid contact with people showing symptoms. Wash your hands often with soap and water. Limit your time in public places, and, when you are out and about, wear a cloth face mask that covers your nose and mouth. Indeed, a mask may be required in some places, such as on an airplane or in a confined space like a theater, where you share the space with a lot of people. You may wish to bring extra supplies, such as disenfecting wipes, hand sanitizer (12-ounce bottles were allowed in carry-on luggage at this writing), and a first-aid kit with a thermometer.

Visitor Information

The New Mexico Department of Tourism can provide general information on the state, but you'll find more specific and useful information by consulting the local tourism offices and convention and visitors bureaus in Santa Fe as well as in other cities and towns throughout north-central New Mexico.

Great Itineraries

THREE DAYS IN SANTA FE

One helpful strategy for exploring Santa Fe is to visit one neighborhood at a time. Over three days, you could devote one day to the Plaza and environs, another to Museum Hill and the East Side, and a third to the Railroad District and points south.

DAY 1

Plan on spending a full day wandering around Santa Fe Plaza, strolling down the narrow lanes, under portals, and along ancient adobe-lined streets. Sip coffee on the tree-shaded Plaza, take in a museum or two (or three), and at some point be sure to marvel at the late 19th-century cathedral. The Palace of the Governors and adjoining New Mexico History Museum are great places to start to gain a sense of the history and cultures that influence this area. It's well-worth taking one of the free docent-led tours offered by the museums—these are a great way to gain invaluable insight into the collections.

Break for lunch, perhaps at casual and historic Tia Sophia's (a terrific spot for breakfast, too). In the afternoon, take a walk through the exceptional New Mexico Museum of Art and singularly fascinating Georgia O'Keeffe Museum. Be sure to set aside some time to visit the many galleries and curio shops lining the streets near the Plaza. A good way to wrap up your adventure is with a cocktail at Secreto Lounge, on the inviting covered patio of the historic Hotel St. Francis.

DAY 2

A few miles south of the Plaza on Museum Hill, you'll find four world-class museums, all quite different and all highly relevant to the culture of Santa Fe and northern New Mexico. There's also the Santa Fe Botanical Garden, which offers a lovely open-air break from touring these mostly indoor attractions. Start at the intimate gem, the Museum of Spanish Colonial Art, where you'll gain a real sense of the Spanish empire's influence on the world beyond Spain. The Museum of International Folk Art is thoroughly engaging for both young and old. Next enjoy the creative lunch fare at the bright and airy Museum Hill Café, before visiting the Museum of Indian Arts and Culture and finally—if time and energy permit—the Wheelwright Museum of the American Indian. There is a path linking all these museums together, and the walk is easy. A tip for arts, crafts, and books collectors: the museum shops are all outstanding.

From Museum Hill, it's a pleasant 10-minute drive or

25-minute walk through a historic residential neighborhood to one of the nation's most impressive gallery districts, Canyon Road, which winds downhill to the eastern edge of downtown and should definitely be explored on foot. Most galleries here are open daily 10–5, so consider heading over early in the afternoon if you're keen on doing a lot of art browsing. However, from May through October, you can also attend a First Friday Art Walk, during which galleries stay open until 7 and often offer refreshments and present special exhibits.

As you're wandering through, take any of the side streets and stroll among the historical homes and ancient *acequias* (irrigation ditches). For a more extensive adventure, keep going up the road past Cristo Rey Church, where the street gets even narrower and is lined with residential compounds. At the top is the Randall Davey Audubon Center, which draws bird-watchers and has a few beautiful, relatively easy hiking trails. For dinner, the venerable El Farol has been going strong since 1835 and offers an extensive menu of tasty tapas and Spanish fare.

DAY 3

Your last day can be spent exploring the lively Railyard District, which bursts with energy and development from bustling Railyard Park and the many galleries and boutiques that surround it. The Santuario de Guadalupe is a great place to start. Head south from there and enjoy the shops, cafés, art galleries, farmers' market (open Saturday, Tuesday, and Wednesday), and Railyard Park. The expanded and impressively redesigned SITE Santa Fe is also here, with its cutting-edge modern art installations, making it a must for art aficionados. Among the many lunch options in the Railyard District, bustling La Choza is a long-time favorite for classic New Mexican fare.

In the afternoon, you can hop into your car and venture out to one of the city's attractions located a bit farther afield, perhaps El Rancho de las Golondrinas or even the Turquoise Trail if you're feeling ambitious. But of all the places you might explore outside Santa Fe's central core, the absolute must-see is Meow Wolf, the electrifyingly imaginative interactive arts space. Drinks and/or a bite to eat in Meow Wolf's inspiring Float Cafe & Bar make for a great end to your visit.

Great Itineraries

ALBUQUERQUE TO TAOS

You only need a week to take in the region's three best cities, along with plenty of outdoor adventures along the way.

DAY 1: ALBUQUERQUE

Start out by strolling through the shops of Old Town Plaza, then visit the New Mexico Museum of Natural History and Science and Albuquerque Museum of Art and History. For lunch, stop by the Indian Pueblo Cultural Center to sample the hearty indigenous-inspired fare at Pueblo Harvest Cafe.

In the afternoon, drive east a couple of miles along Central to reach the University of New Mexico's main campus—with its gracious adobe buildings and outstanding Maxwell Museum of Anthropology—and the nearby Nob Hill District, a hip bastion of offbeat shops and noteworthy restaurants. If it's summer, meaning that you still have some time before the sun sets, it's worth detouring from Old Town to Far Northeast Heights (a 15-minute drive), where you can take the Sandia Peak Aerial Tramway 2.7 miles up to Sandia Peak for spectacular sunset views of the city. Either way, plan to have dinner back in Nob Hill, perhaps at Bosque Brewing Co. Public House.

DAYS 2 AND 3: SANTA FE

On Day 2, head to Santa Fe early in the morning by driving up the scenic Turquoise Trail; once you arrive in town, explore the adobe charms of the Downtown central Plaza. Visit the Palace of the Governors and check out the adjacent New Mexico History Museum. A short drive away at the nearby Museum of Indian Arts and Culture you can see works by talented members of the state's pueblos, and across the courtyard at the Museum of International Folk Art, you can see how different cultures in New Mexico and elsewhere in the world have expressed themselves artistically. Return Downtown and give yourself time to stroll its narrow, adobe-lined streets, and treat yourself to some delicious New Mexican cuisine in the evening, perhaps with a traditional meal at The Shed or a fancier dinner at the Inn of the Anasazi.

On your second day in town, plan to walk a bit. Head east from the Plaza up to Canyon Road and peruse the galleries. If you're up for some exercise, hike the foothills—there are trails beginning at the Randall Davey Audubon Center and also from the free parking area leading into the Dale Ball Trail Network, both a short drive from the Plaza. You might want to try one of Santa Fe's truly stellar, upscale restaurants your final night in town, like Geronimo.

DAY 4: ABIQUIÚ

From Santa Fe, drive north up U.S. 285/84 through Española, and then take U.S. 84 from Española up to Abiquiú, the fabled community where Georgia O'Keeffe lived and painted for much of the final five decades of her life. On your way up, make the detour toward Los Alamos and spend the morning visiting Bandelier National Monument. In Abiquiú, plan to tour Georgia O'Keeffe's home (open early March–late November)—advance reservations are a must.

DAYS 5 AND 6: TAOS

Begin by strolling around Taos Plaza, taking in the galleries and crafts shops. Head south two blocks to visit the Harwood Museum. Then walk north on Paseo del Pueblo to the Taos Art Museum at Fechin House. In the afternoon, drive out to the Rio Grande Gorge Bridge. Return the way you came to see the Millicent Rogers Museum on your way back to town. In the evening, stop in at the Adobe Bar at the Taos Inn and plan for dinner at Love Apple. On the second day, drive out to Taos Pueblo

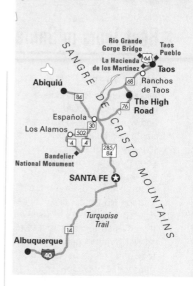

in the morning and tour the ancient village while the day is fresh. Afterwards, head to one of the excellent restaurants in El Prado, just north, for a bite to eat, maybe the Farmhouse Cafe. After lunch drive out to La Hacienda de los Martinez for a look at early life in Taos and then to Ranchos de Taos to see the San Francisco de Asís Church.

DAY 7: THE HIGH ROAD

On your final day, drive back down toward Albuquerque and Santa Fe via the famed High Road, which twists through a series of soaring vistas and tiny, historic villages.

Best Tours in Santa Fe

BIKE TOURS

Routes Bicycle Tours. Based in Albuquerque's Old Town and with a satellite location at Santa Fe's La Fonda Hotel, this full-service repair and rental shop offers a wide range of guided bike tours. In Santa Fe, excursions are offered March through November and include daily two-hour treks focused on the city's art and history as well as weekly tours geared around food and brewpubs. ✉ *Albuquerque* ☎ *505/933–5667* ⊕ *www.routesrentals.com.*

GUIDED TOURS

Food Tour New Mexico. Savor some of the tastiest posole, blue-corn enchiladas, margaritas, craft beers, and sweets on lunch and dinner excursions—some offered with wine pairings—in Santa Fe and Albuquerque, which make four to five stops at locally revered hot spots. ☎ *505/465–9474* ⊕ *www.foodtournewmexico. com.*

Great Southwest Adventures. This reliable group-oriented company conducts guided tours in 7- to 35-passenger van and bus excursions to Bandelier, Pecos National Historical Park, Taos (via the "Low Road" through the Gorge), O'Keeffe country, Chaco Culture National Historical Park, and elsewhere in the region. The company can also arrange single- and multiday custom trips throughout the region for groups of any size. ☎ *505/455–2700* ⊕ *www.swadventures. com.*

Heritage Inspirations. This team of highly knowledgeable, friendly guides offers nearly two dozen engaging, culturally immersive driving, walking, and hiking tours throughout northern New Mexico. Excursions include hikes through Bandelier and Kasha-Katuwe Tent Rocks, a highly popular Santa Fe architecture and wine walk, Taos and Chaco Canyon glamping trips, and agricultural adventures in Albuquerque's Rio Grande Valley. ☎ *888/344–8687* ⊕ *www.heritageinspirations.com.*

Historic Walks of Santa Fe. Get to know the fascinating stories behind many of Santa Fe's most storied landmarks on these engaging strolls through Downtown and along Canyon Road. Other walks focus on ghosts, galleries, shopping, and food; Bandelier, Chimayó, and Taos excursions are also offered. ☎ *505/986–8388* ⊕ *www.historicwalksofsantafe. com.*

New Mexico Wine Tours. Get to know the growing crop of excellent wineries in Santa Fe and north-central New Mexico on these afternoon excursions to several top tasting rooms in the area. These adventures include door-to-door pick-up and transportation and gourmet picnic lunches; tasting room fees are extra. Tours that include white-water rafting or glass-blowing before the tastings are also offered, as are private tours. ⊠ *Santa Fe* 🕾 *505/250–8943* ⊕ *www. newmexicowinetour.com.*

Santa Fe Tour Guides Association. To find an experienced local to lead you on a personal tour, visit the website of this member-based organization of about 25 reliable and vetted independent tour guides, many of whom specialize in specific topics, from art history to hiking. ⊕ *www.santafetourguides.org.*

RIVER RAFTING TOURS

If you want to watch birds and wildlife along the banks, try the laid-back floats along the Rio Chama or the Rio Grande's White Rock Canyon. The season generally runs from April to October. More rugged white-water rafting adventures take place from spring through early summer, farther north along the Rio Grande. Most outfitters have overnight package plans, and all offer half- and full-day trips. Be prepared to get wet, and wear secure water shoes.

Kokopelli Rafting Adventures. This respected outfitter offers half-day, full-day, and multi-day river trips—both relaxing floats and more exhilarating rapids excursions—down the Rio Grande and Rio Chama. ⊠ *South Side* 🕾 *505/983–3734* ⊕ *www.kokopelliraft.com.*

New Wave Rafting. Look to this company founded in 1980 for full-day, half-day, and overnight river trips on the Rio Chama and Rio Grande, as well as fly-fishing trips, from its riverside location in Embudo, on the Low Road to Taos. You can also rent funyaks and paddle easier stretches of rapids yourself. ⊠ *2110 NM 68, mile marker 21, Embudo* 🕾 *800/984–1444* ⊕ *www. newwaverafting.com.*

Santa Fe Rafting Company. This well-known tour company leads day trips down the Rio Grande and the Chama River and customizes rafting tours. Tell them what you want— they'll figure out a way to do it. ⊠ *South Side* 🕾 *505/988–4914, 888/988–4914* ⊕ *www.santaferafting.com.*

On the Calendar

Summer

Contemporary Hispanic Market.
A companion piece to the famed Traditional Spanish Market (which takes place the same weekend), this showcase of contemporary art and crafts featuring local and regional works of painting, photography, jewelry, ceramics, textiles, and more is held on the Plaza. ⊠ *Santa Fe* ⊕ *www.contemporaryhispanicmarket-inc.com.*

Santa Fe Indian Market. This world-class showcase of indigenous art began in 1926 and has grown to feature some 600 booths set up over 14 blocks in the heart of Santa Fe. Taking place over a weekend in mid-August, the market features works by nearly 1,000 indigenous artists from throughout the United States and Canada. Other events over this exciting weekend include fashion shows, films, readings, music performances, and a hugely attended Best of Show Ceremony. A smaller but still outstanding Winter Indian Market is held in Santa Fe in mid-December. ⊠ *Santa Fe* ☎ *505/983–5220* ⊕ *www.swaia.org.*

International Folk Art Market.
Held the second full weekend in July, this market sprawls across Museum Hill parking lots and plazas as the world's largest folk art market. More than 150 master folk artists from every corner of the planet come together to sell their work amid a festive array of huge tents, colorful banners, music, food, and delighted crowds. The feeling of fellowship and celebration here enhances the satisfaction of buying wonderful folk art—it's truly an experience you won't have anywhere else in the world. If you aren't in town during IFAM weekend, the nonprofit has a showroom/store open to the public in its headquarters near the capital at 620 Cerrillos Road. ⊠ *706 Camino Lejo, Museum Hill* ☎ *505/992–7600* ⊕ *www.folkartmarket.org.*

Traditional Spanish Market.
Started in 1926 and administered by the esteemed Spanish Colonial Arts Society, one of the country's most popular arts festivals takes place on the Plaza in late July and features an astounding selection of traditional Spanish-colonial works, including woodcarving, straw appliqué, metalwork, furniture, pottery, and colcha

embroidery. A smaller Winter Spanish Market takes place in Albuquerque each December. ☒ *Santa Fe* ☏ *505/982–2226* ⊕ *www.spanishcolonial.org.*

Fall

Albuquerque International Balloon Fiesta. The most popular festival in Albuquerque, the balloon fiesta draws some 850,000 visitors over nine days in October to watch a variety of events during which hot-air balloons of all shapes and sizes take to the skies. Held in what's considered the world's hot-air ballooning capital, it's a wonderful event for kids and adults, especially the "mass ascensions" that feature hundreds of balloons. ☒ *Albuquerque* ⊕ *www.balloonfiesta.com.*

Fiesta de Santa Fe. Billed the longest continuously running festival in the country, Fiesta de Santa Fe started in 1712 and remains one of the city's top events, drawing thousands over a week in mid-September. It features a mariachi extravaganza, pet parade, concerts, and the famed Burning of Zozobra (the burning of a giant 50-foot-tall effigy of Old Man Gloom). ☒ *Santa Fe* ⊕ *www.santafiesta.org.*

Winter

Christmas in Santa Fe. Santa Fe is a magical destination during the December holiday period, with dozens of events, concerts, and celebrations held throughout the month, including feast days and dances at several of the area's Indian Pueblos and the famous Farolito Walk along Canyon Road on Christmas Eve. ☒ *Santa Fe* ⊕ *www.santafe.org.*

Santa Fe Film Festival. With the film industry booming in New Mexico, this five-day event held in mid-February has become increasingly well attended, and film screenings, workshops, and discussion panels take place at venues around the city. Movie buffs should also mark their calendars for the Santa Fe Independent Film Festival (⊕ *www.santafeindependentfilmfestival.com*), which takes place over five days in mid-October, with an emphasis, of course, on indie flicks. ☒ *Santa Fe* ⊕ *www.santafefilmfestival.com.*

Contacts

Air

AIRPORT INFORMATION
**Albuquerque International
Sunport.** ☎ *505/244–7700*
⊕ *www.abqsunport.com.*
Denver International Airport.
☎ *303/342–2000* ⊕ *www.
flydenver.com.* **Santa Fe Regional
Airport (SAF).** ☎ *505/955–2900*
⊕ *www.santafenm.gov/airport.*

**SHUTTLE CONTACTS Groome
Transportation.** ☎ *505/474–5696*
⊕ *www.groometransportation.
com/santa-fe.* **RoadRunneR.**
☎ *505/424–3367* ⊕ *www.
rideroadrunner.com.* **Taos Rides.**
☎ *575/613–3256* ⊕ *www.
taosrides.com.*

Bus

CONTACTS Greyhound.
☎ *800/231–2222* ⊕ *www.
greyhound.com.* **Santa Fe Trails.**
☎ *505/955–2001* ⊕ *santafenm.
gov/transit.*

Car

**CONTACTS New Mexico
Department of Transportation
Road Advisory Hotline.**
☎ *800/432–4269* ⊕ *www.
nmroads.com.*

Lodging

**CONTACTS New Mexico Bed
and Breakfast Association.**
⊕ *www.nmbba.org.*

Train

CONTACTS Amtrak. ☎ *800/872–
7245* ⊕ *www.amtrak.com.*
New Mexico Rail Runner Express.
☎ *866/795–7245* ⊕ *www.
riometro.org.*

Taxi

CONTACTS Santa Fe Pedicabs.
☎ *505/577–5056* ⊕ *www.
santafepedicabs.com.*

Visitor Information

**CONTACTS Indian Pueblo
Cultural Center.** ☎ *505/843–
7270, 866/855–7902* ⊕ *www.
indianpueblo.org.* **New Mexico
Tourism Department Visitor
Center.** ✉ *Lamy Bldg., 491 Old
Santa Fe Trail, Old Santa Fe Trail
and South Capitol* ☎ *505/827–
7336* ⊕ *www.newmexico.org.*
Tourism Santa Fe. ✉ *Santa Fe
Community Convention Center,
201 W. Marcy St., The Plaza*
☎ *505/955–6200, 800/777–
2489* ⊕ *www.santafe.org.*

THE PLAZA AND DOWNTOWN SANTA FE

Updated by
Zibby Wilder

⊙ Sights 🍴 Restaurants 🛏 Hotels 🛍 Shopping 🍸 Nightlife
★★★★★ ★★★★★ ★★★★★ ★★★★★ ★★★★★

NEIGHBORHOOD SNAPSHOT

TOP EXPERIENCES	QUICK BITES

TOP EXPERIENCES

■ **Shop at the Inn of the Governors:** Meet Native American artists and craftspeople selling their wares under the portal of the Inn of the Governors, one of the oldest buildings in town and where Lew Wallace penned parts of *Ben Hur*.

■ **Attend a festival:** Santa Fe loves its festivals and the Plaza is host to all kinds of special gatherings throughout the year, from free concerts and dances to arts and craft and food events; the most popular are the phenomenal International Folk Art Market, the famed Indian Market, and the two-for-one weekend of the Traditional Spanish Market and Contemporary Hispanic Market.

■ **Snap photos:** This is downtown Santa Fe, after all, and the opportunities for photographs are limitless. The area's buildings, trees, and plants change not just with the seasons but by the hour thanks to New Mexico's famous golden light.

GETTING HERE AND AROUND

Getting to Downtown Santa Fe is easiest by car, although the Rail Runner train connects from downtown Albuquerque to the nearby Santa Fe Railyard. Once in town, there is plenty of metered street parking (it's free on Sunday and federal holidays), but the most convenient parking options are the bevy of municipal parking garages. These are well-located and allow for longer parking periods than the two-hour street meters. Bonus: your first hour is just one dollar. Once here, the neighborhood is easily navigable by foot.

QUICK BITES

■ **Ecco Gelato and Espresso.** This airy café serves delicious and creative gelato flavors (think strawberry-habanero, brandied cherry, and fig-and-walnut). Or try some of the espressos and coffees, pastries, and panini sandwiches. ⊠ *128 E. Marcy St., The Plaza* ⊕ *www. eccogelato.com*

■ **La Lecheria.** Delicious and refreshing craft ice cream is made here, with local ingredients, in flavors ranging from Cracker Jack and citrus basil to habanero vanilla and coconut miso. ⊠ *101 W. Marcy St., Downtown* ⊕ *www. lalecherianm.com*

■ **Madame Matisse On-the-Go.** This take-out spot features tasty sandwiches and baked goods from one of Santa Fe's favorite bakeries. ⊠ *105 E. Marcy St., Downtown*

You haven't been to Santa Fe if you haven't discovered the wonders of its historic Downtown. From territorial Spanish-Pueblo architecture and towering churches to Native jewelry artists and one-of-a-kind museums, Santa Fe's Downtown offers visitors a taste of what makes it "the City Different".

There is no other city like it in the world and its unique blend of art, imagination, and culture has earned it an official Creative City designation from UNESCO and solidified its standing as a favorite filming location for various television shows and movies. To top things off, downtown Santa Fe is home to some of the region's finest restaurants and people-watching, all thanks to its unique local flavor.

Much of the history of Santa Fe, New Mexico, the Southwest, and even the West has some association with Santa Fe's central Plaza, which New Mexico governor Don Pedro de Peralta laid out in 1610. The Plaza was already well established by the time of the Pueblo revolt in 1680. Freight wagons unloaded here after completing their arduous journey across the Santa Fe Trail. The American flag was raised over the Plaza in 1846, during the Mexican War, which resulted in Mexico's loss of all its territories in the present Southwestern United States. For a time the Plaza was a tree-shaded park with a white picket fence. In the 1890s it was an expanse of lawn where uniformed bands played in an ornate gazebo. Particularly festive times on the Plaza are the weekend after Labor Day, during Las Fiestas de Santa Fe, on Indigenous Peoples Day in October (which brings dance celebrations), and during the winter holidays, when all the trees are filled with lights and rooftops are outlined with *farolitos*, votive candles lit within paper-bag lanterns.

It was along the Old Santa Fe Trail that wagon trains from Missouri rolled into town in the 1820s, forever changing Santa Fe's destiny. This street, off the south corner of the Plaza, is one of Santa Fe's most historic and is dotted with houses, shops, markets, and the (relatively modern) state capitol several blocks down.

Though Santa Fe is the oldest capital city in the United States, many considered it little more than a pass-through town of mud and livestock corrals until the early 1900s, when a group of anthropologists, archaeologists, and artists formed a powerful community alliance to lead Santa Fe into a new era of tourism. These scholars and political influencers, which included archaeologists Adolf Bandelier and Kenneth Chapman, led the charge to preserve and promote Santa Fe's characteristic adobe architecture as a way to attract tourists interested in northern New Mexico's unique cultural and historical treasures. This group, also responsible for the founding of the Museum of New Mexico, paved the way for the "City Different" of today.

With its eclectic mix of museums, shops, galleries, restaurants, and more, downtown Santa Fe can take days to explore thoroughly. A good way to plan for a visit is to start in the historic central Plaza and work your way out from there or, plan one day for museums, another for sights, and another for shopping. Downtown Santa Fe is lively both day and night so it's easy to start exploring in the morning and still be going as night falls. To ensure you get a real "taste" of the area, make reservations for dinner as restaurants tend to fill up quickly with both locals and visitors—one of the reasons some call Santa Fe "the city that never stops eating."

The Plaza

Sights

★ Cathedral Basilica of St. Francis of Assisi

RELIGIOUS SITE | This iconic cathedral, a block east of the Plaza, is one of the rare significant departures from the city's nearly ubiquitous Pueblo architecture. Construction was begun in 1869 by Jean Baptiste Lamy, Santa Fe's first archbishop, who worked with French architects and Italian stonemasons. The Romanesque style was popular in Lamy's native home in southwest France. The circuit-riding cleric was sent by the Catholic Church to the Southwest to change the religious practices of its native population (to "civilize" them, as one period document puts it) and is buried in the crypt beneath the church's high altar. He was the inspiration behind Willa Cather's novel *Death Comes for the Archbishop* (1927). In 2005 Pope Benedict XVI declared St. Francis the "cradle of Catholicism" in the Southwestern United States, and upgraded the status of the building from mere cathedral to cathedral basilica—one of just 36 in the country.

A small adobe chapel on the northeast side of the cathedral, the remnant of an earlier church, embodies the Hispanic architectural influence so conspicuously absent from the cathedral itself. The

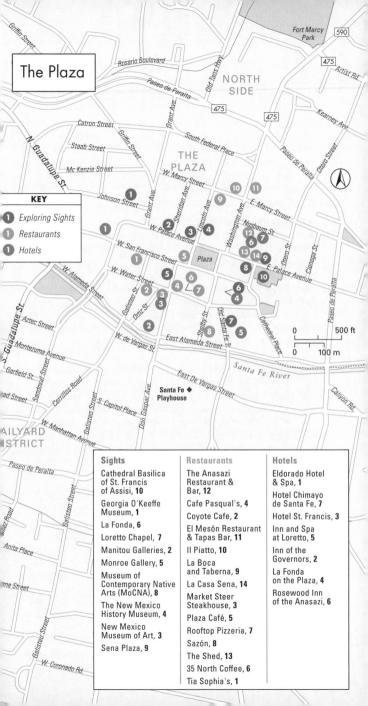

The Plaza

NORTH SIDE

THE PLAZA

KEY

- Exploring Sights
- Restaurants
- Hotels

Sights

Cathedral Basilica of St. Francis of Assisi, **10**

Georgia O'Keeffe Museum, **1**

La Fonda, **6**

Loretto Chapel, **7**

Manitou Galleries, **5**

Monroe Gallery, **5**

Museum of Contemporary Native Arts (MoCNA), **8**

The New Mexico History Museum, **4**

New Mexico Museum of Art, **3**

Sena Plaza, **9**

Restaurants

The Anasazi Restaurant & Bar, **12**

Cafe Pasqual's, **4**

Coyote Cafe, **2**

El Mesón Restaurant & Tapas Bar, **11**

Il Piatto, **10**

La Boca and Taberna, **9**

La Casa Sena, **14**

Market Steer Steakhouse, **3**

Plaza Café, **5**

Rooftop Pizzeria, **7**

Sazón, **8**

The Shed, **13**

35 North Coffee, **6**

Tia Sophia's, **1**

Hotels

Eldorado Hotel & Spa, **1**

Hotel Chimayo de Santa Fe, **7**

Hotel St. Francis, **3**

Inn and Spa at Loretto, **5**

Inn of the Governors, **2**

La Fonda on the Plaza, **4**

Rosewood Inn of the Anasazi, **6**

chapel's *Nuestra Señora de la Paz* (Our Lady of Peace), popularly known as *La Conquistadora,* the oldest Madonna statue in the United States, accompanied Don Diego de Vargas on his recon-quest of Santa Fe in 1692, a feat attributed to the statue's spiritual intervention. Every Friday the faithful adorn the statue with a new dress. Take a close look at the keystone in the main doorway arch: it has a Hebrew tetragrammaton on it. It's widely speculated that Bishop Lamy had this carved and placed to honor the Jewish merchants of Santa Fe who helped provide necessary funds for the construction of the church. ⊠ *131 Cathedral Pl., The Plaza* ☏ *505/982–5619* ⊕ *www.cbsfa.org.*

★ Georgia O'Keeffe Museum

MUSEUM | One of many East Coast artists who visited New Mex-ico in the first half of the 20th century, Georgia O'Keeffe, today known as the "Mother of American Modernism," returned to live and paint in northern New Mexico for the last half of her life, eventually emerging as the demigoddess of Southwestern art. At this museum dedicated to her work, you'll find how O'Keeffe's innovative view of the landscape is captured in *From the Plains,* inspired by her memory of the Texas plains, and in *Jimson Weed,* a study of one of her favorite plants; additional highlights include selections from O'Keeffe's early days as an illustrator, abstract pieces from her time in New York City, and iconic works featur-ing floating skulls, flowers, and bones. Special exhibitions with O'Keeffe's modernist peers, as well as contemporary artists, are on view throughout the year—many of these are exceptional, and just as interesting as the museum's permanent collection, which numbers some 3,000 works. The museum also manages a visitor center and tours of O'Keeffe's famous home and studio in Abiquiú, about an hour north of Santa Fe. ⊠ *217 Johnson St., The Plaza* ☏ *505/946–1000* ⊕ *www.okeeffemuseum.org* ⊠ *$13.*

La Fonda

BUILDING | A *fonda* (inn) has stood on this site, southeast of the Plaza, for centuries and architect Isaac Hamilton Rapp, who put Santa Fe style on the map, built the area landmark that stands there today in 1922. The hotel was sold to the Santa Fe Railway in 1926 and remained a Harvey House hotel until 1968. The property completed its latest major renovation in 2013, its guest rooms receiving a smart but still classic makeover, but the historic public areas retain their original design elements. Because of its prox-imity to the Plaza and its history as a gathering place for every-one from cowboys to movie stars (Errol Flynn stayed here), it's referred to as "The Inn at the End of the Trail." Free guided tours, which touch on the hotel's rich history and detail key pieces in the astounding public art collection, are offered Wednesday through

New Mexico Culture Pass

With a New Mexico Culture Pass (⊕ www.newmexico-culture.org), which you can purchase for $30 online or at any participating museum, you gain admission to each of the 15 state museums and monuments once over a 12-month period. These include a number of attractions elsewhere in the state (Albuquerque's National Hispanic Center and New Mexico Museum of Natural History and Science, the state monuments in Jémez, Coronado, and several other places) as well as the following Santa Fe museums: New Mexico History Museum/Palace of the Governors, New Mexico Museum of Art, Museum of Indian Arts & Culture, and Museum of International Folk Art. Note that the first Sunday of each month, these four museums offer free admission.

Saturday morning at 10:30. Step inside to browse the shops on the main floor or to eat at one of the restaurants, including the impressive greenhouse glass-topped La Plazuela. The dark, cozy bar draws both locals and tourists and has live music many nights. For a real treat have a drink at the fifth-floor Bell Tower Bar (open late spring through late fall), which offers tremendous sunset views. ⊠ *100 E. San Francisco St., at Old Santa Fe Trail, The Plaza* ☎ *505/982–5511* ⊕ *www.lafondasantafe.com.*

Loretto Chapel

RELIGIOUS SITE | A delicate Gothic church modeled after Sainte-Chapelle in Paris, Loretto was built in 1878 by the same French architects and Italian stonemasons who built St. Francis Cathedral, and is known for the "Miraculous Staircase" that leads to the choir loft. Legend has it that the chapel was almost complete when it became obvious that there wasn't room to build a staircase to the choir loft. In answer to the prayers of the cathedral's nuns, a mysterious carpenter arrived on a donkey, built a 20-foot staircase (using only a square, a saw, and a tub of water to season the non-native wood) and then disappeared as quickly as he came. Many of the faithful believed it was St. Joseph himself. The staircase contains two complete 360-degree turns with no central support; no nails were used in its construction. Adjoining the chapel are a small museum and gift shop. ⊠ *207 Old Santa Fe Trail, Old Santa Fe Trail and South Capitol* ☎ *505/982–0092* ⊕ *www.lorettochapel.com* 🖼 *$3* ⊙ *May close without advance notice for special events.*

★ Manitou Galleries

MUSEUM | This respected gallery near the Plaza carries mostly contemporary representational paintings and sculptures by world-class artists such as Jie-Wei Zhou and Martha Pettigrew as well as impressive works by local and Native artists including Hib Sabin, Nocona Burgess, and B. C. Nowlin. There's also a nice collection of photographs by Edward Curtis. Manitou has a second location, every bit as lovely, at 225 Canyon Road. It's hard to miss either location, thanks to the beautiful bronze sculptures outside. ⊠ *123 W. Palace Ave., The Plaza* ☎ *505/986–0440* ⊕ *www.facebook.com/manitougalleries.*

Monroe Gallery

MUSEUM | In this attractive storefront space a couple of blocks from the Plaza, you can admire works by the most celebrated black-and-white photographers of the 20th century, including Margaret Bourke-White, Grey Villet, and Alfred Eisenstaedt. The focus is on humanist and photojournalist-style photography, and many iconic images are available for purchase. ⊠ *112 Don Gaspar Ave., The Plaza* ☎ *505/992–0800* ⊕ *www.monroegallery.com.*

Museum of Contemporary Native Arts (MoCNA)

MUSEUM | This fascinating museum that's part of the esteemed Institute of American Indian Arts (IAIA) is just a block from the Plaza and contains the largest collection—some 7,500 works—of contemporary Native American art in the United States. The collection of paintings, photography, sculptures, prints, and traditional crafts was created by past and present students and teachers. In the 1960s and 1970s it blossomed into the nation's premier center for Native American arts and its alumni represent almost 600 tribes around the country. The museum continues to showcase the cultural and artistic vibrancy of indigenous people and expands what is still an often limited public perception of what "Indian" art is and can be. Be sure to step out back to the beautiful sculpture garden. Artist Fritz Scholder taught here, as did sculptor Allan Houser. Among their disciples were the painter T. C. Cannon and sculptor and painter Dan Namingha. ⊠ *108 Cathedral Pl., The Plaza* ☎ *505/983–8900, 888/922–4242* ⊕ *www.iaia.edu* 🖭 *$10* ⊘ *Closed Tues.*

★ The New Mexico History Museum

MUSEUM | FAMILY | This impressive, modern museum anchors a campus that encompasses the **Palace of the Governors,** the **Palace Print Shop & Bindery,** the **Fray Angélico Chávez History Library,** and **Photo Archives** (an assemblage of more than 1 million images dating from the 1850s). Behind the palace on Lincoln Avenue, the museum thoroughly explores the early history of indigenous

Many of Santa Fe's art galleries, like the Manitou Galleries, are housed in traditional adobe buildings.

people, Spanish colonization, the Mexican Period, and travel and commerce on the legendary Santa Fe Trail. Inside are changing and permanent exhibits. By appointment, visitors can tour the comprehensive Fray Angélico Chávez Library and its rare maps, manuscripts, and photographs (more than 120,000 prints and negatives). The Palace Print Shop & Bindery, which prints books, pamphlets, and cards on antique presses, also hosts bookbinding demonstrations, lectures, and slide shows. The Palace of the Governors is a humble one-story neo-Pueblo adobe on the north side of the Plaza, and is the oldest public building in the United States. Its rooms contain period furnishings and exhibits illustrating the building's many functions over the past four centuries. Built at the same time as the Plaza, circa 1610, it was the seat of four regional governments—those of Spain, Mexico, the Confederacy, and the U.S. territory that preceded New Mexico's statehood, which was achieved in 1912. It served as the residence for 100 Spanish, Mexican, and American governors, including Governor Lew Wallace, who wrote his epic *Ben Hur* in its then drafty rooms, all the while complaining of the dust and mud that fell from its earthen ceiling.

Dozens of Native American vendors gather daily under the portal of the Palace of the Governors to sell pottery, jewelry, bread, and other goods. With few exceptions, the more than 500 artists and craftspeople registered to sell here are Pueblo or Navajo Indians. The merchandise for sale is required to meet strict standards. Prices tend to reflect the high quality of the merchandise but are often significantly less than what you'd pay in a shop. Please remember not to take photographs without permission. ⊠ *Palace Ave., north side of Plaza, 113 Lincoln Ave., The Plaza* ☎ *505/476–5200* ⊕ *www.nmhistorymuseum.org* ⊠ *$12* ⊙ *Closed Nov.–Apr., closed Mon.*

★ New Mexico Museum of Art

MUSEUM | Designed by Isaac Hamilton Rapp in 1917, the museum contains one of America's finest regional collections. It's also one of Santa Fe's earliest Pueblo Revival structures, inspired by the adobe structures at Acoma Pueblo. Split-cedar *latillas* (branches set in a crosshatch pattern) and hand-hewn vigas form the ceilings. The 20,000-piece permanent collection, of which only a fraction is exhibited at any given time, emphasizes the work of regional and nationally renowned artists, including Georgia O'Keeffe; realist Robert Henri; the Cinco Pintores (five painters) of Santa Fe (including Fremont Elis and Will Shuster, the creative mind behind Zozóbra); members of the Taos Society of Artists (Ernest L. Blumenschein, Bert G. Phillips, Joseph H. Sharp, and E. Irving Couse, among others); and the works of noted 20th-century photographers of the Southwest, including Laura Gilpin, Ansel Adams, and Dorothea Lange. Rotating exhibits are staged throughout the year. Many excellent examples of Spanish-colonial-style furniture are on display. Other highlights include an interior *placita* (small plaza) with fountains, WPA murals, and sculpture, and the St. Francis Auditorium, where concerts and lectures are often held. ⊠ *107 W. Palace Ave., The Plaza* ☎ *505/476–5072* ⊕ *www.nmartmuseum.org* ⊠ *$12* ⊙ *Closed Nov.–Apr. and Mon.*

Sena Plaza

PLAZA | Two-story buildings enclose this courtyard, which can be entered only through two small doorways on Palace Avenue or the shops facing Palace Avenue. Surrounding the oasis of flowering fruit trees, a fountain, and inviting benches are a variety of locally owned shops. The quiet courtyard is a good place for repose or to have lunch at La Casa Sena. The buildings, erected in the 1700s as a single-family residence, had quarters for blacksmiths, bakers, farmers, and all manner of help. ⊠ *125 E. Palace Ave., The Plaza.*

🍴 Restaurants

★ The Anasazi Restaurant & Bar

$$$$ | **MODERN AMERICAN** | The expert culinary team at this romantic restaurant with hardwood floors, soft lighting, and Chaco Valley stone–inspired walls balances old-world techniques with Southwestern spice in its approach to the menu. If you want a less formal vibe, dine in the more spacious, convivial bar or on the lively streetside patio. **Known for:** always excellent seasonally changing menu; exceptional craft cocktails; extensive wine and tequila lists. $ *Average main: $36* ⊠ *Rosewood Inn of the Anasazi, 113 Washington Ave., The Plaza* ☎ *505/988–3030* ⊕ *www.rosewoodhotels.com/en/inn-of-the-anasazi-santa-fe/dining/anasazi-restaurant.*

★ Cafe Pasqual's

$$$ | **SOUTHWESTERN** | A perennial favorite, this cheerful cubbyhole dishes up Nuevo Latino and occasional Asian specialties for breakfast, lunch, and dinner. The culinary muse behind Pasqual's is James Beard Award–winning chef and cookbook author Katharine Kagel, who champions organic, local ingredients, and whose expert kitchen staff produces mouthwatering breakfast and lunch specialties like *huevos motuleños* (eggs in a tangy tomatillo salsa with black beans and fried bananas) and the sublime grilled free-range chicken sandwich on toasted-chile corn bread. **Known for:** smoked-trout hash with tomatillo salsa and mole enchiladas; colorful folk art and murals; long waits with reservations only available for dinner. $ *Average main: $30* ⊠ *121 Don Gaspar Ave., The Plaza* ☎ *505/983–9340* ⊕ *www.pasquals.com.*

Coyote Cafe

$$$$ | **SOUTHWESTERN** | A Santa Fe hot spot since it opened in 1987, this pioneer of contemporary Southwestern cuisine is enjoying a bit of a renaissance under the guidance of new-ish (since 2017) owner and long-time bartender/manager Quinn Stephenson. The spot serves some of the most extravagant and delicious cuisine in the city. **Known for:** tellicherry peppered elk tenderloin; Frito pies in the less expensive Coyote Cantina next-door; creative agave and tequila cocktails. $ *Average main: $39* ⊠ *132 W. Water St., The Plaza* ☎ *505/983–1615* ⊕ *www.coyotecafe.com* ☉ *No lunch.*

El Mesón Restaurant & Tapas Bar

$$$ | **SPANISH** | This place is as fun for having drinks and late-night tapas or catching live music (from tango nights to Sephardic music) as it is for enjoying a full meal. The lively tapas bar feels like a Spanish *taberna*, with a menu that includes dishes like classic Tortilla Española with alioli or fried artichoke hearts stuffed with Spanish goat cheese over *romesco* sauce. **Known for:** live jazz, Flamenco, and Tango Tuesdays; paella à la Valenciana with seafood, chorizo, and chicken; nice selection of Spanish wines, including Jerez sherries. $ *Average main: $25* ⊠ *213 Washington Ave., The Plaza* ☎ *505/983–6756* ⊕ *www.elmeson-santafe.com* ☉ *Closed Sun. and Mon. No lunch.*

Il Piatto

$$$ | **ITALIAN** | This chef-owned neighborhood spot near the Plaza charms its legions of fans with pasta dishes like pappardelle with braised duckling ragù and homemade pumpkin ravioli with pine

Dozens of restaurants and shops surround the city's historic Plaza.

nuts and sage brown butter. The menu, which usually features several creative specials, emphasizes locally sourced ingredients. **Known for:** informal trattoria atmosphere; "medium plates" option on pastas and entrées; great late afternoon happy hour. $ *Average main: $27* ✉ *95 W. Marcy St., The Plaza* ☎ *505/984–1091* ⊕ *www.ilpiattosantafe.com* ⊘ *No lunch Sat.–Tues.*

★ La Boca and Taberna

$$$ | SPANISH | A beacon of superbly crafted, authentic yet creatively updated Mediterranean—and especially Spanish—cuisine, La Boca comprises two distinct spaces: an intimate and quieter storefront dining room that's better for a leisurely romantic repast, and in back, spilling out into a cloistered courtyard, Taberna, a bustling tavern with live music, ample seating indoor and out, and late hours. Both spaces feature the delectable small-plates cooking of celebrated chef James Cambpell Caruso. **Known for:** fine Spanish meats and cheeses; extensive selection of authentic Spanish tapas; nice variety of Spanish sherries. $ *Average main: $26* ✉ *72 W. Marcy St., The Plaza* ☎ *505/982–3433* ⊕ *www.labocasantafe. com.*

La Casa Sena

$$$ | CONTEMPORARY | The Southwestern-accented and Continental fare served at La Casa Sena is beautifully presented, and the scenery, especially during the warmer months, is part of the charm. Get a table on the patio surrounded by hollyhocks, flowering shrubs, and centuries-old adobe walls, or for a musical meal (evenings only), sit in the restaurant's adjacent, less-pricey

Cantina, where the talented and perky staff belt out Broadway show tunes. **Known for:** grilled rack of lamb; gorgeous patio; on-site wine shop. $ *Average main: $30* ⊠ *Sena Plaza, 125 E. Palace Ave., The Plaza* ☎ *505/988–9232* ⊕ *lacasasena.com.*

Market Steer Steakhouse

$$$$ | **AMERICAN** | Locals go crazy for this steak house, partly thanks to the chef and co-owner, who earned her chops as a World Champion rodeo roper before moving into the culinary limelight. The steak house brings together flavors from New Mexico and Texas, with a light touch of classic old-world finesse. **Known for:** expertly cooked steak; delicious and creative sides, sauces, and starters; quality cocktails and wines. $ *Average main: $40* ⊠ *Hotel St. Francis, 210 Don Gaspar Ave., The Plaza* ☎ *505/992–6354* ⊕ *www.marketsteersteakhouse.com* ⊗ *Closed Mon.*

Plaza Café

$$ | **SOUTHWESTERN** | **FAMILY** | Run with homespun care by the Razatos family since 1947, this café has been a fixture on the Plaza since 1905. The food runs the gamut, from cashew mole enchiladas to New Mexico meat loaf to chile-smothered burritos to a handful of Greek favorites, but the ingredients tend toward Southwestern. **Known for:** chicken-fried steak and excellent tortilla soup; retro diner charm; breakfast all day. $ *Average main: $17* ⊠ *54 Lincoln Ave., The Plaza* ☎ *505/982–1664* ⊕ *www.plazacafe-santafe.com.*

Rooftop Pizzeria

$$ | **PIZZA** | For sophisticated pizza, head to this slick indoor–outdoor restaurant on the upper level of Santa Fe Arcade. The kitchen here scores high marks for its rich and imaginative pizza toppings: consider the one topped with roasted chicken, green chile, toasted piñons, cotija and asadero cheese, and alfredo sauce on a blue corn crust. **Known for:** unusual pizza toppings; great salads; well-chosen wine and microbrew beer list. $ *Average main: $16* ⊠ *60 E. San Francisco St., The Plaza* ☎ *505/984–0008* ⊕ *rooftop-pizzeria.com.*

★ Sazón

$$$$ | **MODERN MEXICAN** | The realm of Mexico City–born chef Fernando Olea, who's been working his culinary magic at different Santa Fe restaurants since 1991, Sazón offers an upscale take on regional Mexican fare, complete with an exhaustive list of artisan tequilas and mezcals. Within the handsome dining room warmed by a kiva fireplace and filled with Frida Kahlo and Day of the Dead–inspired artwork, the focus is on one of Mexico's greatest dishes, mole. **Known for:** house-made mole sauces; chapulines (baby grasshoppers) on corn taquitos; encyclopedic selection of

artisan mezcals. $ *Average main: $37* ✉ *221 Shelby St., The Plaza* ☎ *505/983–8604* ⊕ *www.sazonsantafe.com* ⊘ *Closed Sun. No lunch.*

★ The Shed

$ | **SOUTHWESTERN** | **FAMILY** | The lines at lunch attest to the status of this Downtown eatery that's been family operated since 1953, serving some of the most flavorful New Mexican food, and margaritas, around. Even if you're a devoted green-chile sauce fan, consider trying the locally grown red chile the place is famous for; it is rich and perfectly spicy. **Known for:** red-chile enchiladas and posole; potent margaritas; historic adobe setting dating from 1692. $ *Average main: $14* ✉ *113½ E. Palace Ave., The Plaza* ☎ *505/982–9030* ⊕ *www.sfshed.com* ⊘ *Closed Sun.*

35 North Coffee

$ | **CAFÉ** | There are plenty of spots near the Plaza for grabbing a latte, but this coffeehouse stands out for brewing exceptional house-roasted, single-origin coffees from Guatamala, Kenya, Sumatra, and other java hot spots around the world. You can order a pour-over made with beans of your choosing, or sample the house-made chai, nitro cold brew, and "latitude adjustment" (coffee blended with organic grass-fed butter, MCT oil, and coconut oil). **Known for:** high-grade single-origin coffees; house-made chai; breakfast croissants. $ *Average main: $6* ✉ *60 E. San Francisco St., The Plaza* ☎ *505/983–6138* ⊕ *www.35northcoffee.com* ⊘ *No dinner.*

Tia Sophia's

$ | **SOUTHWESTERN** | **FAMILY** | This family-run Downtown joint has been starting Santa Feans' days right since 1974, serving some of the area's best New Mexican breakfasts and lunches (it's open until 2 pm most days and 1 on Sunday). Order anything and expect a true taste of local tradition, including perfectly flaky, light sopaipilla; Tia's delicious burritos stuffed with homemade chorizo disappear fast on Saturday so get there early. **Known for:** huge breakfast burritos; popularity with locals; traditional New Mexican cuisine, down to the fiery chiles. $ *Average main: $9* ✉ *210 W. San Francisco St., The Plaza* ☎ *505/983–9880* ⊕ *tiasophias.com* ⊘ *No dinner.*

 Hotels

Eldorado Hotel & Spa

$$ | **HOTEL** | **FAMILY** | This large, yet inviting, hotel comes with individually decorated rooms and stunning mountain views. **Pros:** attractive accommodations three blocks from Plaza; great view from rooftop pool (especially at sunset); fun bar with great

late-night food menu. **Cons:** staff's attention to service varies considerably; can be very expensive during busy periods; convention space can make it feel impersonal. $ *Rooms from: $160* ✉ *309 W. San Francisco St., The Plaza* ☎ *505/988–4455, 800/955–4455* ⊕ *www.eldoradohotel.com* ⤳ *213 rooms* ❏ *No meals.*

Hotel Chimayó de Santa Fe

$$ | HOTEL | FAMILY | Among the handful of midprice, full-service hotels within a couple of blocks of the Plaza, this attractive, Territorial-style adobe hotel with a mix of spacious standard rooms and even bigger suites is a terrific option, especially given the extensive amenities available in many units—wet bars, kitchenettes, spacious sitting areas. **Pros:** unbeatable location; spacious rooms and extensive in-room perks are nice for families or groups; offers free Downtown walking tours May–October. **Cons:** in a crowded part of Downtown; no pool or gym; can have some street noise. $ *Rooms from: $140* ✉ *125 Washington Ave., The Plaza* ☎ *505/988–4900, 855/752–9273* ⊕ *www.hotelchimayo.com* ⤳ *54 rooms* ❏ *No meals.*

Hotel St. Francis

$$ | HOTEL | Just one block south of the Plaza, this stately three-story hotel retains a historic vibe but has been given a modern flair—with expansive stone floors, plaster walls, and spare furnishings lit by massive pillar candles at night, the lobby feels a bit like a Tuscan monastery. **Pros:** stylish, contemporary vibe in a historic building; two blocks from the Plaza and near many shops; excellent dining and nightlife on-site. **Cons:** breakfast not included; some rooms (and especially bathrooms) are quite small; some rooms can have noise from the street. $ *Rooms from: $140* ✉ *210 Don Gaspar Ave., The Plaza* ☎ *505/983–5700* ⊕ *www. hotelstfrancis.com* ⤳ *80 rooms* ❏ *No meals.*

★ Inn and Spa at Loretto

$$ | HOTEL | FAMILY | This plush, oft-photographed, pueblo-inspired property attracts a loyal clientele, many of whom swear by the friendly staff and high decorating standards. **Pros:** ideal location; gorgeous grounds and pool; distinctive architecture. **Cons:** expensive parking and resort fees; bathrooms feel a bit ordinary, small, and dated, and they also lack counter space; some rooms can have noise from the road. $ *Rooms from: $170* ✉ *211 Old Santa Fe Trail, The Plaza* ☎ *505/988–5531* ⊕ *www.hotelloretto.com* ⤳ *134 rooms* ❏ *No meals.*

★ Inn of the Governors

$$ | HOTEL | FAMILY | This rambling, reasonably priced hotel by the Santa Fe River is staffed by a polite, enthusiastic bunch. **Pros:** close to Plaza; year-round, heated pool; free parking (unusual for

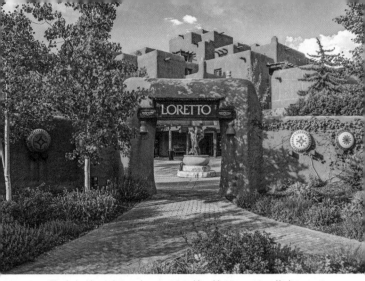

The famed Inn at Loretto has a partnership with tour company Heritage Inspirations, offering guided tours around the area.

Downtown). **Cons:** standard rooms are a bit small; some rooms view parking lot; some traffic noise. ⑤ *Rooms from: $179* ✉ *101 W. Alameda St., The Plaza* ☎ *505/982–4333, 800/234–4534* ⊕ *www.innofthegovernors.com* ⤶ *100 rooms* ◯ *Free Breakfast.*

★ La Fonda on the Plaza

$$$ | HOTEL | FAMILY | This venerable Downtown landmark comes with modern amenities but still retains a warm, artful design—including whimsical painted headboards and handcrafted furniture—that's faithful to the vision of Mary Elizabeth Jane Colter, the vaunted architect responsible for the hotel's elegant Southwestern aesthetic. **Pros:** iconic building steeped in history; Plaza is right outside the door; excellent restaurant, bars, and pool. **Cons:** lobby often packed with tourists and nonguests; fitness facilities are modest for an upscale hotel; busy downtown location means some noise. ⑤ *Rooms from: $269* ✉ *100 E. San Francisco St., The Plaza* ☎ *505/982–5511, 800/523–5002* ⊕ *www.lafondasantafe. com* ⤶ *180 rooms* ◯ *No meals.*

★ Rosewood Inn of the Anasazi

$$$$ | HOTEL | This intimate and artfully designed boutique hotel steps from the Plaza is one of Santa Fe's finest, with superb architectural detail, top-notch service, and a much-celebrated restaurant, bar, and lounge. **Pros:** thoughtful luxurious touches throughout; superb restaurant and charming bar; beautiful, lodgelike public spaces that are ideal for conversation or curling up with a book. **Cons:** standard rooms are a bit small for the price; only a few rooms have balconies; no hot tub or pool. ⑤ *Rooms from: $450*

✉ *113 Washington Ave., The Plaza* ☎ *505/988–3030, 888/767–3966*
⊕ *www.rosewoodhotels.com* ⇌ *58 rooms* ⦿ *No meals.*

Nightlife

Agave Restaurant & Lounge

BARS/PUBS | The bar of the Agave restaurant located within the Eldorado Hotel is stylish and contemporary, making it just as much of a hit with locals and nonguests as with those staying on the property. The well-made cocktails, smart decor, happy hour deals, and stellar late-night bar-food menu—from snacks to burgers—are among Agave's key assets. ✉ *Eldorado Hotel, 309 W. San Francisco St., The Plaza* ☎ *505/995–4530* ⊕ *www.eldoradohotel.com/agave-lounge.*

★ Bell Tower Bar

BARS/PUBS | The lofty rooftop perch at historic Hotel La Fonda is open only from mid-spring through mid-fall, but during the warmer months it's one of the loveliest places in town to sip cocktails while watching the sunset and surrounding mountains. The views make it a popular spot so try and get there during the off-hours to snag a table. Year-round, you can also enjoy outstanding margaritas and tasty bar food in lively La Fiesta Lounge, just off the hotel lobby, which also features live music. ✉ *La Fonda Hotel, 100 E. San Francisco St., The Plaza* ☎ *505/982–5511* ⊕ *www.lafondasantafe.com.*

Del Charro

BARS/PUBS | The laid-back saloon at Downtown's Inn of the Governors serves a fine green-chile cheeseburger, plus quality margaritas and the like. It's less fancy than some of the other hotel bars in town, with old-fashioned Western decor, dark-wood paneling (warmed by the glow of a wood-burning fireplace), and an airy patio. ✉ *Inn of the Governors, 101 W. Alameda St., The Plaza* ☎ *505/954–0320* ⊕ *www.delcharro.com.*

Draft Station

BREWPUBS/BEER GARDENS | **FAMILY** | Beer aficionados can sample a variety of New Mexican craft brews—including selections from Marble Brewery, La Cumbre, Bosque Brewing, and Chama River Brewing—at this no-frills spot with a large balcony overlooking the Plaza. In addition to the fine people-watching from the balcony, you can order tasty pizza from Rooftop Pizzeria, which is just down the hall and makes a great cornmeal crust. ✉ *60 E. San Francisco St., Santa Fe Arcade, 2nd fl., The Plaza* ☎ *505/983–6443* ⊕ *draft-station.com.*

Secreto Lounge

BARS/PUBS | This beautifully designed bar inside the historic Hotel St. Francis has long been known for its creative craft cocktails, including a classic Manhattan with a clove tincture spritzed over the top as well as a smoked-sage margarita. There's a nice selection of appetizers and light entrées and you can also sample superb New Mexico wines at Gruet Winery's Tasting Room, just across the hotel lobby. ⊠ *Hotel St. Francis, 210 Don Gaspar Ave., The Plaza* ☏ *505/983–5700* ⊕ *www.hotelstfrancis.com.*

Tonic

BARS/PUBS | At this intimate, high-ceilinged bar with a dapper art deco interior, you can sip deftly crafted cocktails and listen to some of the best jazz acts in town. It's one of the few late-night spots serving bar food until 1 most evenings. ⊠ *103 E. Water St., The Plaza* ☏ *505/982–1189* ⊕ *www.tonicsantafe.com.*

🎭 Performing Arts

El Flamenco

DANCE | Several organizations produce flamenco concerts around town, including the prestigious Entreflamenco Company, which performs at El Flamenco restaurant a few blocks from the Plaza. ⊠ *135 W. Palace Ave., The Plaza* ☏ *505/209–1302* ⊕ *www.entreflamenco.com.*

★ Lensic Performing Arts Center

CONCERTS | Santa Fe's vintage Downtown movie house has been fully restored and converted into the 850-seat Lensic Performing Arts Center. The grand 1931 building, with Moorish and Spanish Renaissance influences, hosts the Santa Fe Symphony, theater, classic films, lectures and readings, noted world, pop, and jazz musicians, and many other prominent events. ⊠ *211 W. San Francisco St., The Plaza* ☏ *505/988–1234* ⊕ *www.lensic.org.*

Performance Santa Fe

CONCERTS | From September through May, the venerable organization (aka Santa Fe Concert Association) founded in 1937 presents symphony and solo classical concerts, lectures, dance recitals, opera, and family-minded shows at several venues around town, including the Lensic, St. Francis Auditorium, and United Church of Santa Fe. The organization has brought a number of prestigious talents to Santa Fe over the years, including Wynton Marsalis, Patti Lupone, the Russian National Ballet, and the Academy of St. Martin in the Fields Chamber Ensemble. ⊠ *Santa Fe* ☏ *505/984–8759* ⊕ *www.performancesantafe.org.*

Santa Fe Bandstand Concerts

MUSIC | Tuesday through Saturday night throughout July and August, free concerts are staged at the bandstand in Downtown's festive and historic Plaza or occasionally at Swan Park on the South Side (off NM 599). A number of nationally noteworthy artists have appeared for this event, where the music ranges from Spanish guitar to blues to rockabilly. ⊠ *The Plaza* ☎ *505/986–6054* ⊕ *www.santafebandstand.org.*

St. Francis Auditorium

CONCERTS | This historic space with colorful murals inside the Museum of Fine Arts is a top venue for many cultural events, such as theatrical productions and concerts. ⊠ *107 W. Palace Ave., The Plaza* ☎ *505/476–5072* ⊕ *www.nmartmuseum.org.*

Shopping

ANTIQUES

Arrediamo

HOUSEHOLD ITEMS/FURNITURE | One of the top spots in the Southwest for handmade Turkish, Persian, and Afghan rugs, Arrediamo also carries a fine selection of authentic Navajo rugs and textiles. ⊠ *202 Galisteo St., The Plaza* ☎ *505/820–2231* ⊕ *www.arrediamo. com.*

Design Warehouse

ANTIQUES/COLLECTIBLES | A welcome antidote to Santa Fe's preponderance of shops selling Native American and Spanish-colonial antiques, Design Warehouse carries hip, contemporary furniture, kitchenware, home accessories, and other sleek knickknacks, including vaunted brands like Alessi, Knoll, and Normann Copenhagen. Note the select collection of books and magazines focusing on art and design. ⊠ *130 Lincoln Ave., The Plaza* ☎ *505/988–1555* ⊕ *www.designwarehousesantafe.com.*

BOOKS

★ Collected Works Book Store & Coffeehouse

BOOKS/STATIONERY | You'll find a great selection of art and travel books here, including a generous selection of titles on Southwestern art, architecture, and general history, as well as the latest in contemporary literature. In a large, inviting space close to the Plaza, you can also enjoy organic lattes, snacks, and sandwiches by the superb Iconik Coffee Roasters. Author readings and music are frequently scheduled so be sure to check the calendar. The proprietress, Dorothy Massey, and her staff are well loved for their knowledge and helpfulness. ⊠ *202 Galisteo St., The Plaza* ☎ *505/988–4226* ⊕ *www.collectedworksbookstore.com.*

Travel Bug

BOOKS/STATIONERY | Here you'll find a huge array of guides and books about travel along with maps. You'll also find all sorts of gadgets for hikers and backpackers. There's also a cozy coffeehouse (excellent java) with Wi-Fi. On many Saturday evenings the shop hosts presentations on world travel experiences. ☒ *839 Paseo de Peralta, The Plaza* ☎ *505/992–0418* ⊕ *www.mapsofnewmexico.com.*

CLOTHING AND ACCESSORIES

★ Back at the Ranch

CLOTHING | This cozy space in an old, creaky-floored adobe is stocked with perhaps the finest handmade cowboy boots you will ever see—in every color, style, and embellishment imaginable. Other finds, like funky ranch-style furniture, 1950s blanket coats, jewelry, and belt buckles are also sold. The staff is top-notch and the boots are breathtaking. ☒ *209 E. Marcy St., The Plaza* ☎ *505/989–8110* ⊕ *www.backattheranch.com.*

★ O'Farrell Hats

CLOTHING | Scott O'Farrell (son of the shop's late founder, Kevin) and his highly trained staff carry on the tradition of producing carefully designed and constructed classic Western hats. The one-of-a-kind beaver-felt cowboy hats make the ultimate Santa Fe keepsake. This level of quality comes at a cost, but devoted customers—who have included everyone from cattle ranchers to U.S. presidents—swear by O'Farrell's artful creations. ☒ *111 E. San Francisco St., The Plaza* ☎ *505/989–9666* ⊕ *www.ofarrellhatco.com.*

Red River Mercantile

CLOTHING | This small but well-stocked space is one of the best spots in town for rugged and stylish—but casual—men's wear, along with backpacks, computer bags, watches, wallets, and other accessories. Well-established brands like Filson, Pendleton, Howler Brothers, and Grayer's fill the aisles, and the staff is extremely helpful. ☒ *235 Don Gaspar Ave., The Plaza* ☎ *505/992–1233.*

FOOD AND DRINK

★ Todos Santos Chocolates

FOOD/CANDY | This tiny candy shop in the 18th-century courtyard of Sena Plaza sells must-be-seen-to-be-believed works of edible art, including chocolate *milagros* and altar pieces gilded with 23-karat gold or silver leaf. Truffles come in exotic flavors, like tangerine chile, rose caramel, and lemon verbena. The buttery, spicy, handmade chipotle caramels melt in your mouth. Amidst the taste sensations and quirky folk art are amazing and delightful customized

Pez dispensers from Albuquerque folk artist Steve White and astonishing, intricate recycled paper creations from local phenom Rick Phelps. ⊠ *125 E. Palace Ave., The Plaza* ☎ *505/982–3855.*

HOME GOODS AND GIFTS
★ Doodlet's
ANTIQUES/COLLECTIBLES | The whimsical collection of stuff here includes pop-up books, silly postcards, tin art, hooked rugs, and stringed lights. Wonderment is in every display case, drawing the eye to the unusual. There's something for just about everyone at this delightfully quirky, popular shop, and often it's affordable. ⊠ *120 Don Gaspar Ave., The Plaza* ☎ *505/983–3771* ⊕ *doodlets. com.*

Sub Rosa Mercantile
CRAFTS | This charming lifestyle-centric shop features a carefully curated selection of home goods, clothing, cards, bath and body products, jewelry, vintage finds, and more. The focus here is on hand-crafted, small batch items created primarily by women-owned businesses. ⊠ *65 W. Marcy St., The Plaza* ☎ *505/428–9528* ⊕ *www.subrosamercantile.com.*

JEWELRY
LewAllen & LewAllen Jewelry
JEWELRY/ACCESSORIES | Father-and-daughter silversmiths Ross and Laura LewAllen run this impressive shop. Handmade jewelry ranges from whimsical to mystical inside their tiny space just off the Plaza. There's something for absolutely everyone in here, including delightful charms for your pet's collar. ⊠ *105 E. Palace Ave., The Plaza* ☎ *800/988–5112, 505/983–2657* ⊕ *www.lewallenjewelry. com.*

★ Patina Gallery
JEWELRY/ACCESSORIES | In this airy, museum-like space, you'll find outstanding contemporary jewelry, textiles, and sculptural objects of metal, clay, and wood. With a staff whose courtesy is matched by knowledge of the genre, artists-owners Ivan and Allison Barnett have used their fresh curatorial aesthetic to create a showplace for dozens of American and European artists they represent—many of whom are in permanent collections of museums such as MoMA. ⊠ *131 W. Palace Ave., The Plaza* ☎ *505/986–3432* ⊕ *www.patina-gallery.com.*

NATIVE AMERICAN ARTS AND CRAFTS
★ Andrea Fisher Fine Pottery
CERAMICS/GLASSWARE | You can browse, and buy, some of the nation's finest examples of both historic and contemporary Native pottery at this gallery a couple of blocks east of the Plaza. It is

The Plaza is one of the best places in the city to purchase traditional Navajo weavings and blankets, and Shiprock Santa Fe is one of its most popular shops.

especially renowned for its collection of pieces from San Ildefonso Pueblo legend Maria Martinez and her illustrious family. ⊠ *100 W. San Francisco St., The Plaza* ☎ *505/986–1234* ⊕ *www.andreafisherpottery.com.*

Keshi: The Zuni Connection

CRAFTS | Since the early '80s, this gallery specializing in beautiful animal fetishes carved out of turquoise, marble, onyx, and countless other materials has served as a co-op art gallery for western New Mexico's Zuni Pueblo. You'll find fetishes representing an astounding variety of animals, from eagles to mountain lions to turtles, plus fine jewelry and pottery. ⊠ *227 Don Gaspar Ave., The Plaza* ☎ *505/989–8728* ⊕ *www.keshi.com.*

The Rainbow Man

CRAFTS | Established in 1945, this colorful, if a bit touristy, shop does business in an old, rambling adobe complex, part of which dates from before the 1680 Pueblo Revolt and also served as offices for the Manhattan Project. The shop carries early Navajo, Mexican, and Chimayó textiles, along with photographs by Edward S. Curtis, a breathtaking collection of vintage pawn and Mexican jewelry, Day of the Dead figures, Oaxacan folk animals, New Mexican folk art, kachinas, and contemporary jewelry from local artists. The friendly staff possesses an encyclopedic knowledge of the art here. ⊠ *107 E. Palace Ave., The Plaza* ☎ *505/982–8706* ⊕ *www.rainbowman.com.*

★ Shiprock Santa Fe

ANTIQUES/COLLECTIBLES | This rustic and light-filled space showcases a beautifully curated collection of Navajo rugs and blankets, contemporary and vintage Native jewelry, pottery, sculpture, folk art, fine art and more. The vision of fifth-generation art dealer Jed Foutz, who was raised in a family of Indian art traders on the Navajo Nation, the gallery is notable for its dedication to showcasing exquisite vintage pieces alongside vanguard contemporary works. ⊠ *53 Old Santa Fe Trail, 2nd fl., The Plaza* ☎ *505/982–8478* ⊕ *www.shiprocksantafe.com.*

Outside the Plaza

Sights

Barrio de Analco

HISTORIC SITE | Along the south bank of the Santa Fe River, the barrio—its name means "District on the Other Side of the Water"—is one of America's oldest neighborhoods, settled in the early 1600s by the Tlaxcalan Indians (who were forbidden to live with the Spanish near the Plaza) and in the 1690s by soldiers who had helped recapture New Mexico after the Pueblo Revolt. The historic district was named a National Historic Landmark in 1968 and is a great place to experience Santa Fe's unique history of Native American, Spanish, Mexican, and American cultural influence. Plaques on houses on East De Vargas Street will help you locate some of the important structures. Check the performance schedule at the **Santa Fe Playhouse** on De Vargas Street, founded by writer Mary Austin and other Santa Feans in 1922. ⊠ *Old Santa Fe Trail at E. De Vargas St., Old Santa Fe Trail and South Capitol.*

New Mexico State Capitol

GOVERNMENT BUILDING | **FAMILY** | The symbol of the Zía Pueblo, which represents the Circle of Life, was the inspiration for the state's capitol building, also known as the Roundhouse. Doorways at opposing sides of the 1966 structure symbolize the four times of day, the four directions, the four stages of life, and the four seasons. Throughout the building are artworks from the outstanding 600-work collection of the Capitol Art Foundation, historical and cultural displays, and handcrafted furniture—it's a superb and somewhat overlooked array of fine art. The Governor's Gallery hosts temporary exhibits. Six acres of imaginatively landscaped gardens shelter outstanding sculptures. ⊠ *490 Old Santa Fe Trail,*

The Plaza and Downtown Santa Fe OUTSIDE THE PLAZA

3

Outside The Plaza

KEY
- ① Exploring Sights
- ① Restaurants
- ① Hotels

Sights
Barrio de Analco, 4
New Mexico State Capitol, 6
The Oldest House, 3
Peyton Wright, 2
San Miguel Mission, 5
Santa Fe School of Cooking, 1

Restaurants
Bouche, 7
Bumble Bee's Baja Grill, 5
Dolina Cafe & Bakery, 2
Fire & Hops, 4
Restaurant Martin, 9
Sabor Peruano, 1
Santacafé, 8
Taco Fundación, 3
TerraCotta Wine Bistro, 6

Hotels
Campanilla Compound, 4
Casa Culinaria, 10
Drury Plaza Hotel, 6
El Farolito, 9
Fort Marcy Suites, 3
Inn at Vanessie, 2
Inn of the Five Graces, 7
Inn of the Turquoise Bear, 11
Inn on the Paseo, 5
Las Palomas, 1
Pueblo Bonito B&B Inn, 8

Old Santa Fe Trail and South Capitol ☎ *505/986–4589* ⊕ *www. nmlegis.gov/visitors* ⊠ *Free* ☉ *Closed Sun. year-round and Sat. Sept.–late May.*

The Oldest House

BUILDING | FAMILY | This house is said to be the oldest in the United States—a sign on the exterior puts the date at 1646. Some say it's much older, but historians currently can verify only that it dates back to the mid-1700s. Inside, a small gift shop and museum features Harvey House jewelry, kachinas, paintings, pottery, and more. ⊠ *215 E. De Vargas St., Old Santa Fe Trail and South Capitol* ☎ *505/988–2488* ⊕ *www.oldesthousesantafe.com.*

Peyton Wright

MUSEUM | Tucked inside the National Register-listed Spiegelberg house, this gallery represents some of the most talented emerging and established contemporary artists in the country Historic notables featured here include Dorothy Brett, Robert Motherwell, Joseph Stella, and Taro Yamamoto as well as antique, and even ancient, New Mexican, Russian, and Latin works. ⊠ *237 E. Palace Ave., The Plaza* ☎ *505/989–9888* ⊕ *www.peytonwright.com* ☉ *Closed Sun.*

★ San Miguel Mission

RELIGIOUS SITE | FAMILY | Believed to be the oldest church still in use in the United States, this simple earth-hewn adobe structure was built around 1610 by the Tlaxcalan Indians of Mexico, who came to New Mexico as servants of the Spanish. Badly damaged in the 1680 Pueblo Revolt, the structure was restored and enlarged in 1710. On display in the chapel are priceless statues and paintings and the San José Bell, weighing nearly 800 pounds, which is believed to have been cast in Spain in 1356. In winter the church sometimes closes before its official closing hour. Latin mass is held daily at 2 pm, and new mass is on Sunday at 5 pm. ⊠ *401 Old Santa Fe Trail, Old Santa Fe Trail and South Capitol* ☎ *505/983– 3974* ⊕ *www.sanmiguelchapel.org.*

★ Santa Fe School of Cooking

LOCAL INTEREST | If you'd like to bring the flavors of the Southwest to your own kitchen, consider taking one of the wildly popular and fun cooking classes at the Santa Fe School of Cooking. Regular classes are taught during the day, with some evening classes available. More elaborate courses include the three-day Southwest Culinary Boot Camp and five-day New Mexico Culture & Cuisine tour, where participants travel around the state meeting farmers, winemakers, chefs, and more. There are also the ever-popular walking tours of Santa Fe's most notable restaurants, which usually include special visits with the chefs. Reservations are advised. The school also operates an online market where you can purchase all sorts of New Mexico culinary goods and gifts, and virtual classes are also available. ⊠ *125 N. Guadalupe St., West of the Plaza* ☎ *505/983–4511, 800/982–4688* ⊕ *www. santafeschoolofcooking.com*.

 Restaurants

Bouche

$$$ | FRENCH | Talented chef-owner Charles Dale (who previously cooked at Rancho Encantado's Terra, Daniel Boulud's Le Cirque, and at his own James Beard–lauded Renaissance restaurant in Aspen) operates this lively, modern take on a traditional French neighborhood bistro. Choose a cozy table by the fireplace and try the consistently stellar renditions of classic escargots, sautéed sweetbreads with local mushrooms, and pomme frites—prices are more than fair compared with similarly upscale eateries around town. **Known for:** fresh oysters and seafood; charming outdoor patio; tiramisu for dessert. ⑤ *Average main: $30* ⊠ *451 W. Alameda St., West of the Plaza* ☎ *505/982–6297* ⊕ *www.bouchebistro.com* ⊗ *Closed Sun. and Mon. No lunch.*

Bumble Bee's Baja Grill

$ | MEXICAN | FAMILY | A bright, vibrantly colored restaurant with closely spaced tables, piñatas, and ceiling fans whirling overhead, Bumble Bee's (the nickname of the ebullient owner, Bob) delights locals with its superfresh Cal Mex–style food. If you like fish tacos, the mahimahi ones with creamy, nondairy slaw are outstanding; try them with a side of salad instead of beans and rice. **Known for:** Baja-style mahimahi tacos; lots of vegan and vegetarian options; Mexican chocolate brownie. ⑤ *Average main: $10* ⊠ *301 Jefferson St., West of the Plaza* ☎ *505/820–2862* ⊕ *www. bumblebeesbajagrill.com*.

★ Dolina Cafe & Bakery

$ | CAFÉ | Slovakian transplant Annamaria O'Brien's bustling bakery and brunch spot is as bright and crisp as her food. The menu borrows a bit from the chef's Eastern European roots with favorites such as paprikash, langos, and goulash, but also features regional American dishes like cornmeal waffles with buttermilk fried chicken and a surprising bone broth "morning soup". **Known for:** Eastern European pastries; eclectic and hearty breakfast-brunch fare; farm-fresh local ingredients. ⑤ *Average main: $12* ⊠ *402 N. Guadalupe St., West of the Plaza* ☎ *505/982–9394* ⊕ *www.dolina-santafe.com* ⊗ *No dinner.*

The interior of San Miguel Mission, the oldest church in America, still reflects its 1610 origins.

★ Fire & Hops

$ | **ECLECTIC** | Tucked inside a cozy house on busy Guadalupe Street, Fire & Hops turns out some of the most flavorful, local, seasonal, and affordable gastropub-style food in Santa Fe while also offering a stellar list of craft beers from regional breweries such as Bosque, Bow & Arrow, Le Cumbre, Marble, and Ex Novo. Fire & Hops also features an extensive wine and cider list, and reserves a tap for hard kombucha crafted by celebrated local producer HoneyMoon Brewery. **Known for:** upscale pub food with an Asian flair; small plates like crispy fried Brussels sprouts; house-made ice cream in unusual flavors. $ *Average main: $14* ✉ *222 N. Guadalupe St., West of the Plaza* ☎ *505/954–1635* ⊕ *www. fireandhopsgastropub.com* ☽ *No lunch.*

★ Restaurant Martin

$$$$ | **MODERN AMERICAN** | Having cooked at some of the best restaurants in town (Geronimo, the Old House, Anasazi), acclaimed James Beard–nominated chef Martin Rios now flexes his culinary muscles in his own place, a simple, elegant restaurant with a gorgeous patio. Rios prepares progressive American cuisine, which is heavily influenced by his French culinary training. **Known for:** daily-changing vegetarian tasting plate; lovely Sunday brunch; attractively landscaped patio. $ *Average main: $32* ✉ *526 Galisteo St., Old Santa Fe Trail and South Capitol* ☎ *505/820–0919* ⊕ *www. restaurantmartin.com* ☽ *Closed Mon. year-round and Tues. Jan.–May.*

Sabor Peruano

$ | PERUVIAN | FAMILY | Among the more unlikely locales for a exceptionally good Peruvian lunch or early dinner, this lively eatery decorated with colorful Andes textiles, paintings, and crafts occupies a windowless (but well-lighted) space inside humdrum DeVargas shopping center. The authentic food here relies heavily on organic ingredients, and many vegetarian and vegan options are offered, including avocados stuffed with olives, peppers, cherry tomatoes, and other vegetables. **Known for:** excellent causa rellena limena (a layered dish of potatoes, lime, yellow chiles, chicken, and avocado); on-site boutique selling Peruvian arts and crafts; early closing at 5 pm. ⑤ *Average main: $12* ⌧ *DeVargas Center, 163 Paseo de Peralta, West of the Plaza* ☎ *505/358–3829* ⊕ *www.saborperuanosf.com* ⊗ *Closed Sun.*

Santacafé

$$$ | MODERN AMERICAN | Owner Quinn Stephenson (who also owns fine dining institution Coyote Cafe) recently reopened this long-acclaimed member of Santa Fe's culinary vanguard with a lighter menu focused on fresh, fusion cuisine, and it remains one of Santa Fe's must-eat destinations. The minimalist, elegant restaurant is located two blocks north of the Plaza in the historic Padre Gallegos House and offers inventive dishes such as Maine lobster rolls with tarragon butter, spring pea and mint soup, and pan-seared salmon with roasted orange and fennel. **Known for:** one of the city's old-world dining institutions; fantastic patio popular with locals and visitors alike; fun happy hour. ⑤ *Average main: $28* ⌧ *231 Washington Ave., The Plaza* ☎ *505/984–1788* ⊕ *www.santacafe.com* ⊗ *No lunch Sun.*

Taco Fundación

$ | MEXICAN | FAMILY | Tasty and affordable regional Mexican-style tacos, with soft corn tortillas, are the name of the game at this hip fast-food joint where you order at the counter and enjoy your meal in the tiny no-frills dining area or outside at a wooden picnic table or covered bench (or, as many locals do, in your car). You'll find nearly 20 taco fillings—fried squash blossom, goat, bison, al pastor (roasted marinated pork with pineapple), and shrimp are among the best—plus rice bowls, burritos, and sides of guacamole and pinto beans. **Known for:** huge variety of taco fillings; Mexican soft-serve ice cream; no alcohol and early 7 pm closing (5 pm on Sunday). ⑤ *Average main: $9* ⌧ *235 N. Guadalupe St., West of the Plaza* ☎ *505/982–8286* ⊕ *www.facebook.com/tacofundacionsf.*

TerraCotta Wine Bistro

$$ | **WINE BAR** | This reasonably priced, warmly decorated bistro and wine bar occupies a cozy late-19th-century Territorial-style house near the O'Keeffe Museum. The menu favors snacking and sharing—salmon salad with pomegranate vinaigrette, bruschetta with Brie and fig-port jam, flatbread pizzas, panini, grilled flank steak. **Known for:** bruschetta with a variety of toppings; panini sandwiches; terrific wine list. ⑤ *Average main: $21 ⊠ 304 Johnson St., The Plaza ☎ 505/989–1166 ⊕ www.terracottawinebistro.com ⊘ No lunch Sun.*

 Hotels

Casa Culinaria

$$$ | **B&B/INN** | Known as the "Gourmet Inn," this is one of the city's most charming little finds, an exquisitely landscaped and attractively decorated compound on a pretty residential street a half-mile south of the Plaza. **Pros:** some units have fully equipped kitchens; the owners offer superb breakfasts and cooking classes; lush gardens. **Cons:** occasional noise from nearby elementary school; about a 10-minute walk from Downtown; not too much to do in the immediate vicinity. ⑤ *Rooms from: $217 ⊠ 617 Don Gaspar Ave., Old Santa Fe Trail and South Capitol ☎ 505/986–8664, 888/986–8664 ⊕ www.ccsantafe.com ➷ 12 rooms ⑩ Free Breakfast.*

★ Campanilla Compound

$$$ | **RENTAL** | **FAMILY** | This luxurious, secluded, yet centrally located tract of about 15 spacious one- and-two-bedroom vacation rentals is located on a hill just north of Downtown. **Pros:** perfect for extended stays; beautiful furnishings and high-end appliances; close to Plaza but still very private. **Cons:** the walk from Plaza is uphill; there's a two-night minimum stay; can book up well in advance in summer. ⑤ *Rooms from: $250 ⊠ 334 Otero St., North Side ☎ 505/988–7585 ⊕ www.campanillacompound.com ➷ 15 units ⑩ No meals.*

Drury Plaza Hotel

$$$ | **HOTEL** | **FAMILY** | One of Downtown Santa Fe's largest and most impressive hotels, this LEED-certified upscale property with a expansive rooftop bar and pool is located next to St. Francis Cathedral inside the masterfully transformed Territorial Revival–style former St. Vincent's Hospital. **Pros:** beautiful, light-filled public spaces; steps from Canyon Road and the Plaza; spacious rooms. **Cons:** parking is valet only and costs $16; some room amenities are a bit ordinary for an upscale hotel; large events can make things a bit busy. $ *Rooms from: $259* ✉ *828 Paseo de Peralta, The Plaza* ☎ *505/424–2175* ⊕ *www.druryhotels.com* ⤵ *182 rooms* ⦿ *Free Breakfast.*

El Farolito

$$ | B&B/INN | All the beautiful Southwestern and Mexican furniture in this small, upscale compound is custom-made, and all the art and photography is original. **Pros:** excellent breakfast; half of the casitas have private patios, and half have shared patio areas; ample free off-street parking. **Cons:** no on-site pool or hot tub; about a 10-minute walk to the Plaza; a bit of neighborhood noise. $ *Rooms from: $195* ✉ *514 Galisteo St., Old Santa Fe Trail and South Capitol* ☎ *505/988–1631, 888/634–8782* ⊕ *www.farolito. com* ⤵ *8 rooms* ⦿ *Free Breakfast.*

Fort Marcy Suites

$$ | RENTAL | FAMILY | On a bluff just a 10-minute walk northeast of the Plaza with great views, this large, older compound comprises individually furnished units that accommodate two to six guests and come with full kitchens and wood fireplaces. **Pros:** nice views of the Sangre de Cristo range; handy amenities for extended stays; good value. **Cons:** not especially fancy; some decor is a bit dated; uphill walk from the Plaza. $ *Rooms from: $135* ✉ *321 Kearney Ave., North Side* ☎ *505/988–2800* ⊕ *www.allseasonsresortlodging.com* ⤵ *100 units* ⦿ *No meals.*

Inn at Vanessie

$$ | B&B/INN | The large rooms in this handsome adobe compound 2½ blocks from the Plaza are decorated with reed shutters, antique pine beds, viga-beam ceilings, hand-stenciled artwork, wood or brick floors, and a blend of cowboy, Hispanic, and Native American art and artifacts. **Pros:** elegant decor; free parking; popular restaurant and live-music venue next door. **Cons:** overlooks a parking lot; pet-friendly rooms are suites only; comes with resort fee. $ *Rooms from: $140* ✉ *427 W. Water St., West of the Plaza* ☎ *505/984–1193* ⊕ *www.vanessiesantafe.com* ⤵ *21 rooms* ⦿ *Free Breakfast.*

★ Inn of the Five Graces

$$$$ | B&B/INN | There isn't another property in Santa Fe to compare to this sumptuous yet relaxed inn with an unmistakable East-meets-West feel. **Pros:** tucked into a quiet, ancient neighborhood; loads of cushy perks and in-room amenities; fantastic staff—attentive but not overbearing. **Cons:** very steep rates; a short walk to downtown; can hear faint city noise from certain rooms. $ *Rooms from: $675* ✉ *150 E. DeVargas St., Old Santa Fe Trail and South Capitol* ☎ *505/992–0957, 866/992–0957* ⊕ *www.fivegraces.com* ⤵ *26 rooms* ⦿ *Free Breakfast.*

★ Inn of the Turquoise Bear

$$$ | B&B/INN | In the 1920s, poet Witter Bynner played host to an eccentric circle of artists and intellectuals, as well as some wild parties in his mid-19th-century Spanish–Pueblo Revival home, which is now a superb bed-and-breakfast with a great location a few blocks from the capitol; in sum, it's the quintessential Santa Fe inn. **Pros:** gorgeous grounds and a house steeped in local history; gracious, knowledgeable staff; generous gourmet breakfasts. **Cons:** no pool or hot tub on-site; quirky layout of some rooms isn't for everyone; about a 15-minute walk to the Plaza. $ *Rooms from: $220* ⊠ *342 E. Buena Vista, Old Santa Fe Trail and South Capitol* ☎ 505/983–0798, 800/396–4104 ⊕ *www.turquoisebear.com* ⤵ *9 rooms* ❖ *Free Breakfast.*

Inn on the Paseo

$$ | B&B/INN | This handily situated inn has fairly simple, if in some cases compact, rooms, but they're clean and light, some have hardwood floors, and all have pleasing Southwestern furnishings and color schemes—the best units even have fireplaces and private patios. **Pros:** just a few blocks from the Plaza; friendly, helpful staff; old buildings have unique Southwest character. **Cons:** some rooms facing the road; can have some traffic noise; certain rooms can be small. $ *Rooms from: $155* ⊠ *630 Paseo de Peralta, The Plaza* ☎ 505/984–8200 ⊕ *https://www.innonthepaseo.com* ⤵ *18 rooms* ❖ *Free Breakfast.*

Las Palomas

$$$ | B&B/INN | It's a pleasant 10-minute walk west of the Plaza to reach this group of properties consisting of a few historic, luxurious compounds, one of them Spanish Pueblo–style adobe, another done in the Territorial style, and others ranging from rooms in renovated Victorian houses to contemporary condos with up to three bedrooms. **Pros:** kid-friendly, with swings and a play yard; free Downtown shuttle service; most units feel very private and self-contained. **Cons:** big variations among the accommodations; no hot tub or pool on-site (guests may use pool at the Hotel Santa Fe); location requires transport to most local sights. $ *Rooms from: $250* ⊠ *460 W. San Francisco St., West of the Plaza* ☎ 505/982–5560, 855/982–5560 ⊕ *www.laspalomas.com* ⤵ *50 casitas* ❖ *Free Breakfast.*

Pueblo Bonito B&B Inn

$$ | B&B/INN | Rooms in this reasonably priced 1873 adobe compound have handmade and hand-painted furnishings, Navajo weavings, brick and hardwood floors, sand paintings and pottery, locally carved *santos* (Catholic saints), and Western art. **Pros:** intimate, cozy inn on peaceful grounds; excellent value; hearty

breakfasts. **Cons:** bathrooms tend to be small; on a slightly noisy street; short walk to major sights. ⑤ *Rooms from: $150* ⊠ *138 W. Manhattan Ave., Old Santa Fe Trail and South Capitol* ☎ *505/984–8001, 800/461–4599* ⊕ *www.pueblobonitoinn.com* ⊅ *19 rooms* ⦿ *Breakfast.*

 Performing Arts

Center for Contemporary Arts (CCA)

ART GALLERIES—ARTS | The city's most interesting multiuse arts venue, the Center for Contemporary Arts (CCA) presents indie and foreign films, art exhibitions, provocative theater, and countless workshops and lectures. ⊠ *1050 Old Pecos Trail, Old Santa Fe Trail and South Capitol* ☎ *505/982–1338* ⊕ *www.ccasantafe.org.*

Santa Fe Playhouse

THEATER | The oldest extant theater company west of the Mississippi, the Santa Fe Playhouse occupies a converted 19th-century adobe stable and has been presenting an adventurous mix of avant-garde pieces, classical drama, and musical comedy since 1922—the season runs year-round. The Fiesta Melodrama—a spoof of the Santa Fe scene—pokes sly fun from late August to mid-September. ⊠ *142 E. De Vargas St., Old Santa Fe Trail and South Capitol* ☎ *505/988–4262* ⊕ *www.santafeplayhouse.org.*

THE EAST SIDE WITH CANYON ROAD AND MUSEUM HILL

Updated by
Zibby Wilder

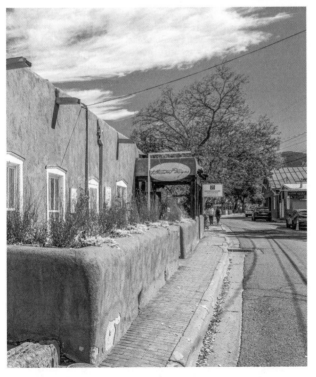

⊙ Sights　🍴 Restaurants　🛏 Hotels　🛍 Shopping　🍸 Nightlife
★★★★★　★★★☆☆　★★★☆☆　★★★★☆　★★☆☆☆

NEIGHBORHOOD SNAPSHOT

TOP EXPERIENCES

■ **Stroll down Canyon Road:** Spend the day walking up and down Canyon Road enjoying the street's many art galleries, sculpture gardens, lifestyle shops, and some of the city's best restaurants.

■ **Take a hike:** The East Side's Dale Ball Trail system—with options for both short and long hikes—makes for a great way to experience Santa Fe's wild beauty.

■ **Spend an afternoon in a museum (or four):** Family-friendly Museum Hill offers something intriguing for nearly every age and interest.

■ **Appreciate the natural beauty:** Make time for a visit to the Santa Fe Botanical Garden, which features beautiful and unexpected plant combinations showcasing the vast possibilities of low-water landscaping.

GETTING HERE AND AROUND

The winding roads of this historic area are great for walking, but some sections can be a bit of a hike from Downtown. Parking is limited on Canyon Road itself, but there are a few small lots drivers can use. Another good option is to park along Alameda, which is parallel to Canyon and has some access bridges. The attractions on Museum Hill have plenty of free parking and are far enough from Downtown that driving is the best option, though some hotels offer free shuttles to the area. A great alternative for both areas is the city's free "Santa Fe Pick-Up" shuttle, which runs Canyon Road and Museum Hill routes daily from Downtown, approximately every 30 minutes.

QUICK BITES

■ **Craft Donuts and Coffee.** This stationary food truck can have long lines, but it's worth the wait for the made-to-order doughnuts and delicious coffee. ⊠ *502 Old Santa Fe Trail* ⊕ *www.craft-donutsf.com*

■ **Downtown Subscription.** A great, friendly spot to people-watch, this café-news-stand sells coffees, snacks, and pastries, plus one of the largest assortments of newspapers and magazines in town. It has lovely outdoor spaces to sit during warm weather. ⊠ *376 Garcia St.*

■ **Santa Fe BBQ.** This big red food truck is a constant along Old Santa Fe Trail, serving up quick and delicious New Mexico–style BBQ. ⊠ *502 Old Santa Fe Trail* ⊕ *www.santafebbq.com*

The historic neighborhoods of the East Side are infinitely walkable and a slow stroll makes for a great way to experience Santa Fe's famous pueblo revival architecture.

While most buildings in the city are required to adhere to this style, it is in the East Side neighborhoods where you will find true historic adobe homes, made of earthen bricks, versus newer concrete and stucco finishes. Even where facades are crumbling, a peek of adobe just adds to the charm. Topping these East Side neighborhoods, Museum Hill has spectacular vistas and, of course, is a culture haven thanks to its impressive museums; it also serves as a gateway to the many walking and hiking trails that line the foothills of the Sangre de Christos.

The East Side is anchored by Canyon Road. Once a trail used by indigenous people to access water and the lush forest in the foothills east of town, then a route for Hispanic woodcutters and their burros, and for most of the 20th century a prosaic residential street with only a gas station and a general store, Canyon Road today is lined with nearly 100 mostly upscale art galleries along with a handful of shops and restaurants. The narrow road begins at the eastern curve of Paseo de Peralta and stretches for about 2 miles uphill at a moderate incline. Upper Canyon Road (past East Alameda) is narrow and residential, with access to hiking and biking trails along the way, and the Randall Davey Audubon Center at the far east end.

There are few places as festive as Canyon Road on Christmas Eve, when thousands of *farolitos* illuminate walkways, walls, roofs, and even trees. In May the scent of lilacs wafts over the adobe walls, and in August red hollyhocks enhance the surreal color of the blue sky on a dry summer day.

What used to be the outskirts of town became the site of gracious, neo-Pueblo style homes in the mid-20th century, many of them designed by the famed architect John Gaw Meem. Elsewhere on neighboring streets in the East Side, you'll find a few bed-and-breakfasts as well as the beautifully situated campus of St. John's College, but this part of town is mostly residential. Old Santa Fe Trail, part of the long-traveled commercial route that connected the region to the Midwest and Mexico City (via El Camino

Real), takes you to Camino Lejo, aka Museum Hill, where you'll find four excellent museums, a botanical garden, and a café.

Sights

Art of Russia Gallery

MUSEUM | The art communities of Santa Fe and Taos have a surprisingly strong connection with those of Russia, and this Canyon Road space carries a particularly strong collection of works by contemporary and historic Russian artists, including a number of Impressionist paintings. A highlight here is the selection of USSR propaganda posters. ⊠ *225 Canyon Rd., #5, East Side and Canyon Road* ☎ *505/466–1718* ⊕ *www.artofrussiagallery.com* ۞ *Closed Sun. and Tues.*

Bellas Artes

GARDEN | A sophisticated gallery with a serene sculpture garden, Bellas Artes has a captivating collection of ceramics, paintings, photography, and sculptural work, and represents internationally renowned artists like Judy Pfaff, David Kimball Anderson, and Olga de Amaral. The vanguard modernist work of sculptor Ruth Duckworth is also well represented. ⊠ *653 Canyon Rd., East Side and Canyon Road* ☎ *505/983–2745* ⊕ *www.bellasartesgallery.com* ۞ *Closed Sun. and Mon.*

Cristo Rey Church

RELIGIOUS SITE | Built in 1940 and designed by legendary Santa Fe architect John Gaw Meem to commemorate the 400th anniversary of Francisco Vásquez de Coronado's exploration of the Southwest, this church is the largest Spanish adobe structure in the United States and is considered by some to be the finest example of Pueblo-style architecture anywhere. The church was constructed in the old-fashioned way by parishioners, who mixed the more than 200,000 mud-and-straw adobe bricks and hauled them into place. The 225-ton white stone *reredos* (altar screen) is magnificent. ⊠ *1120 Canyon Rd., East Side and Canyon Road* ☎ *505/983–8528* ⊕ *www.cristoreyparish.org* ⊠ *Free.*

El Zaguan

GARDEN | Headquarters of the **Historic Santa Fe Foundation (HSFF)**, this 19th-century Territorial-style house has a small exhibit on Santa Fe architecture and preservation, but the real draw is the small but stunning garden abundant with lavender, roses, and mid-19th-century trees. You can relax on a wrought-iron bench and take in the fine views of the hills northeast of town. The HSFF is a wealth of information on Santa Fe's historic properties, offering a great brochure for self-guided walking tours. They also

The Art of Santa Fe

The artistic roots of Santa Fe stretch back to the landscape and the devotion of those who roamed and settled here long before the Santa Fe Trail transplanted goods and people from the eastern half of the nation. The intricate designs on Native American pottery and baskets, the embroidery on the ritual dance wear, the color and pattern on Rio Grande weavings, and the delicate paintings and carvings of devotional images called santos all contributed to the value and awareness of beauty that Santa Fe holds as its cultural birthright. The rugged landscape, the ineffable quality of the light, and the community itself continue to draw to Santa Fe a plethora of musicians, writers, and visual artists.

While holding strong in its regional art identity, Santa Fe has also steadily emerged into a more international art scene. Native American and Hispanic arts groups now include the work of contemporary artists who have pressed beyond the bounds of tradition. Bold color and the oft-depicted New Mexico landscape are still evident, but you're just as likely to see mixed-media collages by a Chinese artist currently living in San Francisco. And just as Santa Fe welcomed early modernist painters who responded to the open landscape and the artistic freedom it engendered, contemporary artists working with edgier media, such as conceptual, performance, and installation art, are finding welcoming venues in Santa Fe, specifically at SITE Santa Fe museum and the contemporary galleries in the surrounding Railyard District.

sponsor monthly Salon El Zaguán lectures and rotating exhibits. ⊠ *545 Canyon Rd., East Side and Canyon Road* ☎ *505/983–2567* ⊕ *www.historicsantafe.org* 🎟 *Free* ⊙ *Office closed weekends, garden closed Sun.*

Gerald Peters Gallery

MUSEUM | While under construction, this 32,000-square-foot building was dubbed the "ninth northern pueblo," its scale supposedly rivaling that of the eight northern pueblos around Santa Fe. The suavely designed Pueblo-style gallery is now Santa Fe's premier showcase for American and European art from the 19th century to the present. It feels like a museum, but all the works are for sale. ⊠ *1005 Paseo de Peralta, East Side and Canyon Road* ☎ *505/954–5700* ⊕ *www.gpgallery.com* 🎟 *Free* ⊙ *Closed Sun.*

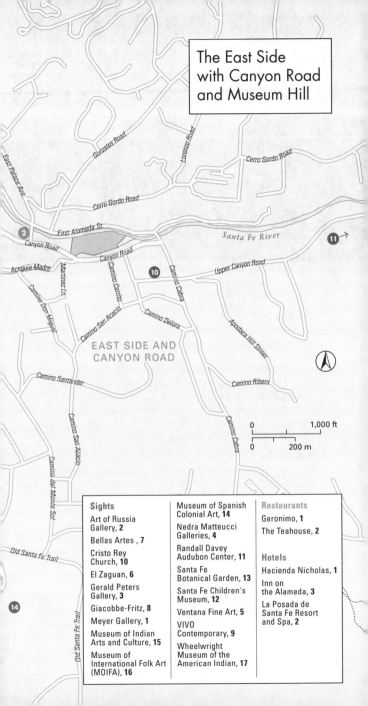

The East Side
with Canyon Road
and Museum Hill

EAST SIDE AND CANYON ROAD

| 0 | | 1,000 ft |
| 0 | | 200 m |

Sights

Art of Russia Gallery, **2**

Bellas Artes , **7**

Cristo Rey Church, **10**

El Zaguan, **6**

Gerald Peters Gallery, **3**

Giacobbe-Fritz, **8**

Meyer Gallery, **1**

Museum of Indian Arts and Culture, **15**

Museum of International Folk Art (MOIFA), **16**

Museum of Spanish Colonial Art, **14**

Nedra Matteucci Galleries, **4**

Randall Davey Audubon Center, **11**

Santa Fe Botanical Garden, **13**

Santa Fe Children's Museum, **12**

Ventana Fine Art, **5**

VIVO Contemporary, **9**

Wheelwright Museum of the American Indian, **17**

Restaurants

Geronimo, **1**

The Teahouse, **2**

Hotels

Hacienda Nicholas, **1**

Inn on the Alameda, **3**

La Posada de Santa Fe Resort and Spa, **2**

The Museum of International Folk Art features a wide variety of art, much of it handmade and often reflecting shared cultural traditions.

Giacobbe-Fritz

MUSEUM | Stop inside this late-1890s adobe building to admire a truly diverse collection of paintings, drawings, and sculpture, much of it with a regional and traditional approach, including impressionist New Mexico landscapes by Connie Dillman and whimsical bronze sculptures of burros, bats, and other animals by Copper Tritscheller. The owners also operate the excellent GF Contemporary, across the street, which focuses more on modern and abstract works. ⊠ *702 Canyon Rd., East Side and Canyon Road* ☎ *505/986–1156* ⊕ *www.giacobbefritz.com.*

Meyer Gallery

MUSEUM | One of the oldest and most prestigious galleries in the Southwest, Meyer's location at the bottom of Canyon Road makes it a good place to begin a stroll up the historic street. The work shown in this expansive gallery gives a good sense of the traditional Santa Fe art scene along with an eclectic selection of modern works focused on contemporary realism, including the likes of Milt Kobayashi and William C. Hook. ⊠ *225 Canyon Rd., #14, East Side and Canyon Road* ☎ *800/779–7387* ⊕ *www.meyergalleries.com.*

Museum of Indian Arts and Culture

MUSEUM | An interactive, multimedia exhibition tells the story of Native American history in the Southwest, merging contemporary Native American experience with historical accounts and artifacts. The collection includes some of New Mexico's oldest works of art: pottery vessels, fine stone and silver jewelry, intricate textiles, and other arts and crafts created by Pueblo,

Navajo, and Apache artisans. Changing exhibitions feature arts and traditions of historic and contemporary Native Americans. You can also see art demonstrations and a video about the life and work of Pueblo potter Maria Martinez. ⊠ *710 Camino Lejo, Museum Hill* ☎ *505/476–1269* ⊕ *www.indianartsandculture.org* ⊠ *$12* ☉ *Closed Mon. in Nov.–May.*

★ Museum of International Folk Art (MOIFA)

MUSEUM | **FAMILY** | A delight for adults and children alike, this museum is the best institution of its kind in the world, with a permanent collection of more than 130,000 objects from about 100 countries. In the Girard Wing, you'll find thousands of amazingly inventive handmade objects, like a tin Madonna, a devil made from bread dough, dolls from around the world, and miniature village scenes. The Hispanic Heritage Wing rotates exhibitions of art from throughout Latin America, dating from New Mexico's Spanish-colonial period (1598–1821) to the present. The exhibits in the Neutrogena Wing rotate, showing subjects ranging from outsider art to the magnificent quilts of Gee's Bend. Lloyd's Treasure Chest, the wing's innovative basement section, provides a behind-the-scenes look at the museum's permanent collection and explores the question of what exactly constitutes folk art. The innovative Gallery of Conscience explores topics at the intersection of folk art and social justice. Each exhibition also includes educational activities for both kids and adults. Allow time to visit the outstanding gift shop and bookstore. ⊠ *706 Camino Lejo, Museum Hill* ☎ *505/476–1200* ⊕ *www.internationalfolkart.org* ⊠ *$12* ☉ *Closed Mon. in Nov.–Apr.*

Museum of Spanish Colonial Art

MUSEUM | This 5,000-square-foot adobe museum occupies a classically Southwestern former home designed in 1930 by acclaimed regional architect John Gaw Meem. The Spanish Colonial Art Society formed in Santa Fe in 1925 to preserve traditional Spanish-colonial art and culture, and the museum, which sits next to the Museum of International Folk Art and the Museum of Indian Arts and Culture complex, displays the fruits of the society's labor: one of the most comprehensive collections of Spanish-colonial art in the world. The more than 3,700 objects here, dating from the 16th century to the present, include retablos, elaborate santos, tinwork, straw appliqué, furniture, ceramics, and ironwork. The contemporary collection of works by New Mexico Hispanic artists helps put all this history into regional context. The museum also hosts national traveling shows and its gift shop features artwork from participants in Santa Fe's yearly Spanish Market. ⊠ *750 Camino Lejo, Museum Hill* ☎ *505/982–2226* ⊕ *www.spanishcolonial. org* ⊠ *$10* ☉ *Closed Mon. in Sept.–May.*

Nedra Matteucci Galleries

MUSEUM | One of the Southwest's premier galleries, Matteucci Galleries exhibits works by California regionalists, members of the early Taos and Santa Fe schools, and masters of American impressionism and modernism. Spanish-colonial furniture, Indian antiquities, and a fantastic sculpture garden are other draws of this well-respected establishment. The old adobe building that the gallery is in is a beautifully preserved example of Santa Fe–style architecture. Matteucci also owns Morning Star Gallery around the corner at 513 Canyon Road. ⊠ *1075 Paseo de Peralta, East Side and Canyon Road* ☎ *505/982–4631* ⊕ *www.matteucci.com* ⊗ *Closed Sun.*

★ Randall Davey Audubon Center

NATURE PRESERVE | **FAMILY** | At the end of Upper Canyon Road, located at the mouth of the canyon as it wends into the foothills, the 135-acre Randall Davey Audubon Center harbors diverse birds (nearly 200 species have been identified) and other wildlife. Free guided nature walks are given most Saturday mornings at 8:30; there are also two major hiking trails that you can tackle on your own. The home and studio of Randall Davey, a prolific early Santa Fe artist, can be toured on Friday afternoons. There's also a nature bookstore. ⊠ *1800 Upper Canyon Rd., East Side and Canyon Road* ☎ *505/983–4609* ⊕ *randalldavey.audubon.org* ▨ *Docent-led tours of the historic Randall Davey House and Studio $5* ⊗ *Closed Sun.*

Santa Fe Botanical Garden

GARDEN | This 14-acre garden across the street from Milner Plaza's parking lot provides another great reason for exploring the Museum Hill neighborhood outside of the collections in its four world-class museums. Situated on a bluff with fantastic views of the surrounding mountains, the facility is divided into four sections that emphasize distinct elements of New Mexico's flora and terrain: the Orchard Gardens, Ojos y Manos: Eyes and Hands, the Courtyard Gardens, and the Arroyo Trails. You can gain a much fuller sense of what's planted and why by embarking on one of the free guided tours, offered daily (call for hours). The organization also operates 35-acre Leonora Curtin Wetland Preserve on 27283 I–25 West Frontage Road (next to El Rancho de las Golondrinas), which is open spring through fall—check the SFBG website for more information. ⊠ *725 Camino Lejo, Museum Hill* ☎ *505/471–9103* ⊕ *www.santafebotanicalgarden.org* ▨ *Apr.–Oct. $10; Nov.–Mar. $7* ⊗ *Closed Mon.–Wed. in Nov.–Mar.*

Santa Fe Children's Museum

MUSEUM | **FAMILY** | Stimulating hands-on exhibits, a solar greenhouse, oversize geometric forms, and an 18-foot indoor

The exterior of the Wheelwright Museum of the American Indian is shaped like a traditional octagonal Navajo hogan.

rock-climbing wall all contribute to this museum's popularity with kids. Outdoor gardens with climbing structures, forts, and hands-on activities are great for whiling away the time in the shade of big trees. Puppeteers and storytellers perform often. ⊠ *1050 Old Pecos Trail, Old Santa Fe Trail and South Capitol* ☎ *505/989–8359* ⊕ *www.santafechildrensmuseum.org* 🖃 *$8* ⊘ *Closed Mon. year-round and Tues. Sept.–May.*

Ventana Fine Art

MUSEUM | Set in a dramatic and expansive Victorian redbrick schoolhouse on Canyon Road, Ventana has been at the forefront of Santa Fe's constantly shifting contemporary art scene since the mid-1980s. The gallery represents notable talents like Doug Dawson, John Axton, John Nieto, and Marshall Noice, and is surrounded by lovely sculpture gardens. ⊠ *400 Canyon Rd., East Side and Canyon Road* ☎ *505/983–8815, 800/746–8815* ⊕ *www. ventanafineart.com.*

VIVO Contemporary

ART GALLERIES | Distinct in that it focuses solely on Santa Fe artists who produce contemporary works, VIVO also offers some very interesting programming from its handsome two-level space on Canyon Road, including an annual show featuring paintings and poems together. Ilse Bolle's fiber art constructions and Warren Keating's playfully voyeuristic paintings are among the gallery's highlights. ⊠ *725 Canyon Rd., East Side and Canyon Road* ☎ *505/982–1320* ⊕ *www.vivocontemporary.com.*

★ Wheelwright Museum of the American Indian

MUSEUM | A private institution in a building shaped like a traditional octagonal Navajo hogan, the Wheelwright opened in 1937. Founded by Boston scholar Mary Cabot Wheelwright and Navajo medicine man Hastiin Klah, the museum originated as a place to house ceremonial materials. Those items were returned to the Navajo in 1977, but what remains is an incredible collection of 19th- and 20th-century baskets, pottery, sculpture, weavings, metalwork, photography, paintings, including contemporary works by Native American artists, and typically fascinating changing exhibits. The Case Trading Post on the lower level is modeled after the trading posts that dotted the Southwestern frontier more than 100 years ago. It carries an outstanding selection of books and contemporary Native American jewelry, kachina dolls, weaving, and pottery. ⊠ *704 Camino Lejo, Museum Hill* ☎ *505/982–4636* ⊕ *www.wheelwright.org* ▣ *$8.*

 Restaurants

★ Geronimo

$$$$ | **MODERN AMERICAN** | This bastion of dazzling, sophisticated contemporary cuisine occupies the historic Borrego House, built in 1756 by Geronimo Lopez, a massive-walled Canyon Road adobe with intimate white dining rooms, beamed ceilings, wood floors, fireplaces, and cushioned *bancos* (banquettes). It's one of the loveliest venues in New Mexico for a special meal, perhaps local rack of lamb with roasted leeks and a Merlot–natural jus reduction or mesquite grilled Maine lobster tails with a creamy garlic chile sauce. **Known for:** complex and sophisticated contemporary fare; setting in beautiful 18th-century Canyon Road adobe; sublime service. ⑤ *Average main: $42* ⊠ *724 Canyon Rd., East Side and Canyon Road* ☎ *505/982–1500* ⊕ *www.geronimorestaurant.com* ☉ *No lunch.*

The Teahouse

$$ | **CAFÉ** | **FAMILY** | A delightful spot toward the end of gallery row at the intersection of Canyon Road and East Palace Avenue, the Teahouse has several bright dining rooms throughout the converted adobe home, and a tranquil outdoor seating area in a rock garden. In addition to fine teas from all over the world, you can find extremely well-prepared breakfast, lunch, and dinner options, including baked polenta with poached eggs and romesco sauce, bagels and lox, and wild-mushroom panini. **Known for:** fine teas and coffees; serene garden seating; delicious breakfasts. ⑤ *Average main: $15* ⊠ *821 Canyon Rd., East Side and Canyon Road* ☎ *505/992–0972* ⊕ *www.teahousesantafe.com.*

Hotels

⭐ Hacienda Nicholas

$$ | **B&B/INN** | This classic Santa Fe hacienda is just blocks from the Plaza yet set in a quiet residential area and sheltered from outside noises by thick adobe walls. **Pros:** reasonable rates for such a lovely, upscale inn; the inn uses eco-friendly products and practices; delicious food. **Cons:** no hot tub or pool, but guests have privileges for a minimal charge at El Gancho Health Club (a 15-minute drive); located in residential area so not much around; some rooms are a bit small. ⓢ *Rooms from: $175 ⊠ 320 E. Marcy St., East Side and Canyon Road* ☎ *505/986–1431, 888/284–3170* ⊕ *www.haciendan-icholas.com* ⌅ *7 rooms* ⅠⓄⅠ *Free Breakfast.*

⭐ Inn on the Alameda

$$ | **HOTEL** | Within an easy walk of both the Plaza and Canyon Road, this midpriced charmer with spacious Southwest-style rooms is one of the city's best small hotels. **Pros:** the solicitous staff is first-rate; excellent, expansive breakfast buffet and afternoon snacks and wine; free parking. **Cons:** rooms closest to Alameda can be a bit noisy; no pool; grounds can be a challenge for strollers or wheelchairs. ⓢ *Rooms from: $189 ⊠ 303 E. Alameda St., East Side and Canyon Road* ☎ *505/984–2121, 888/984–2121* ⊕ *www.innonthealameda.com* ⌅ *72 rooms* ⅠⓄⅠ *Free Breakfast.*

La Posada de Santa Fe Resort and Spa

$$$ | **RESORT** | **FAMILY** | Rooms on the beautiful, quiet grounds of this Tribute Portfolio resort and spa vary greatly in size and configuration, but the level of luxury befits the somewhat steep rates, especially given the considerable amenities and appealing East Side location. **Pros:** numerous amenities, including a top-notch spa and restaurant; a few blocks from Plaza and similarly close to Canyon Road; a large pool. **Cons:** resort can sometimes feel crowded; daily resort fee; some rooms have street noise. ⓢ *Rooms from: $285 ⊠ 330 E. Palace Ave., East Side and Canyon Road* ☎ *505/986–0000, 855/210–7210* ⊕ *www.laposadadesantafe.com* ⌅ *157 rooms* ⅠⓄⅠ *No meals.*

🅨 Nightlife

⭐ El Farol

BARS/PUBS | With its long front portal and expansive back patio, this ancient adobe restaurant is a lovely spot to enjoy the afternoons and evenings of summer. The roomy, rustic lounge has a true Old West atmosphere—there's been a bar on the premises since 1835—and you can order some fine Spanish brandies and sherries in addition to cold beers, sangria, and margaritas, and the kitchen turns out authentic Spanish fare, from hearty paellas to lighter tapas. There's a daily happy hour from 3 to 5 pm, and it's a great place to see a variety of music, including first-rate flamenco dinner shows; the dance floor fills up with a friendly crowd. ⊠ *808 Canyon Rd., East Side and Canyon Road* ☎ *505/983–9912* ⊕ *www. elfarolsantafe.com.*

Shopping

ANTIQUES, GIFTS, AND HOME FURNISHINGS

★ Cielo Handcrafted

LOCAL SPECIALTIES | This family-run lifestyle gallery specializes in goods produced by local artists and craftspeople including pottery, clothing, art, furniture, and home goods. Of particular interest is the stunning jewelry created by local artist Gloria Olazabal as well as the beautiful wood cutting boards and serving trays featuring inlaid turquoise by Wild Edge Woodworks. ⊠ *836 Canyon Rd., East Side and Canyon Road* ☎ *575/551–8390* ⊕ *www.cielohandcrafted.com.*

★ Hecho a Mano

CRAFTS | Focusing on handmade items from both local crafts-people and artists in Oaxaca, this lifestyle gallery offers beautiful prints, ceramics, jewelry, and more, at all price points. Owner and "Creative Conductor" Frank Rose also sells an impressive collection of prints by Mexican artists including Diego Rivera and Rufino Tamayo. ⊠ *830 Canyon Rd., East Side and Canyon Road* ☎ *505/916–1341* ⊕ *www.hechoamano.org.*

La Mesa

ANTIQUES/COLLECTIBLES | This shop has become well known for showcasing contemporary handcrafted, mostly functional, works by more than two dozen, mostly local, artists including Kathy O'Neill, Gregory Lomayesva, and Ritchie Mole. Collections include dinnerware, glassware, pottery, lighting, fine art, and accessories. ⊠ *225 Canyon Rd., East Side and Canyon Road* ☎ *505/984–1688* ⊕ *www.lamesaofsantafe.com.*

BOOKS

Garcia Street Books

BOOKS/STATIONERY | **FAMILY** | This outstanding independent shop is strong on art, architecture, cookbooks, literature, and regional Southwestern works—it's a block from the Canyon Road galleries and hosts frequent talks by authors in person and via interviews posted to the shop's website. ⊠ *376 Garcia St., East Side and Canyon Road* ☎ *505/986–0151* ⊕ *www.garciastreetbooks.com.*

4

CLOTHING
★ Homefrocks

CLOTHING | This shop features simple, yet exquisite, women's clothing designed by local artist Nancy Traugott. The natural silk and linen fabrics are colored by hand with botanical dyes, making each classic piece truly one-of-a-kind. ⊠ *550 Canyon Rd., East Side and Canyon Road* ☎ *505/986–5800* ⊕ *www.homefrocks.com.*

Nathalie

CLOTHING | There are many fans of Parisian-born owner Nathalie Kent's distinctive style and carefully curated collection of vintage and new pieces. Though Kent's passion clearly leans toward traditional Western wear, from cowboy boots to velvet skirts to exquisite Old Pawn jewelry, you'll also find gorgeous pieces from all over the globe—antique Moroccan treasures line up next to 100-year-old Navajo bracelets like long lost pals. Her home furnishings are stupendous, too. ⊠ *503 Canyon Rd., East Side and Canyon Road* ☎ *505/982–1021* ⊕ *www.nathaliesantafe.com.*

FOOD AND DRINK
★ Kakawa

FOOD/CANDY | **FAMILY** | You're unlikely to ever have tasted anything like the divine, agave-sweetened, artisanal creations that emerge from this shop. Historically accurate chocolate drinks, like the Aztec Warrior Elixir, divine caramels, and agave-sweetened, gluten-free chocolate baked goods are served in this cozy, welcoming establishment that's as much an educational experience as a chance to indulge in exceptional sweets. Another location is found south of town on Rufina Street, near Meow Wolf. ⊠ *1050 Paseo de Peralta, Santa Fe* ☎ *505/982–0388* ⊕ *www.kakawachocolates. com.*

NATIVE AMERICAN ARTS AND CRAFTS
★ Morning Star Gallery

ART GALLERIES | Owned by the prestigious Nedra Matteucci Galleries, this is a veritable museum of Native American art. An adobe shaded by a huge cottonwood tree houses antique basketry, pre-1940 Navajo silver jewelry, Northwest Coast Native American carvings, Navajo weavings, and art of the Plains Indians. Prices and quality span the spectrum, making this a great stop for both new and experienced collectors. ⊠ *513 Canyon Rd., East Side and Canyon Road* ☎ *505/982–8187* ⊕ *www.morningstargallery.com.*

★ Robert Nichols Gallery

CRAFTS | This long-running establishment on Canyon Road represents a remarkable group of Native American ceramics artists doing primarily nontraditional work. Diverse artists include Glen Nipshank, whose organic, sensuous shapes would be right at home in MoMA, and Diego Romero, whose Cochiti-style vessels are detailed with graphic-novel-style characters and sharp social commentary. It is a treat to see cutting-edge work that is clearly informed by indigenous traditions. ⊠ *419 Canyon Rd., East Side and Canyon Road* ☎ *505/982–2145* ⊕ *www.robertnicholsgallery. com.*

Activities

HIKING

Hiking around Santa Fe can take you into high-altitude alpine country or into lunaresque high desert as you head south and west to lower elevations. For winter hiking, the gentler climates to the south are less likely to be snow packed, while the alpine areas tend to require snowshoes or cross-country skis. In summer, wildflowers bloom in the high country, and the temperature is generally at least 10 degrees cooler than in town. The mountain trails accessible at the base of the Ski Santa Fe area and at nearby Hyde Memorial State Park (near the end of NM 475) stay cool on even the hottest summer days. Weather can change with one gust of wind, so be prepared with extra clothing, rain gear, food, and lots of water. Keep in mind that the sun at 10,000 feet is very powerful, even with a hat and sunscreen.

★ Atalaya Trail

HIKING/WALKING | Spurring off the Dale Ball Trail system, the steep but rewarding (and dog-friendly) Atalaya Trail runs from the visitor parking lot of St. John's College, up a winding, ponderosa pine–studded trail to the peak of Mt. Atalaya, which affords incredible 270-degree views of Santa Fe. The nearly 6-mile round-trip hike climbs almost 2,000 feet (to an elevation of 9,121 feet), so pace yourself. The good news: the return to the parking area is nearly all downhill. ⊠ *1160 Camino de Cruz Blanca, East Side and Canyon Road.*

Dale Ball Foothills Trail Network

HIKING/WALKING | A favorite spot for a ramble, with a vast system of trails, is the Dale Ball Foothills Trail Network, a 24-mile network of paths that winds and wends up through the foothills east of town and can be accessed at a few points, including Hyde Park Road (en route to the ski valley), the upper end of Canyon Road at Cerro Gordo, and from Camino de Cruz Blanca near St. John's College. There are trail maps and signs at these points, and the trails are very well marked. ⊠ *East Side and Canyon Road* ⊕ *www. sfct.org/dale-ball-trails.*

Chapter 5

THE RAILYARD DISTRICT

Updated by
Zibby Wilder

⊙ Sights   🍴 Restaurants   🛏 Hotels   🛍 Shopping   🍸 Nightlife

★★★★☆   ★★★★☆   ★★☆☆☆   ★★★★☆   ★★★★☆

NEIGHBORHOOD SNAPSHOT

TOP EXPERIENCES

■ **Search for vintage items:** One-of-a-kind treasures are waiting to be discovered at the many well-curated secondhand shops along Guadalupe Street.

■ **Shop like a local:** Around the Railyard you'll find dozens of specialty boutiques selling everything from colorful cowboy boots to local art.

■ **Plan your next meal:** Try whatever is fresh, local, and delicious at the famous Santa Fe Farmers' Market.

■ **Enjoy the city's nightlife:** Dance the night away to live music at local watering holes or the Railyard's free summer concert series.

■ **Appreciate art:** Art abounds in the Railyard District, whether it's within a big gallery, a local artist's studio, or the excellent SITE Santa Fe.

GETTING HERE AND AROUND

The Railyard District is easily accessible by car and within walking distance of Downtown. While most parking is metered street parking, there is a large parking garage, as well as a few small lots, at the Railyard itself. Walk the winding streets around the area to see some of the historic homes and buildings. The free "Santa Fe Pick-Up" shuttle also offers a historic district loop that runs around Downtown and to the Railyard, with pick-ups/drop-offs approximately every 15 minutes.

QUICK BITES

■ **El Chile Toreado.** Considered one of Santa Fe's best food trucks, El Chile Toreado offers hearty, delicious, and affordable New Mexican breakfast and lunch. ⊠ *807 Early St.* ⊕ *elchiletoreado. com*

■ **Revolution Bakery.** This gluten-free bakery serves baked goods, soups, sandwiches, and other goodies (with lots of vegan options) that are so delicious you won't miss the gluten. ⊠ *The Design Center, 418 Cerrillos Rd.* ⊕ *www.revolution-bakery.com*

■ **Whoo's Donuts.** Whoo's has developed a near-fanatical following for its traditional and creative doughnuts (think blue corn blueberry lavender and green chile apple fritter). ⊠ *851 Cerrillos Rd.* ⊕ *www.whoosdo-nuts.com*

The most significant development in Santa Fe in recent years has taken place in the Railyard District, a neighborhood just south of the Plaza that was for years called the Guadalupe District (and is occasionally still known by that name).

Comprising a few easily walked blocks along Guadalupe Street between Agua Fria and Paseo de Peralta, the district has been revitalized with a snazzy park and outdoor performance space, a permanent indoor–outdoor home for the farmers' market, and quite a few notable restaurants, shops, and galleries.

This historic warehouse and rail district endured several decades of neglect after the demise of the train route through town. But rather than tearing the buildings down (this is a city where 200-year-old mud-brick buildings sell at a premium, after all), the city, with extensive input from residents, worked with developers to gradually convert the low-lying warehouses into artists' studios, antiques shops, bookstores, indie shops, and restaurants. The Rail Runner commuter train to Albuquerque has put the rail tracks as well as the vintage mission-style depot back into use.

A central feature of the district's redevelopment is Railyard Park, at the corner of Cerrillos Road and Guadalupe Street, which was designed to highlight native plants and provide citizens with a lush, urban space. The buildings just north, in the direction of the Plaza, contain the vibrant Santa Fe Farmers' Market, the stunning SITE Santa Fe museum, art galleries, shops, restaurants, and live-work spaces for artists. This dramatic development reveals the fascinating way Santa Feans have worked to meet the needs of an expanding city while paying strict attention to the city's historic relevance.

On weekends, the Railyard District is a lively spot thanks to the ever-popular Santa Fe Farmers' Market and the Sunday Artisan Market. One could easily spend an entire day perusing the many contemporary galleries, vintage shops, and quirky boutiques that surround the Railyard. In the evenings, you can often dance the night away at free community concerts or to a live band at local nightlife staple, the Cowgirl BBQ.

Sights

Charlotte Jackson Fine Art

ARTS VENUE | This Railyard District notable focuses primarily on monochromatic "radical" painting and sculpture and is set in a fantastic, open space in a renovated warehouse. Many of the pieces here are large-scale, with "drama" the guiding force. Joe Barnes, William Metcalf, Constance DeJong, and Winston Roeth are among the artists producing minimalist works dealing with light and space. ⊠ *554 S. Guadalupe St., Railyard District* ☎ *505/989–8688* ⊕ *www.charlottejackson.com* ⊘ *Closed Sun. and Mon.*

El Museo Cultural de Santa Fe

ARTS VENUE | **FAMILY** | More an arts, educational, and community-ty gathering space than a museum, the 31,000-square-foot El Museo celebrates Santa Fe's—and New Mexico's—rich Hispanic heritage by presenting a wide range of events, from children's theater to musical concerts. It also hosts the Antique American Indian Art Show, during which dozens of craftspersons and artists exhibit their work in early August along with the Mercado, held on weekends from late September through late May and featuring an exceptional array of vendors selling folk, tribal, and Western art and memorabilia. A small gallery shows contemporary art by Hispanic artists. ⊠ *555 Camino de la Familia, Railyard District* ☎ *505/992–0591* ⊕ *www.elmuseocultural.org* ✉ *Free; prices vary for events and shows* ⊘ *Closed Sun. and Mon.*

EVOKE Contemporary

ARTS VENUE | In a striking, high-ceilinged space in the Railyard District, EVOKE ranks among the more diverse contemporary galleries in town, with works by renowned landscape painters such as Lynn Boggess and the late Louisa McElwain, outsider folk art by Nicholas Herrera, surrealist portraits by self-taught painter Jorge Santos, colorful contemporary works by "street to studio" artist Thomas Vigial, and intricate sgraffito by Alice Leora Briggs. ⊠ *550 S. Guadalupe St., Railyard District* ☎ *505/995–9902* ⊕ *www.evokecontemporary.com.*

★ LewAllen Galleries

MUSEUM | Set in a dramatic 14,000-square-foot neo-industrial building beside the farmers' market in the Railyard District, this leader in both contemporary and modern art carries works by such icons as Alexander Calder, Claes Oldenburg, and Pablo Picasso. You'll also find a dazzling collection of abstract sculpture, photography, and paintings by up-and-coming regional and international talents. ⊠ *1613 Paseo de Peralta, Railyard District* ☎ *505/988–3250* ⊕ *www.lewallengalleries.com* ⊘ *Closed Sun.*

The Santuario de Guadalupe honors the patron saint of Mexico, Our Lady of Guadalupe.

Railyard Park

CITY PARK | A 12-acre expanse that helped redefine the neighborhood, Railyard Park is an urban park with orchards, a community garden, w bird and butterfly garden, children's play areas, picnic areas, and some fantastic public art. The park runs past SITE Santa Fe to the Railyard Plaza via the walkable and bikeable "Rail Trail". ✉ *740 Cerrillos Rd., Railyard District* ☎ *505/316–3596* ⊕ *www. railyardpark.org.*

Santuario de Guadalupe

RELIGIOUS SITE | A massive-walled adobe structure built by Franciscan missionaries between 1776 and 1795, this is the oldest shrine in the United States to Our Lady of Guadalupe, Mexico's patron saint. The church's adobe walls are nearly 3 feet thick, and among the sanctuary's religious art and artifacts is a beloved image of Nuestra Virgen de Guadalupe, painted by Mexican master Jose de Alzibar in 1783. Highlights are the traditional New Mexican carved and painted altar screen called a reredos, an authentic 19th-century sacristy, a pictorial-history archive, a library devoted to Archbishop Jean Baptiste Lamy that is furnished with many of his belongings, and a garden with plants from the Holy Land. ✉ *100 Guadalupe St., Railyard District* ☎ *505/988–2027* ✎ *Donations accepted* ☉ *Closed Sun. year-round and Sat. Nov.–Apr.*

SITE Santa Fe

ARTS CENTERS | The events at this 18,000 square foot nexus of international contemporary art include lectures, concerts, author readings, films, performance art, and gallery shows. The facility also hosts a biennial exhibition, SITElines, staged every even-numbered year. Exhibitions are often provocative, and the immense, open space provides an ideal setting for the many larger-than-life installations. The on-site museum store, Curated, offers a tasteful selection of unique, artist-made items. ⊠ *1606 Paseo de Peralta, Railyard District* ☎ *505/989–1199* ⊕ *sitesantafe. org* 🎫 *$10, free on Fri.*

Zane Bennett Contemporary Art

MUSEUM | The sleek design of this airy, two-story gallery with a skylighted atrium is a fitting venue for the cutting-edge photography, paintings, sculptures, and mixed-media works within. Zane Bennett has carried works by icons (think Helen Frankenthaler, Sol LeWitt, and Richard Serra) but also presents rotating shows, including Native artist Jaune Quick-to-See Smith, the iconic feminist works of Judy Chicago, and pieces by noted American pop artist Jim Dine. ⊠ *435 S. Guadalupe St., Railyard District* ☎ *505/982–8111* ⊕ *www.zanebennettgallery.com* ☾ *Closed Sun. and Mon.*

 Restaurants

Andiamo!

$$ | **ITALIAN** | A longtime locals' favorite, Andiamo! scores high marks for its friendly staff, consistently good northern Italian food, and comfortable dining room. Produce from the farmers' market down the street adds to the seasonal surprises of this intimate restaurant set inside a sweet cottage in the Railyard District. **Known for:** crispy duck leg confit with polenta; great pizzas; charming cottage setting. ⑤ *Average main: $17* ⊠ *322 Garfield St., Railyard District* ☎ *505/995–9595* ⊕ *www.andiamosantafe.com* ☾ *No lunch weekends.*

★ Joseph's Culinary Pub

$$$ | **MODERN AMERICAN** | Chef-restauranteur Joseph Wrede has garnered countless accolades since the 1990s at various restaurants in Taos and then Santa Fe, and his current eatery—a stylish gastropub set in a vintage adobe with low beamed ceilings, slate floors, and a cozy patio—continues to showcase his considerable talents, featuring a menu of deliciously updated comfort fare. Dishes you're already familiar with receive novel twists, including caviar-topped duck fat-fried potato chips with crème fraîche, pickled onion, cured egg yolk, and caviar; and posole verde with chicken, a farm egg, tomatillos, and avocado. **Known for:** duck fat fries; excellent steak au poivre; stellar beer and wine selection. ⑤ *Average main: $30* ⊠ *428 Agua Fria St., Railyard District* ☎ *505/982–1272* ⊕ *www.josephsofsantafe.com* ☾ *No lunch.*

★ La Choza

$ | **SOUTHWESTERN** | **FAMILY** | The off-the-beaten-path and less expensive sister to the Shed located Downtown, La Choza (which means "the shed" in Spanish), serves supertasty, supertraditional New Mexican fare. It's hard to go wrong here: chicken or pork *carne adovada* (marinated in red chile and slow-cooked until tender) burritos, white clam chowder spiced with green chiles, green chile stew, and the classic huevos rancheros are exceptional. **Known for:** stuffed sopaipilla; outstanding and extensive margarita and premium-tequila list; long waits unless you make a reservation. $ *Average main: $14* ✉ *905 Alarid St., Railyard District* ☎ 505/982–0909 ⊕ *www.lachozasf.com* ⊗ *Closed Sun.*

★ Opuntia

$$ | **CAFÉ** | This modern café offers a calm breath of fresh air from the hustle and bustle of the Railyard, thanks in part to its sweeping views of downtown Santa Fe and the surrounding landscape. With a focus on house-made, locally sourced, and seasonal ingredients, the dishes aren't tied to any specific cuisine, but are crafted more to compliment Opuntia's carefully curated selection of fine teas. **Known for:** incredible selection of tea, Belgian beers, sake, wine, and ciders; creative design aesthetic that blurs indoors and outdoors; fun on-site cactus and succulent shop. $ *Average main: $16* ✉ *1607 Alcadesa St., 2nd fl., Railyard District* ☎ 505/780–5796 ⊕ *www.opuntia.cafe* ⊗ *No dinner Mon.*

★ Paloma

$$ | **MODERN MEXICAN** | A fun go-to for happy hour or an intimate dinner, this bright and bustling modern take on a Mexican cantina offers an impressive mezcal-focused cocktail program, plenty of shareable small plates, and seasonal entrées such as squash blossom enmoladas and a perfectly roasted half chicken with grilled chard, charro beans, and a classic mole poblano sauce. Street tacos—crispy Baja-style sea bass, cauliflower with marcona almonds, or lamb barbacoa with smoky adobo sauce—are another specialty, as is the remolacha salad of hibiscus beets, citrus, seasonal fruits, and frisee. **Known for:** street-food-style tacos; craft cocktails; Mexican and Tex-Mex classics. $ *Average main: $21* ✉ *401 S. Guadalupe St., Railyard District* ☎ 505/467–8624 ⊕ *www. palomasantafe.com* ⊗ *Closed Mon.*

★ Radish & Rye

$$$ | **MODERN AMERICAN** | Set in a rustic yet modern space, Radish & Rye stands out both for its deftly crafted American food and one of the best small-batch bourbon selections in the Southwest. The kitchen focuses on "farm-inspired" victuals—seasonally rotating dishes like roasted beets and labneh cheese with piñon

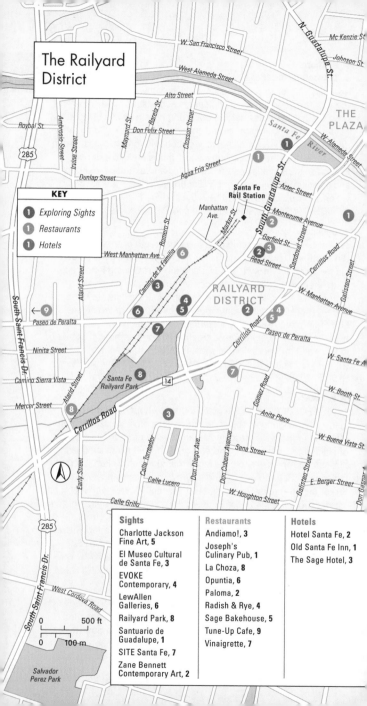

The Railyard District

W. San Francisco Street
N. Guadalupe St.
Mc Kenzie St.
Johnson St.
West Alameda Street
Alto Street
Roybal St.
Maynard St.
Barela St.
Clisson Street
Ambrosio Street
Irvine Street
THE PLAZA
Santa Fe River
W. Alameda Street
Don Felix Street
285
Dunlap Street
Agua Fria Street
Aztec Street
Santa Fe Rail Station
Santa Fe Rail Station
Manhattan Ave.
Montezuma Avenue
Market St.
South Guadalupe St.
Sandoval Street
Garfield St.
Cerrillos Road
West Manhattan Ave.
Camino de la Familia
Primero St.
Read Street
W. Manhattan Avenue
RAILYARD DISTRICT
Galisteo Street
Alarid Street
Cerrillos Road
Paseo de Peralta
Paseo de Peralta
W. Santa Fe A
South Saint Francis Dr.
Ninita Street
Cerrillos Road
W. Booth St.
Camino Sierra Vista
Santa Fe Railyard Park
14
Gomez Road
Mercer Street
Alarid Street
Anita Place
W. Buena Vista St.
Cerrillos Road
Don Diego Ave.
Sena Street
Don Cubero Avenue
E. Berger Street
Early Street
Calle Torreador
Galisteo Street
Don Gaspar
Calle Lucero
W. Houghton Street
Calle Grillo
285
West Cordova Road
0   500 ft
0   100 m
Salvador Perez Park

KEY
- **1** Exploring Sights
- **1** Restaurants
- **1** Hotels

Sights
Charlotte Jackson Fine Art, **5**

El Museo Cultural de Santa Fe, **3**

EVOKE Contemporary, **4**

LewAllen Galleries, **6**

Railyard Park, **8**

Santuario de Guadalupe, **1**

SITE Santa Fe, **7**

Zane Bennett Contemporary Art, **2**

Restaurants
Andiamo!, **3**

Joseph's Culinary Pub, **1**

La Choza, **8**

Opuntia, **6**

Paloma, **2**

Radish & Rye, **4**

Sage Bakehouse, **5**

Tune-Up Cafe, **9**

Vinaigrette, **7**

Hotels
Hotel Santa Fe, **2**

Old Santa Fe Inn, **1**

The Sage Hotel, **3**

vinaigrette, and grilled local pork chops with bacon, polenta, and wild mushrooms. **Known for:** local and seasonal ingredients; bourbon pecan pie; encyclopedic list of small-batch bourbons. $ *Average main: $29* ⊠ *505 Cerillos Rd., Railyard District* ☎ *505/930–5325* ⊕ *www.radishandrye.com* ⊗ *Closed Mon. No lunch.*

Sage Bakehouse

$ | **BAKERY** | **FAMILY** | This artisanal bakery produces some of the best bread you'll ever taste along with delectable pastries, panini, tartines, quiches, soups, and salads. While many items are made to grab n' go, taking the time to enjoy a fresh-made meal in the small café is a nice break from a busy day. **Known for:** artisanal bread and baked goods; seasonal soups, panini, and tartines; charming ambience. $ *Average main: $8* ⊠ *535 Cerillos Rd., Railyard District* ☎ *505/820–7243* ⊕ *www.sagebakehouse.com* ⊗ *Closed Sun. No dinner.*

★ Tune-Up Cafe

$ | **SOUTHWESTERN** | This cozy locals' favorite has colorful walls and wood details, booths, a few tables, and a community table. The shaded patio out front is a great summertime spot to enjoy the toothsome Southwest-inspired cooking, from breakfast through dinner. **Known for:** breakfast rellenos; vegetarian, vegan, and gluten-free options; homemade cakes and pies. $ *Average main: $11* ⊠ *1115 Hickox St., West of the Plaza* ☎ *505/983–7060* ⊕ *www. tuneupsantafe.com.*

Vinaigrette

$$ | **AMERICAN** | **FAMILY** | A novel and noble alternative to the many Santa Fe restaurants that favor filling (and often fattening) dishes, Vinaigrette is all about the greens, which are sourced organically, with the majority of produce raised on owner Erin Wade's 10-acre farm in nearby Nambé. This isn't mere rabbit food, however—the hearty salads make a satisfying meal, especially when you add toppings like grilled flank steak, lemon-herb chicken breast, or griddled tofu. **Known for:** hearty (and expensive) salads; daily house-made fruit pies; baked panko-crusted goat cheese (which can be added to any salad). $ *Average main: $18* ⊠ *709 Don Cubero Alley, Old Santa Fe Trail and South Capitol* ☎ *505/820–9205* ⊕ *www.vinaigretteonline.com* ⊗ *Closed Sun.*

 Hotels

★ Hotel Santa Fe

$$$ | **HOTEL** | Picurís Pueblo has controlling interest in this handsome Pueblo-style three-story hotel on the Railyard District's edge and a 15-minute walk from the Plaza. **Pros:** lots of amenities,

including spa and pool; easy access to Railyard District's trendy shopping and dining; interesting focus on Native American history and culture. **Cons:** standard rooms are a bit small; room rates vary greatly; a bit far from Downtown. ⑤ *Rooms from: $250* ⊠ *1501 Paseo de Peralta, Railyard District* ☎ *855/825–9876* ⊕ *www.hotel-santafe.com* ⌕ *158 rooms* ❑ *No meals.*

★ Old Santa Fe Inn

$$ | **HOTEL** | This contemporary motor court–style inn looks from the outside like an attractive, if fairly ordinary, adobe motel, but it has stunning and spotless rooms with elegant Southwestern decor. **Pros:** rooms are more inviting than several more-expensive Downtown hotels; short walk to the Plaza; free parking. **Cons:** rooms set around parking lot; noise from other rooms; decor can be a bit drab in places. ⑤ *Rooms from: $139* ⊠ *201 Montezuma Ave., Railyard District* ☎ *505/995–0800* ⊕ *www.oldsantafeinn.com* ⌕ *58 rooms* ❑ *Free Breakfast.*

The Sage Hotel

$$ | **HOTEL** | **FAMILY** | On the southern edge of the Railyard District, this smart motel offers affordable comfort, modern bohemian Southwestern decor, and a location that's just about a 5-minute walk to the Railyard and a 15-minute walk from the Plaza. **Pros:** comfortable and affordable; small but nice pool; close to Railyard District attractions and galleries. **Cons:** rooms nearest the street can be noisy; parking lot views; extra $15 fee to use all amenities. ⑤ *Rooms from: $199* ⊠ *725 Cerrillos Rd., Railyard District* ☎ *505/982–5952* ⊕ *www.thesagesf.com* ⌕ *145 rooms* ❑ *Free Breakfast.*

Nightlife

Bosque Brewing Co.

BREWPUBS/BEER GARDENS | One of the state's most celebrated craft brewing companies, Bosque Brewing Co.'s Santa Fe taproom offers rotating taps including favorites such as the Jetty Jack Amber and Elephants on Parade wheat ale. The kitchen serves up beer-friendly foods ranging from nachos and deep-fried cheese curds to street tacos, burgers, and fish-and-chips. It's a great spot to relax and people watch. ⊠ *500 Market St., Railyard District* ☎ *505/433–3889* ⊕ *www.bosquebrewing.com.*

Cowgirl BBQ

BARS/PUBS | **FAMILY** | This rollicking barbecue, burger, and Southwestern soul food joint is one of the most popular places in town for live blues, country, rock, folk, and even karaoke. The bar is friendly and the cheap happy hour margaritas provide a lot of bang for your buck. The fun pool hall and central outdoor patio can get wild as the night gets late. ⊠ *319 S. Guadalupe St., Railyard District* ☎ *505/982–2565* ⊕ *www.cowgirlsantafe.com.*

★ Santa Fe Spirits Downtown Tasting Room

BARS/PUBS | One of the Southwest's most acclaimed microdistilleries, Santa Fe Spirits operates a convivial tasting room from a small adobe home. Known for its award-winning Colkegan Single Malt Whiskey, Wheeler's Gin, and Apple Brandy, among several other robust elixirs, it's a great place to sip drinks on the lovely patio on warm evenings. Distillery tours, by reservation, are available at the main production facility out near the airport. ⊠ *308 Read St., Railyard District* ☎ *505/780–5906* ⊕ *www.santafespirits.com.*

Second Street Brewery

BARS/PUBS | This long-popular brewpub has three locations in town, with the Railyard location being especially popular thanks to the easy walking distance from Downtown hotels. There's great live music (usually rock or folk) or DJs most nights along with a rotating selection of terrific beers. A substantial food menu includes good burgers and pub favorites. ⊠ *1607 Paseo de Peralta, Suite 10, Railyard District* ☎ *505/989–3278* ⊕ *www.second-streetbrewery.com.*

🎭 Performing Arts

★ Jean Cocteau Cinema

FILM | Author and longtime Santa Fe resident George R.R. Martin, of *Game of Thrones* fame, restored this intimate, funky Railyard District art-movie house into a busy neighborhood favorite. The single-screen theater is a great place to catch first-run films, indie flicks, cult classics, and traveling selections from international film festivals. The lobby has a small bar and coffee shop to complete the indie vibe. Next door, Martin also operates Beastly Books which focuses, of course, on science fiction and fantasy. ⊠ *418 Montezuma Ave., Railyard District* ☎ *505/466–5528* ⊕ *www. jeancocteaucinema.com.*

Violet Crown Cinema

FILM | **FAMILY** | This state-of-the-art multiscreen cinema shows everything from blockbusters to indie and vintage movies and offers a restaurant and bar featuring craft brews and ciders, fine wine, and sophisticated food options, which you can eat in the theaters. The food and drink selection is actually so good that many people choose the Violet Crown simply to hang out—you'll frequently see locals meeting in the bar for a weekly game of cards. Reserved seating means never having to settle for a bad row and each screening room has air-conditioning, making it a great hot weather escape. ⊠ *1606 Alcaldesa St., Railyard District* ☎ *505/216–5678* ⊕ *santafe.violetcrown.com.*

Shopping

BOOKS

The Ark

BOOKS/STATIONERY | Santa Fe is well-known for its mystical side and the Ark is where locals go to feed their spiritual souls. Mainly a metaphysical bookstore, the Ark also offers a diverse selection of cards, gemstones, and crystals as well as gifts of all kinds, from Tibetan prayer flags and wind chimes to yoga mats and clothing. ⊠ *133 Romero St., Railyard District* ☎ *505/988–3709* ⊕ *www. arkbooks.com.*

Beastly Books

BOOKS/STATIONERY | Famed Santa Fe resident George R. R. Martin owns both this fantasy-and-science-fiction-focused bookstore as well as Jean Cocteau Cinema next-door. Named after Cocteau's 1946 classic *Beauty and the Beast* (which was also a television show the *Game of Thrones* author worked on in the 1980s), the shop features books of all genres, each signed by its writer. This of course includes Martin's many offerings, but also books by Diana Gabaldon, Leonard Maltin, Erica Jong, and Walter Jon Williams. ⊠ *418 Montezuma Ave., Railyard District* ☎ *505/395–2628* ⊕ *www.jeancocteaucinema.com/beastlybooks.*

CLOTHING AND ACCESSORIES

★ Double Take

CLOTHING | This rambling 25,000-square-foot shop ranks among the best consignment stores in the West, carrying elaborately embroidered vintage cowboy shirts, hundreds of pairs of boots, funky old prints, antique Southwestern-style furniture, and amazing vintage Indian pawn and Mexican jewelry. The store comprises several sections that also include contemporary clothing and accessories for men and women and a pottery showroom. ⊠ *320 Aztec St., Railyard District* ☎ *505/989–8886* ⊕ *www.santafedoubletake.com.*

FOOD AND DRINK

★ Modern General Feed & Seed

FOOD/CANDY | With a clean, orderly aesthetic that seems right out of the pages of *Kinfolk,* this updated, upscale take on a general store carries gorgeous kitchenware and table linens, from salvaged-olive-wood cutting boards to handwoven dish towels. Fine hardware, garden tools, and books related to kitchen and home are also on offer. It's adjacent to and run by the team at Vinaigrette

The weekly Santa Fe Farmers' Market is one of the Railyard District's biggest draws.

restaurant, and you can dine here, too—there's a juice bar and a small café proffering delicious breakfast fare, sandwiches, pies, and more. Owner Erin Wade is well-known in the restaurant community for her creative sustainability solutions, such as reusable take-out containers, to-go cups, and composting initiatives. ⊠ *637 Cerrillos Rd., Railyard District* ☎ *505/930–5462* ⊕ *www.modern-generalfeedandseed.com.*

HOME FURNISHINGS

Array

GIFTS/SOUVENIRS | In this cozy Railyard District shop you'll find a well-curated selection of home goods—tableware, candles and folk art from Mexico, tote bags, toys, and even a few antiques. Note the very nice selection of lotions and body-care products made in New Mexico. ⊠ *322 S. Guadalupe St., Railyard District* ☎ *505/699–2760.*

Casa Nova

ANTIQUES/COLLECTIBLES | A spacious shop that sells functional and decorative art from around the world, Casa Nova deftly mixes colors, textures, and cultural icons—old and new—from stylish pewter tableware from South Africa to vintage hand-carved ex-votos (votive offerings) from Brazil. There is a major emphasis here on goods produced by artists and cooperatives focused on sustainable economic development. ⊠ *530 S. Guadalupe St., Railyard District* ☎ *505/983–8558* ⊕ *www.casanovagallery.com.*

JEWELRY

Eidos

JEWELRY/ACCESSORIES | Check out "concept-led" minimalist contemporary jewelry from European designers and Deborah Alexander and Gordon Lawrie, who own the store. It's a lovely, contemporary space with a fascinating array of materials, good range of prices, and helpful staff. ✉ *508A Camino de la Familia, Railyard District* ☎ *505/992–0020* ⊕ *www.eidosjewelry.com.*

MARKETS

★ Santa Fe Farmers' Market

OUTDOOR/FLEA/GREEN MARKETS | **FAMILY** | Browse through the vast selection of local produce, meat, flowers, honey, wine, jams, and cheese—much of it organic—at the thriving Santa Fe Farmers' Market. Dozens of stalls are arranged inside a snazzy, modern building in the Railyard and adjacent to it; it's open year-round on Saturday morning (7 am to 1 pm in summer, 8 am to 1 pm in winter) and additionally on Tuesday morning May through mid-December. The lively space also hosts an artisan market on Sunday from 10 to 3. It's a great people-watching venue, with entertainment for kids as well as food vendors selling terrific breakfast burritos, green-chile bread, Taos Cow ice cream, and other goodies. For those staying on the Southside of town, be sure to check out the satellite Del Sur Market, Tuesday from 3 to 6, July through September, at the Presbyterian Medical Center at 4801 Buckner Road. ✉ *1607 Paseo de Peralta, Railyard District* ☎ *505/983–4098* ⊕ *www.santafefarmersmarket.com.*

GREATER SANTA FE

Updated by
Zibby Wilder

● Sights	ⓥ Restaurants	⬠ Hotels	● Shopping	⍦ Nightlife
★★★★☆	★★★★☆	★★★☆☆	★★★☆☆	★★★☆☆

NEIGHBORHOOD SNAPSHOT

TOP EXPERIENCES

■ **Take a ski and spa day:** Work up a sweat on the slopes of Ski Santa Fe then head down the mountain to soak it out at one of the area's many luxury spas, like Ten Thousand Waves.

■ **Embrace the mystery and magic of Meow Wolf:** As Santa Fe's top tourist attraction of late, Meow Wolf's mind-bending House of Eternal Return puts your mind to work solving an expansive mystery while allowing your inner child to run free.

■ **Experience open-air opera:** The famous Santa Fe opera performs regularly in a gorgeous indoor–outdoor amphitheater carved into a hillside.

■ **Dine with the locals:** The popular eateries along busy Cerillos Road (also part of historic Route 66) are always filled to the brim with locals and tourists alike.

GETTING HERE AND AROUND

The north, west, and south sides of Santa Fe are easily reachable by car. Areas in the north are more rural so parking is rarely an issue. The same goes for the south side as it is highly developed, therefore parking lots abound. The area to the west of town, save for DeVargas Center, can pose a bit more of a parking problem as the historic streets are narrow and most parking is reserved for residents. Your best bet is to park in one of the nearby city parking garages and walk while exploring the area.

QUICK BITES

■ **Blake's Lotaburger.** This old-school, regional fast-food chain serves tasty breakfast burritos and juicy burgers. ✉ 404 N. Guadalupe St., West Side ⊕ www.lotaburger.com

■ **Jambo Hapa.** The Hapa is the food truck of this popular East African-Caribbean fusion eatery, a local favorite known for its jerk chicken sandwiches and creative curries. ✉ 2010 Cerillos Rd., Southside ⊕ www.jambocafe.net

■ **Posa's El Merendero Tamale Factory & Restaurant.** Famous for its tamales, this is also a great spot for a quick sit-down or grab-and-go traditional New Mexico meal. ✉ 1514 Rodeo Rd., Southside ⊕ www.santafetamales.com

Beyond Santa Fe's commercial core, you'll find a bevy of other notable attractions, restaurants, shops, and inns around the easy-to-access north, west, and south sides of town.

The north claims some of the area's most stunning scenery including the winding drive along Bishop's Lodge Road to the village of Tesuque. Among the area's rolling hills and sage-brush-dotted mesas sits the famed Santa Fe Opera, the Tesuque Casino, and the distinctive Four Seasons Rancho Encantado. A trip northeast through the verdant foothills of the Sangre de Christos is the way to go if you're looking for day hikes, beautiful vistas, enchanting spa experiences, or an adrenaline rush down the slopes of Ski Santa Fe.

West of Downtown, the area along Guadalupe Street between Alameda Street and Paseo de Peralta (and the historic blocks just west) nurtures many independent businesses, from hip record stores and cozy inns to breweries and gastropubs. At the intersection of Paseo de Peralta and Guadalupe, you'll find the expansive DeVargas Center shopping mall, which has a few notable shops and eateries, a bustling bowling alley/family activity center/lounge, and some larger grocery and big-box stores that can come in handy if you just need basic supplies (and are still within walking distance of the Plaza).

The majority of Santa Feans live on the Southside, which encompasses a vast stretch of relatively level mesa land. What this somewhat sprawly part of town lacks in scenic beauty—especially along traffic-choked and strip-mall-lined Cerrillos Road (a stretch of the original Route 66)—it makes up for in convenient services, good food, and creative experiences. This is where you're going to find most of the area's midrange and budget chain accommodations and fast-food restaurants, along with an increasing number of genuinely notable eateries, from down-home neighborhood favorites like Horseman's Haven and El Parasol to inspired contemporary spots like Rowley's Farmhouse Ales and Dr. Field Goods Kitchen. One burgeoning sub-neighborhood on the Southside, the Midtown Innovation District, has sprung up along Siler Road—just off Cerrillos Road—and is anchored by experiential art collective Meow Wolf as well as a growing number of hip breweries, eateries, galleries, and art studios.

At El Rancho de las Golondrinas, you'll see what life was like in the area from the 17th to 19th centuries, including the use of traditional kiva stoves.

If you've got a car, exploring Santa Fe's surrounding neighborhoods is worth a day on your itinerary. Head down south of town to stock up supplies at one of the many grocery stores, delis, or eateries specializing in New Mexican cuisine, then cruise the winding roads for a picnic and hike near Ski Santa Fe. On the way back, stop for a soak or book a treatment at the zen-inspiring spa at Ten Thousand Waves. Or, head north to Tesuque and explore the sculpture garden at Shidoni and the vistas of the famous Santa Fe Opera before winding down at a popular eatery like El Nido. If you time it right, the hills surrounding Santa Fe are prime spots to enjoy one of Santa Fe's spectacular sunsets.

Sights

El Rancho de las Golondrinas

MUSEUM VILLAGE | Sometimes dubbed the "Colonial Williamsburg of the Southwest," El Rancho de las Golondrinas ("Ranch of the Swallows") is a reconstruction of a small agricultural village with buildings from the 17th to 19th centuries. Travelers on El Camino Real would stop at the ranch before making the final leg of the journey north, a half-day ride from Santa Fe in horse-and-wagon time. By car, the ranch is only a 25-minute drive from the Plaza. It's also a 10-minute drive from where the Turquoise Trail (NM 14) intersects with Interstate 25, making it a fun stop—especially for kids—on your way to or from Albuquerque. Self-guided tours interpret the lives of locals in those bygone eras while farm animals roam through the barnyards on the 200-acre complex. During the ranch's many festivals—Spring & Fiber Fest, the Herb & Lavender Festival, Viva México, La Panza Llena New Mexico Food Fest, Santa Fe Wine Festival, and others—music, dance, food, and crafts are offered. In April, May, and October, the museum is open weekdays, by advance reservation only. ⊠ *334 Los Pinos Rd., South Side* ☎ *505/471–2261* ⊕ *www.golondrinas.org* ⊠ *$6* ⊗ *Closed weekends Nov.–Mar. and Mon. and Tues. June–Sept.*

★ Meow Wolf

ARTS VENUE | FAMILY | Both the name of an ambitious visual and musical arts collective and of the dazzling multimillion-dollar arts complex the group created out of a former bowling alley (with much of the funding coming from Santa Fe–based *Game of Thrones* author George R. R. Martin), visitors now flock to the arts complex's first permanent exhibition, the self-billed "immersive art installation" *House of Eternal Return*, which has become one of the city's leading attractions. Give yourself at least a couple of hours to tour this sci-fi-inspired, 20,000-square-foot interactive exhibit in which you'll encounter hidden doorways, mysterious corridors, ambient music, and clever, surrealistic, and often slyly humorous artistic renderings. It's a strange, almost impossible to describe, experience, but it is absolutely family-friendly, and although wildly imaginative and occasionally eerie, the subject matter isn't at all frightening. Tickets are good throughout the day—you can leave and reenter the installation, and perhaps break up the experience by enjoying a light bite and craft beer at the lobby bar/café. Be aware that the experience is highly sensory and can be a little overstimulating for those who are sensitive to noise, changing lighting, and crowds. Meow Wolf is open until 8 most evenings and 10 on Friday and Saturday. The collective also presents concerts and other events both at the Meow Wolf arts complex and at other venues around the city. ⊠ *1352 Rufina Cir., South Side* ☎ *505/395–6369* ⊕ *www.meowwolf.com* ⊠ *$35* ⊗ *Closed Tues.*

★ Santa Fe Opera

MUSIC | To watch opera in this strikingly modern structure—a 2,128-seat, indoor–outdoor amphitheater with excellent acoustics and sight lines—is a memorable visual and auditory experience. Carved into the natural curves of a hillside 7 miles north of the Plaza, the opera overlooks mountains, mesas, and sky. Add some of the most acclaimed operatic talents from Europe and the United States, and you begin to understand the excitement that builds every June. This world-renowned company presents five works in repertory each summer—a blend of seasoned classics, neglected

Sights

El Rancho de las Golondrinas, **4**

Meow Wolf, **1**

Santa Fe Opera, **2**

Shidoni Gallery and Sculpture Garden, **3**

Restaurants

Arroyo Vino, **17**

Chocolate Maven, **6**

Clafoutis, **3**

Counter Culture, **4**

Dr. Field Goods Kitchen, **13**

El Nido, **15**

El Parasol, **8**

Harry's Roadhouse, **20**

Horseman's Haven Cafe, **19**

Iconik Coffee Roasters, **5**

Izanami, **16**

Jambo, **11**

Madame Matisse, **9**

Mariscos la Playa, **2**

The Pantry, **7**

Paper Dosa, **1**

Ranch House, **18**

Rowley Farmhouse Ales, **12**

San Marcos Cafe & Feed Store, **21**

Santa Fe Bite, **10**

Terra, **14**

Hotels

Bobcat Inn, **7**

El Rey Court, **2**

Four Seasons Resort Rancho Encantado Santa Fe, **4**

Ojo Santa Fe, **6**

Residence Inn, **3**

Silver Saddle Motel, **1**

Ten Thousand Waves, **5**

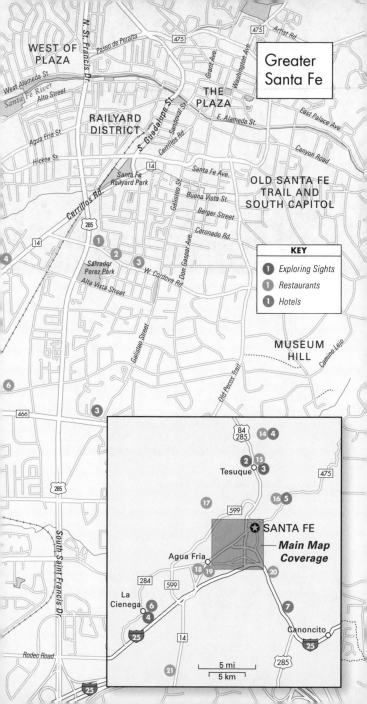

At Meow Wolf, you can experience the immersive, psychedelic art installation known as "House of Eternal Return".

masterpieces, and world premieres. Many evenings sell out far in advance, but less expensive standing-room tickets are often available on the day of the performance. A favorite pre-opera pastime is tailgating in the parking lot before the evening performance—many guests set up elaborate picnics of their own, but you can also preorder picnic meals at the opera website by calling 24 hours in advance or ordering a take-out meal from one of the many local restaurants that offer opera meals. In the off-season, the opera house hosts shows by contemporary artists such as Bonnie Raitt, St. Vincent, The Shins, and The National. ⊠ *301 Opera Dr., North Side* ☎ *505/986–5900, 800/280–4654* ⊕ *www. santafeopera.org.*

Shidoni Gallery and Sculpture Garden

ART GALLERIES | FAMILY | This picturesque compound on the grounds of an old chicken ranch in rural Tesuque is home to a rambling sculpture garden and art gallery. On sunny afternoons, there are few more picturesque places to admire art than the tranquil garden, in which you'll find dazzling large-scale works in bronze and other metals. The gallery shows a variety of crafts and other works, from wood carvings to fiber. ⊠ *1508 Bishop's Lodge Rd., 5 miles north of the Plaza, North Side* ☎ *505/988–8001* ⊕ *www. shidoni.com* ☉ *Closed Sun. and Mon.*

🍴 Restaurants

★ Arroyo Vino

$$$ | **MODERN AMERICAN** | It's worth making the trek out to Santa Fe's western mesa to dine at this outstanding bistro–cum–wine-shop with a devout following among locals. At the store, stock up on often hard-to-find vintages from all over the world (for a $30 corkage fee, you can also enjoy your new Bordeaux or Albariño in the airy dining room or, when weather allows, the charming outdoor patio), and enjoy the menu of sublime contemporary American fare that changes regularly and is based on the incredible variety of seasonal produce grown on Arroyo Vino's on-site farm. **Known for:** garden-fresh seasonal produce; excellent chicken liver pâté; stellar wine shop and selection. ⑤ *Average main: $29 ⊠ 218 Camino la Tierra, off NM 599, 4 miles west of U.S. 285/84, West of the Plaza* 🕾 *505/983–2100* ⊕ *www.arroyovino.com* ⓥ *Closed Sun. and Mon. No lunch.*

Chocolate Maven

$ | **CAFÉ** | **FAMILY** | Although the name of this cheery bakery suggests sweets, and it does sweets especially well, Chocolate Maven also produces impressive savory breakfast and lunch fare. Meals are "farmers' market–inspired" and feature seasonal dishes, including wild-mushroom-and-goat-cheese focaccia sandwiches, eggs ménage à trois (one each of eggs Benedict, Florentine, and Madison—the latter consisting of smoked salmon and poached egg), and Caprese salad of fresh mozzarella, basil, and tomatoes. **Known for:** excellent breakfast burritos; delicious baked goods and desserts; local, seasonal ingredients. ⑤ *Average main: $13 ⊠ 821 W. San Mateo St., South Side* 🕾 *505/984–1980* ⊕ *www.chocolatemaven.com* ⓥ *No dinner.*

Clafoutis

$ | **CAFÉ** | **FAMILY** | Undeniably French, this bustling café serves authentic, delicious food. Walk through the door of this bright, open space and you'll almost certainly be greeted with a cheery *"bonjour"* from Anne-Laure, who owns it with her husband, Philippe. **Known for:** bounteous salads and French omelets; famous clafoutis for dessert; some of the best baguettes and pastries in the city. ⑤ *Average main: $11 ⊠ 333 W. Cordova Rd., Old Santa Fe Trail and South Capitol* 🕾 *505/988–1809* ⓥ *Closed Sun. No dinner.*

Counter Culture

$ | **CAFÉ** | **FAMILY** | This low-key, slightly off-the-beaten-path café is worth finding for its delicious breakfasts, lunches, dinners, or even just afternoon coffee breaks—there's a spacious covered patio (that's dog-friendly) beyond the dining room with long communal tables and a few smaller, more private ones. Inside the hip industrial space, tuck into plates of huevos rancheros and other eggy fare in the morning, and a mix of Southwestern and Asian dishes later in the day. **Known for:** smothered breakfast burritos; well-prepared espresso drinks; cash-only policy. ⑤ *Average main: $13* ⌧ *930 Baca St., South Side* ☎ *505/995–1105* ⊕ *www.counterculturesantafe.com* ▭ *No credit cards* ⊙ *No dinner Sun. and Mon.*

Dr. Field Goods Kitchen

$$ | **ECLECTIC** | **FAMILY** | Ardent foodies regularly trek 4 miles south along traffic-choked Cerrillos Road to experience one of the more memorable "down home" farm-to-table dining adventures in Santa Fe. Situated in a nondescript shopping center, chef/owner Josh Gerwin serves up boldly flavored comfort cuisine that is a favorite of both locals and tourist, thanks to appearances on TV shows such as *Diners, Drive-Ins, and Dives*. **Known for:** the famous "Bad Ass BLT" sandwich; house-smoked meats; brick-oven pizza. ⑤ *Average main: $16* ⌧ *2860 Cerrillos Rd., South Side* ☎ *505/471–0043* ⊕ *www.drfieldgoods.com.*

★ El Nido

$$$ | **CONTEMPORARY** | This stylish, upscale restaurant located in the heart of little Tesuque village specializes in "live fire"—cooking directly over wood or coal on a specially made grill. The menu is rustic and seasonally influenced so it's rare to find the same dish on the menu for more than a few weeks, but summer favorites can include sage smoked rainbow trout wood-grilled with artichoke, lobster sofrito, and preserved lemon or a Black Angus rib eye grilled over pecan wood with chimichurri fire-roasted veggies and green chile demi. **Known for:** pre-Santa Fe Opera dinners; impressive wine list; wood-fire grilled favorites. ⑤ *Average main: $30* ⌧ *1577 Bishop's Lodge Rd., Tesuque* ☎ *505/954–1272* ⊕ *www.elnidosantafe.com* ⊙ *Closed Mon. No lunch.*

El Parasol

$ | **SOUTHWESTERN** | **FAMILY** | This no-frills, family-owned local chain might not look like much from the outside, but its fast, fresh New Mexican cuisine is a standard favorite among most northern Mew Mexicans. Consistently praised for its superior chile, tacos, carne adovada, and breakfast burritos by locals and national media like, it's worth a stop for those looking for a true New Mexican food experience. **Known for:** excellent breakfast burritos and tacos; casual, family-friendly atmosphere; quick lunch spot. ⑤ *Average main: $8* ⌧ *1833 Cerrillos Rd., South Side* ☎ *505/995–8015* ⊕ *www.elparasol.com.*

★ Harry's Roadhouse

$ | **ECLECTIC** | **FAMILY** | This busy, friendly, art-filled compound 6 miles southeast of Downtown consists of several inviting rooms, from a diner-style space with counter seating to a cozier nook with a fireplace, and an enchanting courtyard out back with juniper trees and flower gardens. The varied menu of contemporary diner favorites, pizzas, New Mexican fare, and bountiful salads is supplemented by a long list of daily specials, which often include delicious international dishes and an array of scrumptious home-made desserts. **Known for:** friendly neighborhood hangout; stellar margaritas; house-made desserts. $ *Average main: $13* ⊠ *96-B Old Las Vegas Hwy., 1 mile east of Old Pecos Trail exit off I–25, East Side and Canyon Road* ☎ *505/989–4629* ⊕ *www.harrysroad-housesantafe.com.*

Horseman's Haven Cafe

$ | **SOUTHWESTERN** | Tucked behind the Giant gas station, this no-frills diner-style restaurant close to the many chain hotels along lower Cerrillos Road has long been a standout for some of the spiciest and tastiest northern New Mexican fare in town, includ-ing superb green chile-bacon-cheeseburgers, blue-corn tacos packed with beef or chicken, huevos rancheros, and the hearty *plato sabroso* (a 12-ounce rib steak with rolled enchilada, beans, posole, rice, and hot sopaipilla with honey). Grab one of the comfy red-leatherette corner booths or a stool at the counter, and enjoy the people-watching. **Known for:** blue corn tacos with beef or chicken; green-chile bacon cheeseburgers; hearty New Mexican breakfasts. $ *Average main: $10* ⊠ *4354 Cerrillos Rd., South Side* ☎ *505/471–5420* ⊕ *www.facebook.com/horsemans.haven* ☉ *No dinner Sun.*

Iconik Coffee Roasters

$ | **CAFÉ** | First and foremost a lively coffeehouse that turns out expertly prepared pour-overs, lattes, cold brews, and other delicious espresso drinks using house-roasted beans, this funky, inviting space also serves tasty and eclectic salads, sandwiches, and tapas. The menu spans the globe, featuring breakfast tacos, Korean steak bowls, ramen, and poached-egg salads. **Known for:** pour-over single-origin coffees; chocolate milk stout on tap; ramen with miso-coconut broth. $ *Average main: $10* ⊠ *1600 Lena St., Suite A2, South Side* ☎ *505/428–0996* ⊕ *www.iconikcoffee.com.*

Izanami

$$ | **JAPANESE** | Set in the pine-scented foothills northeast of town, the ethereal boutique resort and spa Ten Thousand Waves has always cultivated a tranquil Japanese aesthetic, and its on-site restaurant is no exception. The menu is izakaya-style and features an extensive list of sakes and shareable small plates—two or three per person is typically sufficient; highlights include oyster mushrooms in a rich tamari butter sauce, grilled avocado with nori sea salt and fresh wasabi, and fall-off-the-bone smoked pork ribs in a sweet chile glaze. **Known for:** omakase chef's choice tasting menu; beautiful forest views; an outstanding selection of first-rate sakes. $ *Average main: $16* ⊠ *Ten Thousand Waves, 21 Ten Thousand Waves Way, North Side* ☎ *505/982–9304* ⊕ *www. tenthousandwaves.com/food* ☯ *No lunch Tues.*

Jambo

$ | **AFRICAN** | **FAMILY** | Ahmed Obo, the Kenyan-born owner who regularly tops the local paper's "best chef" list, applies great skill and enthusiasm to the Afro-Caribbean food at this casual, homey eatery in a shopping center a couple of miles south of the Plaza. Flavors of coconut, peanuts, and curry influence everything from shrimp to goat stew. **Known for:** Caribbean goat stew; East African coconut lentil stew; African music and art. $ *Average main: $14* ⊠ *2010 Cerrillos Rd., South Side* ☎ *505/473–1269* ⊕ *www.jambo-cafe.net* ☯ *Closed Sun.*

Madame Matisse

$ | **FRENCH** | This bright, modern bakery and café is a welcome change from the hustle and bustle of busy Cerrillos Road. The interior is crisp and clean with Matisse-inspired pops of color, and the food is inspired as well, with spot-on executions of French favorites for every meal including crepes, eggs Benedict, salads, sandwiches, and pastas. **Known for:** delectable baked goods; classic French cuisine; tasty omelets. $ *Average main: $12* ⊠ *1291 San Felipe Ave., South Side* ☎ *505/772–0949* ⊕ *www.facebook. com/MadamematisseSantaFe* ☯ *No dinner Sun.*

Mariscos la Playa

$$ | **MEXICAN** | **FAMILY** | Yes, even in landlocked Santa Fe it's possible to find incredibly fresh and well-prepared seafood served in big portions. This cheery, colorful Mexican restaurant surrounded by strip malls is just a short hop south of Downtown. **Known for:** delightfully friendly staff; ceviche tostadas; trout grilled with butter and paprika. $ *Average main: $15* ⊠ *537 W. Cordova Rd., Old Santa Fe Trail and South Capitol* ☎ *505/982–2790* ⊕ *www.facebook. com/mariscoslaplayanm.*

The Pantry

$ | **DINER** | **FAMILY** | Since 1948, this beloved, family-owned greasy spoon with a familiar blue neon sign has been pleasing budget-minded locals and visitors with consistently tasty, New

Mexican–style diner fare. Popular choices here include buck-wheat pancakes, *huevos consuelo* (a corn tortilla topped with two eggs, spicy chile, and cheese, with the Pantry's famous home fries), green-chile stew, tortilla burgers, and chicken-fried steak. **Known for:** excellent huevos consuelo; great value; down-home atmosphere. $ *Average main: $9* ✉ *1820 Cerrillos Rd., South Side* ☎ *505/986–0022* ⊕ *www.pantrysantafe.com.*

★ Paper Dosa

$$ | **MODERN INDIAN** | **FAMILY** | Begun as a catering business that threw occasional pop-up dinners, Paper Dosa became so beloved for its boldly flavored southern Indian cuisine that the owners opened what has become a tremendously popular brick-and-mortar restaurant. Dosas (large, thin crepes made with fermented rice and lentils and stuffed with different fillings) are the specialty here and come in about 10 varieties, from paneer and peas to a locally inspired version with green chile and three cheeses. **Known for:** dosas with interesting fillings; chile-dusted mango salad; a thoughtful, diverse wine list. $ *Average main: $17* ✉ *551 W. Cordova Rd., Old Santa Fe Trail and South Capitol* ☎ *505/930–5521* ⊕ *www.paper-dosa.com* ⊗ *Closed Mon.*

Ranch House

$$ | **BARBECUE** | **FAMILY** | Given New Mexico's deep ties to its easterly neighbor, the Lone Star State, it's hardly surprising that the region has some top-notch barbecue joints, including this spacious, contemporary adobe building with two large patios. It looks a bit fancy but still turns out superb, fall-off-the-bone barbecue brisket, baby-back ribs, pulled pork, and smoked half-chicken. **Known for:** barbecue brisket; steaks and fish tacos; daily happy hour from 4 to 6. $ *Average main: $18* ✉ *2571 Cristo's Rd., South Side* ☎ *505/424–8900* ⊕ *www.theranchhousesantafe.com.*

★ Rowley Farmhouse Ales

$ | **AMERICAN** | **FAMILY** | Tiny Rowley Farmhouse Ales has won several awards at the Great American Beer Festival, including three medals for its sour style ales, so if you like beer (any kind of beer) a stop at Rowley is a must. In addition to offering its own brews, Rowley also has an extensive list of local and imported beers and ciders that it finds inspiring, along with comfort foods like shrimp po'boys, cast iron skillet green chile mac n' cheese, and chicken and waffles. **Known for:** award-winning small-batch sour ales; creative pub food; extensive international beer list. $ *Average main: $12* ✉ *1405 Maclovia St., South Side* ☎ *505/428–0719* ⊕ *www.rowleyfarmhouse.com.*

★ San Marcos Cafe & Feed Store

$ | **CAFÉ** | **FAMILY** | In Lone Butte, about 20 miles south of Downtown Santa Fe along the northern end of the scenic Turquoise Trail, this funky spot is known for its creative fare and nontraditional setting: an actual feed store selling propane, hardware, tools, and farm animal feed, with roosters, turkeys, and peacocks running about outside. In one of the two bric-a-brac–filled dining rooms, sample rich cinnamon rolls and such delectables as burritos stuffed with roast beef and potatoes and topped with green chile. **Known for:** the Feed Store burrito (with hash browns, bacon, cheese, chile, and egg); offbeat farmyard setting; long waits on weekend mornings. $ *Average main: $9 ⊠ 3877 NM 14, South Side* ☎ *505/471–9298* ⊙ *Closed Tues. No dinner.*

Santa Fe Bite

$ | **BURGER** | **FAMILY** | John and Bonnie Eckre, the former owners of the legendary but now defunct Bobcat Bite burger joint, now serve their juicy green-chile cheeseburgers and humongous 16-ounce "Big Bite" burgers—along with hefty steaks, enchiladas, and tacos—in this kitsch-filled strip mall space south of town. There's breakfast, too: morning highlights include huevos rancheros, gluten-free buttermilk waffles, and traditional steak-and-eggs. **Known for:** green-chile cheeseburgers; hearty breakfast fare; malted milkshakes. $ *Average main: $14 ⊠ 1616 St. Michaels Dr., South Side* ☎ *505/428–0328* ⊕ *www.santafebite.com* ⊙ *Closed Mon.*

Terra

$$$$ | **MODERN AMERICAN** | Among the many reasons guests of the Four Seasons Rancho Encantado often find it difficult to ever leave the gloriously situated property is this handsome yet down-to-earth restaurant that serves tantalizingly delicious and creative contemporary American and Southwestern cuisine. A specialty here is the exquisitely plated seafood, from ahi tuna and beef carpaccio to grilled prawns with cucumber "spaghetti," wild mushrooms, prickly pear pesto, macadamia crumbs, and bacon. **Known for:** creatively prepared seafood; romantic atmosphere; stunning mountain views. $ *Average main: $39 ⊠ Four Seasons Rancho Encantado, 198 NM 592, North Side* ☎ *505/946–5700* ⊕ *www.fourseasons.com/santafe.*

 Hotels

Bobcat Inn

$$ | **B&B/INN** | A delightful, affordable, country hacienda that's a 15-minute drive southeast of the Plaza, this adobe bed-and-breakfast sits amid 10 secluded acres of piñon and ponderosa pine,

with grand views of the Ortiz Mountains and the area's high-desert mesas. **Pros:** gracious inn and secluded location; wonderful hosts; spectacular views. **Cons:** located outside of town; small bathrooms in some rooms; breakfast not served until 8:30 am. ⑤ *Rooms from: $165* ✉ *442 Old Las Vegas Hwy., South Side* ☎ *505/988–9239* ⊕ *www.bobcatinn.com* ⇆ *8 rooms* ⊚ *Free Breakfast.*

El Rey Court

$$ | **HOTEL** | A circa 1936 motor court along Cerillos Road, El Rey Court was redesigned and now attracts design aficianados and Instagram influencers with its hip take on modern, 1950s-inspired Southwest decor. **Pros:** Instagramable modern Southwestern design; fun on-site bar; friendly and laid-back vibe. **Cons:** some noise from the bar; rates vary widely; no restaurant on-site. ⑤ *Rooms from: $200* ✉ *1862 Cerrillos Rd., South Side* ☎ *505/982– 1931* ⊕ *www.elreycourt.com* ⇆ *86 rooms* ⊚ *No meals.*

★ Four Seasons Resort Rancho Encantado Santa Fe

$$$$ | **RESORT** | This secluded and stunning luxury compound on a dramatic, sunset-facing bluff in the Sangre de Cristo foothills exemplifies the Four Seasons brand's famously flawless sense of gracious hospitality and efficiency. **Pros:** freestanding couples spa suites; complimentary minibar (nonalcoholic beverages only); stunning rooms and views. **Cons:** several of the private terraces overlook parking lots; remote location; large property requires walking but on-site transport is readily available. ⑤ *Rooms from: $700* ✉ *198 NM 592, North Side* ☎ *505/946–5700, 855/674–5401* ⊕ *www.fourseasons.com/santafe* ⇆ *65 rooms* ⊚ *No meals.*

★ Ojo Santa Fe

$$$ | **RESORT** | This tranquil 70-acre resort offers 32 rooms overlooking verdant gardens and 20 casitas with gas fireplaces and secluded patios, plus a first-rate spa focused on energy healing and integrative medicine, a variety of open-air soaking tubs, a large outdoor pool, yoga and fitness studios, a sweat lodge, and an outstanding restaurant—Blue Heron—serving healthy, locally sourced contemporary fare. **Pros:** great restaurant using organic vegetables and herbs grown on-site; unbelievably soothing cottonwood-shaded soaking tubs; superb spa with an extensive list of treatments (including playing with puppies!). **Cons:** 20-minute drive away from Downtown; located in very rural setting; property size requires a lot of walking. ⑤ *Rooms from: $270* ✉ *242 Los Pinos Rd., South Side* ☎ *877/977–8212* ⊕ *ojosantafe.ojospa.com* ⇆ *52 rooms* ⊚ *No meals.*

Residence Inn

$$ | HOTEL | This compound consists of clusters of three-story town houses with pitched roofs and tall chimneys. **Pros:** complimentary full breakfast; evening socials; grocery-shopping service. **Cons:** not within easy walking distance of many restaurants or attractions; near hospital so there can be siren noise; very busy business area. ⑤ *Rooms from: $179* ✉ *1698 Galisteo St., South Side* ☎ *505/988–7300, 800/331–3131* ⊕ *www.marriott.com/safnm* ⇱ *120 suites* ⦿ *Free Breakfast.*

★ Silver Saddle Motel

$ | HOTEL | This low-slung adobe property significantly transcends the generally sketchy quality of the several other budget motels along Cerrillos Road, thanks to the tireless efforts of its owner. **Pros:** superaffordable; good-size rooms, some with refrigerators; friendly, helpful staff. **Cons:** rooms toward the front get noise from Cerrillos Road; very few frills; a 15-minute drive from the Plaza. ⑤ *Rooms from: $75* ✉ *2810 Cerrillos Rd., South Side* ☎ *505/471–7663* ⊕ *www.santafesilversaddlemotel.com* ⇱ *27 rooms* ⦿ *Free Breakfast.*

★ Ten Thousand Waves

$$$ | RESORT | Devotees appreciate the authentic *onsen* (Japanese-style baths) atmosphere of this award-winning 20-acre Japanese-inspired spa and boutique resort in the picturesque foothills a few miles northeast of town. **Pros:** sleek, stylish decor; outstanding restaurant; a soothing, spiritual vibe. **Cons:** a bit remote; the spa and baths can get crowded with day visitors; some areas can be difficult to access. ⑤ *Rooms from: $290* ✉ *3451 Hyde Park Rd., 4 miles northeast of the Plaza, North Side* ☎ *505/982–9304* ⊕ *www.tenthousandwaves.com* ⇱ *14 cottages* ⦿ *Free Breakfast.*

Nightlife

The Alley

GATHERING PLACES | FAMILY | This hybrid family fun center/date night/sports bar/bowling alley in DeVargas Center truly has something for everyone (or at least everyone who loves fun). Both food and bar service are available throughout the facility, whether you're knocking down pins on the 12-lane bowling alley, cracking some bocce balls on one of two indoor courts, or chalking up your cue stick at one of the various pool tables. A couple of shuffleboard tables and some arcade games round out the experience. A great option for families needing a break from sightseeing or a little indoor fun on a rainy day, it's also a lot of fun at night, when things really get hopping. ✉ *DeVargas Center, 153 Paseo de Peralta, West of the Plaza* ☎ *505/557–6789* ⊕ *www.thealleysantafe.com.*

HoneyMoon Brewery

BARS/PUBS | **FAMILY** | The Southwest's first producer of artisanal alcoholic kombucha is impressive not just for the quality of its fermented brews, but also for its upstart business plan, garnering seed capital from both Los Alamos National Laboratory's Venture Acceleration Fund and Miller Lite's "Tap the Future" Business Plan Competition. The laid-back tasting room, located in a convenient shopping center, welcomes visitors to bring their own food from neighboring restaurants or the co-op grocery store and is both family-friendly and good for a date night. If you haven't tried "hard" kombucha, this is your chance. Kombuchas are available in tasting flights, as well as by glass or to-go. For those with differing tastes, beer and wine are also available. Live music and a chill atmosphere make this a great spot to try something new and relax with a creative group of locals. ⊠ *Solana Shopping Center, 907 W. Alameda St., Suite B, South Side* ☎ *505/303–3139* ⊕ *www.honeymoonbrewery.com.*

Santa Fe Brewing Company

BREWPUBS/BEER GARDENS | **FAMILY** | A little off the beaten path, about a 20-minute drive south of the Plaza right where the Turquoise Trail intersects with Interstate 25, this respected craft brewery—the state's oldest—serves fine ales as well as offering tours at its two-story flagship, the Beer Hall at HQ. A variety of beer-friendly food is served via a creative shipping container kitchen and can be eaten indoors or out in the expansive seating area. Santa Fe Brewing Company also has a cozy, smaller tasting room called the Brakeroom, in a historic building on Galisteo Street, and hosts live music at its indoor/outdoor music venue, the Bridge. ⊠ *35 Fire Pl., off NM 14, South Side* ☎ *505/424–3333* ⊕ *www. santafebrewing.com.*

Second Street Brewery Rufina Taproom

BREWPUBS/BEER GARDENS | **FAMILY** | The newest taproom of local favorite Second Street Brewery is located in a 20,000 square foot building that houses a production brewery and canning line. But it's most popular for its consistent live music line-up, an extensive pub food menu (including everything from tater tots to ramen), and its large, dog-friendly deck. Located near Meow Wolf and other arts-focused start-ups and non-profits, it's one of the best places to rub elbows with Santa Fe's hippest. ⊠ *2920 Rufina St., Santa Fe* ☎ *505/954–1068* ⊕ *www.secondstreetbrewery.com.*

Tumbleroot Brewery and Distillery

BARS/PUBS | **FAMILY** | Within this large industrial building in a quiet neighborhood south of town, you'll find a lively community gathering place that hosts regular live music acts, fundraisers, DJs, and more. Families can take advantage of the large outdoor area for kids to play and there is plenty of space for large groups inside the building. Also inside you'll find some of the region's best scratch-made beers and spirits, from Juicy IPA and Honey Hibiscus Wheat to gin and whiskey crafted with local ingredients. Pub fare is available from the on-site kitchen as well as the East Root food truck, which specializes in Asian-influenced bites. On busy weekends, it can get pretty crowded and the line for a drink can have you waiting over an hour; get there early to enjoy a cocktail before the place starts jumping. ⌧ *2791 Agua Fria St., South Side* ☎ *505/780–5730* ⊕ *www.tumblerootbreweryanddistillery.com.*

Shopping

BOOKS

★ Photo-eye Bookstore and Gallery

BOOKS/STATIONERY | The place to go for an almost unbelievable collection of new, rare, and out-of-print photography books; the staff is made up of photographers who are excellent sources of information and advice on great spots to shoot in and around Santa Fe. The store has an impressive gallery in the Railyard District (541 S. Guadalupe St.) that presents fine photography. ⌧ *1300 Rufina Circle, Suite A3, South Side* ☎ *505/988–5152* ⊕ *www.photoeye.com.*

FOOD AND DRINK

Las Cosas Kitchen Shoppe & Cooking School

SPECIALTY STORES | **FAMILY** | In DeVargas shopping center, Las Cosas Kitchen Shoppe stocks a fantastic selection of cookery, tableware, and kitchen gadgetry and gifts. The shop is also renowned for its cooking classes taught by local personality chef Johnny Vee, which touch on everything from high-altitude baking and northern New Mexican specialties to Chinatown classics and Vietnamese street food. For those looking to really up their culinary game, Johnny Vee also offers regular classes on techniques such as braising, grilling, and fundamentals including knife skills and pressure cooking. Classes are Tuesday and Friday night, as well as Saturday morning. If you've got a tight schedule or a big group, Las Cosas and chef Johnny are happy to schedule something just for you. ⌧ *De Vargas Center, 181 Paseo de Peralta, at N. Guadalupe St., West of the Plaza* ☎ *505/988–3394* ⊕ *www. lascosascooking.com.*

GIFTS AND HOME FURNISHINGS

★ Jackalope

ANTIQUES/COLLECTIBLES | **FAMILY** | You could easily spend a couple of hours wandering through this legendary indoor–outdoor bazaar, which sprawls over 7 acres, incorporating pottery barns, a

While New Mexico is often thought of as a desert locale, there are still some stunning ski slopes, including the ones at Ski Santa Fe.

furniture store, endless aisles of knickknacks from Latin America and Asia, and a glassblowing studio. There's also an area where craftspeople, artisans, and others sell their wares—sort of a mini–flea market. ⊠ *2820 Cerrillos Rd., South Side* ☎ *505/471–8539* ⊕ *www.jackalope.com.*

Pandora's

HOUSEHOLD ITEMS/FURNITURE | Beautiful, carefully curated items for the home—some produced regionally and others from Peru, Uzbekistan, the Congo, and other far-flung lands—are the specialty of this colorful boutique in DeVargas Center. Keep an eye out for quilts made by a weaving co-op in Vietnam and brightly colored Missoni bath linens. ⊠ *173 Paseo de Peralta, West of the Plaza* ☎ *505/982–3298* ⊕ *www.pandorasantafe.com.*

Activities

HIKING

★ Aspen Vista

HIKING/WALKING | **FAMILY** | Especially in autumn, when golden aspens shimmer on the mountainside, this trail up near Santa Fe's ski area makes for a lovely hike. After walking a few miles through thick aspen groves you come to panoramic views of Santa Fe. The path, which is well marked and gradually inclines toward Tesuque Peak, becomes steeper with elevation—also note that snow has been reported on the upper portions of the trail as late as July. In winter, after heavy snows, the trail is great for intermediate–advanced cross-country skiing. The full hike to the peak makes for a long, rigorous day—it's 12 miles round-trip and sees an elevation gain of 2,000 feet, but it's just 3½ miles to the spectacular overlook. Note that the Aspen Vista Picnic Site is also the trailhead for the Alamo Vista Trail, which leads to the summit of the ski area. ⊠ *Hyde Park Rd. (NM 475), 2 miles before ski area, North Side* ✛ *Parking lot at Aspen Vista Picnic Site.*

HORSEBACK RIDING

New Mexico's rugged countryside has been the setting for many Hollywood Westerns. Whether you want to ride the range that Gregory Peck and Kevin Costner tamed or just head out feeling tall in the saddle, you can do so year-round.

SKIING

Ski Santa Fe

SKIING/SNOWBOARDING | **FAMILY** | Open roughly from late November through early April, this is a somewhat underrated, midsize ski and snowboard operation that receives an average of 225 inches of snow a year and plenty of sunshine. It's one of America's highest ski areas—the 12,075-foot summit has unbelievable views and a varied terrain which make its 1,725 feet of vertical rise and 660 acres seem even bigger. There are some great powder stashes, tough bump runs, and many wide, gentle cruising runs. The 87 trails are ranked 20% beginner, 40% intermediate, and 40% advanced; there are seven lifts: one quad, two triples, two doubles, and two surface lifts. Chipmunk Corner provides day care and supervised kids' skiing. The ski school is excellent. Rentals, a ski shop, and a good restaurant round out the amenities at bright and modern La Casa Lodge base-camp, and Totemoff's Bar and Grill is a welcome midmountain option with frequent live music during the season. While Ski Santa Fe doesn't offer cross-country skiing, there are many Nordic trails available off of Hyde Park Road just before the downhill ski area. Ski Santa Fe is also fun for hiking during the summer months and the Super Chief Quad Chair operates from late August through mid-October, catering to hikers and shutterbugs eager to view the high-mountain fall foliage, including acres of shimmering golden aspens. ⊠ *End of NM 475, 18 miles northeast of Downtown, North Side* ☎ *505/982–4429 general info, 505/983–9155 snow report* ⊕ *www.skisantafe.com.*

DAY TRIPS FROM SANTA FE

Updated by
Yvonne Pesquera

Sights ★★★★★   Restaurants ★★★☆☆   Hotels ★☆☆☆☆   Shopping ★★★☆☆   Nightlife ★★★☆☆

Santa Fe makes a great base for exploring the entire north-central Rio Grande Valley, a region rich in Spanish-colonial and Native American heritage and abounding with scenic drives, dazzling geographical formations, colorful villages, and important historic sites. Every community and attraction covered here could be visited as a day trip and as a road trip, following along state and local roads and passing lush scenery, pretty rivers, and expansive blue skies that nourish the soul.

There is also some impressive history to take in. Tucked in the pockets of New Mexico's mountains and desert, you'll discover the 1717 mission church ruins in Pecos National Historical Park; the ancestral Pueblo petroglyphs and dwellings at Bandelier National Monument; the dazzling artistry of Georgia O'Keeffe; and the world-changing history of the atomic bomb at Manhattan Project National Historical Park in Los Alamos.

Keep in mind that the day trips listed here are in high-elevation areas, in a climate where the winters are snowy and summer days are hot. Take time to prepare before hitting the road by stocking up on water and snacks as gas stations and convenience stores are few and far between. It's also practical to embark on some of these trips en route to Albuquerque or Taos. For example, you could drive the Turquoise Trail or visit Tent Rock National Monument on the way to Albuquerque. The side trips to points north—such as the High Road, Bandelier and Los Alamos, and Abiquiú and Georgia O'Keeffe Country—are worth investigating on your way to Taos.

Top Reasons to Go

Hiking stunning landscapes. From the sandstone rock formations of Kasha-Katuwe Tent Rocks National Monument to one of the world's largest calderas in Valles Caldera National Preserve, this area is filled with opportunities for gorgeous hikes.

Georgia O'Keeffe's homestead. Perhaps the most famous artist of the American Southwest, Georgia O'Keeffe spent the final decades of her life at her house in Abiquiú, painting the scenery seen from her cabin in nearby Ghost Ranch.

Native American culture and history. Pecos National Historic Park is filled with the fascinating ruins of a Pueblo village while Bandelier National Monument holds the remnants of a community of Ancestral Puebloan peoples.

Scenic road trips. Take your time driving down famed road trip routes like the Turquoise Trail and the High Road to Taos, appreciating the beautiful scenery and interesting small towns along the way.

Local art and artists. Former mining towns like Madrid and rural villages like Chimayó and Truchas have become renowned for their local artwork, selling everything from paintings and sculptures to weavings and religious imagery.

The Turquoise Trail

The most prominent side trip south of the city is along the fabled Turquoise Trail, an excellent—and leisurely—alternative route from Santa Fe to Albuquerque that's far more interesting than Interstate 25. Etched out in the early 1970s, the scenic Turquoise Trail (or more prosaically, NM 14) is a National Scenic Byway that's dotted with ghost towns now popular with writers, artists, and other urban refugees. This 70 miles of piñon-studded mountain back road along the eastern flank of the sacred Sandia Mountains is a gentle roller coaster that also affords panoramic views of the Ortiz, Jémez, and Sangre de Cristo mountains. It's believed that 2,000 years ago Native Americans mined turquoise in these hills. The Spanish took up turquoise mining in the 16th century, and the practice continued into the early 20th century, with Tiffany & Co. removing a fair share of the semiprecious stone. Today, turquoise is the official state gem of New Mexico, and its allure to the region has remained. In addition, gold, silver, tin, lead, and coal have been mined here.

There's plenty of opportunity for picture taking and picnicking along the way. You can drive this loop in three hours with minimal stops, or make a full day of it, if you stop to explore the main attractions along the way, through the towns of Cerrillos, Madrid, Golden, Sandia Park, Cedar Crest, and Tijeras. You can even take a little side trip on NM State Road 536, which will lead you up to Sandia Crest (with its elevation of 10,378 feet). At the crest's rim there are easy walking paths to get out and stretch your legs as well as wide-open, panoramic views of Albuquerque in the near distance and the expanse of the New Mexico desert beyond. You'll find plenty of great information including events and road conditions, online at ⊕ *www.turquoisetrail.org*.

Madrid

27 miles south of Santa Fe.

Abandoned when its coal mine closed in the 1950s, Madrid (locals put the emphasis on the first syllable: *mah*-drid) has gradually been rebuilt and is now—to the dismay of some longtime locals—actually a bit trendy. The entire town was offered for sale for $250,000 back in the 1950s, but there were no takers. Finally, in the early 1970s, a few artists fleeing big cities settled in and began restoration. Weathered houses and old company stores have been repaired and turned into boutiques and galleries, some of them selling high-quality furniture, paintings, and crafts. Big events here include the CrawDaddy Blues Fest in mid-May, the Madrid and Cerrillos Studio Tour in early October, and Madrid Christmas Open House, held weekends in December, when galleries and studios are open and the famous Madrid Christmas lights twinkle brightly.

As you continue south down NM 14 from Madrid, after about 11 miles you pass through the sleepy village of **Golden,** the site of the first gold rush (in 1825) west of the Mississippi. It has a rock shop and a mercantile store. The rustic adobe church and graveyard are popular with photographers.

 Sights

Old Coal Town Museum

MUSEUM | FAMILY | Part of the historic complex that houses the beloved Mine Shaft Tavern, this fascinating trove of local history recounts Madrid's legacy as a booming mining town and then a ghost town. Memorabilia from the mine operations, old photos,

The town of Madrid along the Turquoise Trail has lots of shops selling local goods.

the historic Engine 769, and occasional variety shows and other performances in the old Engine House Theatre make this a fun diversion, especially with kids. ⊠ *2846 NM 14* ☎ *505/473–0743* ⊕ *www.themineshafttavern.com/madrid-old-coal-town-museum* ⊠ *$5*.

🍴 Restaurants

The Hollar

$ | SOUTHERN | Stop by this funky restaurant set inside a converted freight car for well-prepared Southern and Southwestern comfort food, from fried green tomatoes to crispy-shrimp and grits. There's a good-size patio from which you can watch the colorful parade of tourists and art buyers strolling through town. **Known for:** biscuits with pulled pork; live music on the patio many days; good selection of local beers. ⑤ *Average main: $12* ⊠ *2849 NM 14* ☎ *505/471–4821* ⊕ *www.thehollar.com*.

Java Junction

$ | CAFÉ | Aged hippies, youthful hipsters, and everyone in between congregate at Java Junction for lattes, chai, sandwiches, breakfast burritos, bagels, pastries, and other treats. You can also pick up a number of house-made gourmet goods, from hot sauces to jalapeño-raspberry preserves. **Known for:** hip crowd; upstairs room for rent; homemade gourmet goods. ⑤ *Average main: $6* ⊠ *2855 NM 14* ☎ *505/438–2772* ⊕ *www.java-junction.com* ⏰ *No dinner*.

★ Mineshaft Tavern

$ | **SOUTHWESTERN** | A rollicking old bar and restaurant adjacent to the Old Coal Mine Museum, this boisterous place—there's live music many nights—was a miners' commissary back in the day. Today it serves a popular green-chile cheeseburger (available with beef, Wagyu, buffalo, or mushroom-veggie), along with plenty of ice cold beers on tap and a selection of other pub favorites and comfort foods. **Known for:** green-chile cheeseburgers; live music; fried green-chile appetizer. $ *Average main: $12* ⊠ *2846 NM 14* ☎ *505/473–0743* ⊕ *www.themineshafttavern.com.*

Shopping

Johnsons of Madrid

ART GALLERIES | Among the most prestigious galleries in a town with quite a few good ones, Johnsons carries paintings, photography, sculpture, and textiles created by some of the region's leading artists. ⊠ *2843 NM 14* ☎ *505/471–1054.*

Seppanen & Daughters Fine Textiles

TEXTILES/SEWING | You could spend hours browsing the fine rugs and furnishings at this well-established shop. They stock custom Zapotec textiles from Oaxaca, Navajo weavings, and Tibetan carpets, as well as fine arts and crafts tables, sofas, and chairs. ⊠ *2879 NM 14* ☎ *505/424–7470* ⊕ *www.finetextiles.com.*

Sandia Park

24 miles southwest of Madrid, 22 miles northeast of Albuquerque.

The southern stretch of the Turquoise Trail, as you continue from Golden and begin encountering upscale housing developments around Paa-Ko Ridge Golf Club, is more densely populated than the northern section—it's almost suburban in character, with the towns of Sandia Park (population 260), Cedar Crest (population 1,000), and several smaller nearby communities considered part of metro Albuquerque. The Turquoise Trail meanders along the eastern flanks of the Sandia Mountains before intersecting with Interstate 40, which leads east for the final 10 miles into Albuquerque proper.

Sights

Sandia Crest

VIEWPOINT | For awesome views of Albuquerque and half of New Mexico, take NM 536 up the back side of the Sandia Mountains through Cibola National Forest to Sandia Crest. At the 10,378-foot summit, explore the foot trails along the rim (particularly in summer) and take in the breathtaking views of Albuquerque down below, and of the so-called Steel Forest—the nearby cluster of radio and television towers. Always bring an extra layer of clothing, even in summer—the temperature at the crest can be anywhere from 15 to 25 degrees cooler than down in Albuquerque. ⊠ *NM 536.*

🏃 Activities

Sandia Peak

SKIING/SNOWBOARDING | Although less extensive and challenging than the ski areas farther north in the Sangre de Cristos, Sandia Peak is extremely popular with locals from Albuquerque and offers a nice range of novice, intermediate, and expert downhill trails; there's also a ski school. Snowboarding is welcome on all trails, and there's cross-country terrain as well, whenever snow is available. Snowfall can be sporadic, so call ahead to check for cross-country; Sandia has snow-making capacity for about 30 of its 200 acres of downhill skiing. The season runs from mid-December to mid-March, and lift tickets cost $55. Keep in mind that you can also access the ski area year-round via the Sandia Peak Aerial Tramway, which is faster from Albuquerque than driving all the way around. In summer, the ski area converts into a fantastic mountain-biking and hiking terrain. The ski area offers a number of packages with bike and helmet rentals and lift tickets. Other summer activities at Sandia Peak include sand volleyball, horseshoes, and picnicking. ⊠ *NM 536* 🕾 *505/242–9052 ski area, 505/857–8977 snow conditions* ⊕ *www.sandiapeak.com.*

Kasha-Katuwe Tent Rocks National Monument

36 miles west of Santa Fe.

Hoodoos and slot canyons form an enchanted hiking getaway that can be accessed from Interstate 25 on the drive between Albuquerque and Santa Fe. If you have time for just one hike, this is an excellent choice. The national monument was established by President Clinton in 2001 in order to protect the remarkable volcanic rock formations that are shaped like tents. The monument is managed in cooperation with Cochiti Pueblo, whose people call the area Kasha-Katuwe.

Sights

★ Kasha-Katuwe Tent Rocks National Monument

NATURE SITE | FAMILY | The sandstone rock formations here are a visual marvel, resembling stacked tents in a stark, water- and wind-eroded box canyon. Tent Rocks offers superb hiking year-round, although it can get hot in summer, when you should bring extra water. The drive to this magical landscape offers its own delights, as the road heads west toward Cochiti Dam and through the cottonwood groves around the pueblo. It's a good hike for kids. The round-trip hiking distance is only 2 miles, about 1½ leisurely hours, but it's the kind of place where you'll want to hang out for a while. Take a camera, but leave your pets at home—no dogs are allowed. There are no facilities here, just a small parking area with a posted trail map and a self-pay admission box; you can get gas and pick up picnic supplies and bottled water (along with some locally made Pueblo items) at Pueblo de Cochiti Convenience Store. ✉ *Cochiti Pueblo, Indian Service Rte. 92, Cochiti Lake* ✥ *Follow signs to Kasha-Katuwe Tent Rocks National Monument* ☎ *505/331–6259* ⊕ *www.blm.gov/visit/kktr* 💲 *$5 per vehicle.*

The Santa Fe Trail and Pecos National Historical Park

27 miles east of Santa Fe.

In the mid-19th century, this vast tract of grasslands and prairies, along with the eastern foothills of the Sangre de Cristo range, became the gateway to New Mexico for American settlers

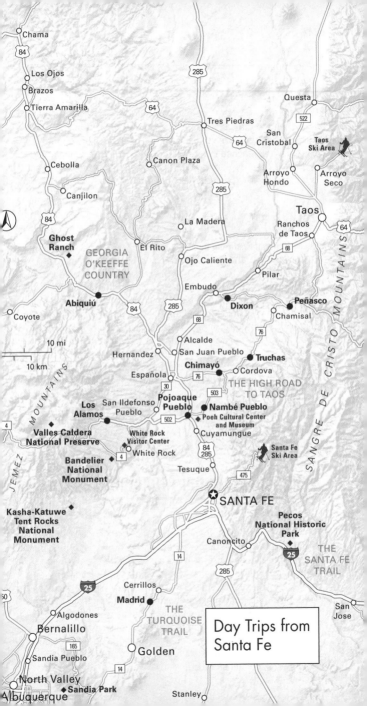

Day Trips from Santa Fe

headed here from the Midwest. Towns along the Santa Fe Trail's modern offspring, Interstate 25 remain popular stops for road-tripping fans of Old West history.

From ancestral Pecos Pueblo Indians, to the Spaniards in the 1600s, and to the Santa Fe Trail wagon travelers in the 1800s (Pecos was the last major encampment that travelers on the Santa Fe Trail reached before Santa Fe), all of these groups lived in this area and passed through this region. Today the little village is mostly a starting point for exploring the Pecos National Historic Park.

Sights

Pecos National Historical Park
ARCHAEOLOGICAL SITE | The centerpiece of this national park is the ruins of Pecos, once a major Pueblo village with more than 1,100 rooms. About 2,500 people are thought to have lived in this structure, as high as five stories in places. Pecos, in a fertile valley between the Great Plains and the Rio Grande Valley, was a trading center centuries before the Spanish conquistadors visited in about 1540. The Spanish later returned to build two missions. The pueblo was abandoned in 1838, and its 17 surviving occupants moved to the Jémez Pueblo. Anglo travelers on the Santa Fe Trail observed the mission ruins with a great sense of fascination. You can view the mission ruins and the excavated pueblo on a 1¼-mile self-guided tour, a Civil War battlefield on a 2½-mile trail, and the small but outstanding visitor center museum containing photos, pottery, and artifacts from the pueblo. ⊠ *NM 63, Pecos* ☎ *505/757–7241* ⊕ *www.nps.gov/peco* ⊠ *Free.*

Bandelier National Monument

40 miles west of Santa Fe.

Seven centuries before the Declaration of Independence was signed, compact city-states existed in the Southwest. Remnants of one of the most impressive examples can be seen at Frijoles Canyon in Bandelier National Monument. At the canyon's base, near a gurgling stream, the remains of cave dwellings, ancient ceremonial kivas, and other stone structures stretch out for more than a mile beneath the sheer walls of the canyon's tree-fringed rim. For hundreds of years the Ancestral Puebloan people, relatives of today's Rio Grande Pueblo Indians, thrived on wild game, corn, and beans. Suddenly, for reasons still undetermined, the settlements were abandoned.

◉ Sights

★ Bandelier National Monument

ARCHAEOLOGICAL SITE | A fascinating trip back in time, Bandelier National Monument is home to a stunning collection of preserved petroglyphs and cave dwellings of the Ancestral Puebloan people. Along a paved, self-guided trail, steep wooden ladders and narrow doorways lead to a series of cave dwellings and cell-like rooms. There is one kiva in the cliff wall that is large, and tall enough to stand in. Bandelier National Monument, named after author and ethnologist Adolph Bandelier (his novel *The Delight Makers* is set in Frijoles Canyon), contains 33,000 acres of backcountry wilderness, waterfalls, and wildlife. Some 70 miles of trails traverse the park; the short Pueblo Loop Trail is an easy, self-guided walk. Pick up the $2 trail guide at the monument's main building to read about the 21 numbered sites along the trail. A small museum in the visitor center focuses on the area's prehistoric and contemporary Native American cultures, with displays of artifacts from 1200 to modern times.

Note that from mid-May to mid-October, visitors arriving by car between 9 am and 3 pm must park at the White Rock Visitor Center 10 miles east on NM 4 and take a free shuttle bus into the park. ⊠ *15 Entrance Rd., Los Alamos* ☎ *505/672–3861* ⊕ *www. nps.gov/band* ☜ *$15 on foot or bicycle; $25 per car.*

White Rock Visitor Center

INFO CENTER | This sleek, eco-friendly building is a one-stop shop for finding out about the many things to see and do in the area, from Bandelier and Los Alamos to the Jémez Mountain Trail National Scenic Byway, the hiking at nearby White Rock Overlook, and Valles Caldera National Preserve. You can also catch free shuttle buses into Bandelier (in fact, you can only visit the park in this way from mid-May to mid-October, daily 9–3) and downtown Los Alamos. The region's nicest chain hotel, the Hampton Inn & Suites Los Alamos, is next door. Discover Los Alamos operates a second visitor center in Los Alamos at 109 Central Park Square. ⊠ *115 NM 4, White Rock* ☎ *505/672–3183* ⊕ *www.visitlosalamos. org* ☜ *Free.*

Los Alamos

35 miles north of Santa Fe.

Look at old books on New Mexico and you rarely find a mention of Los Alamos, now a busy town of about 18,000 that has the highest per capita income in the state. Like so many other Southwestern communities, Los Alamos was created expressly as a company town; only here the workers weren't mining iron, manning freight trains, or hauling lumber—they were busy toiling at America's foremost nuclear research facility, Los Alamos National Laboratory (LANL). The facility still employs some 10,000 full-time workers.

A few miles from ancient cave dwellings, scientists led by J. Robert Oppenheimer built Fat Man and Little Boy, the atom bombs that in August 1945 decimated Hiroshima and Nagasaki, respectively. LANL was created in 1943 under the auspices of the intensely covert Manhattan Project, whose express purpose it was to expedite an Allied victory during World War II. Indeed, Japan surrendered—but a full-blown Cold War between Russia and the United States ensued for another four and a half decades.

 Sights

Bradbury Science Museum

MUSEUM | FAMILY | Los Alamos National Laboratory's public show-case, the Bradbury provides a balanced and provocative examination of such topics as atomic weapons and nuclear power. You can experiment with lasers; witness research in solar, geothermal, fission, and fusion energy; learn about DNA fingerprinting; and view fascinating exhibits about World War II's Project Y (the Manhattan Project, whose participants developed the atomic bomb). ⊠ *1350 Central Ave.* ☎ *505/667–4444* ⊕ *www.lanl.gov/museum* ⊠ *Free.*

Fuller Lodge Art Center

BUILDING | New Mexican architect John Gaw Meem designed Fuller Lodge, a short drive up Central Avenue from the Bradbury Science Museum. The massive log building was erected in 1928 as a dining and recreation hall for a small private boys' school; the area was so remote that a large part of the school curriculum focused on wilderness training and outdoor adventures. In 1942 the federal government purchased the school and made it the base of operations for the Manhattan Project. It became the site of socializing for the scientists and their spouses as well as the location for meetings, talks, and lectures about the bomb's progress. Today, part of the lodge contains an art center that shows the works of northern New Mexican artists; there's a gorgeous rose garden on the grounds. This is a bustling center with drop-in art classes, nine art shows per year, and an outstanding gallery gift shop featuring works by nearly 100 local artisans. ⊠ *2132 Central Ave.* ☎ *505/662–1635* ⊕ *www.fullerlodgeartcenter.com* ⊠ *Free* ☾ *Closed Sun.*

Los Alamos History Museum

MUSEUM | Here you will find succinct, informative indoor and outdoor exhibits tracing the history of human activity on the site of The Atomic City, from a 13th-century Ancestral Pueblo, to a Boy Scout–influenced prep school for young men from prominent families (including Gore Vidal and William S. Burroughs), to the Manhattan Project and beyond. Permanent exhibits in the Ranch School's former guesthouse set the scene. Steps away, the Hans Bethe House re-creates home life for the top-level scientists working on the atomic bomb. The house next door, home to project coordinator J. Robert Oppenheimer, remains a private residence, but can be viewed from the outside. ⊠ 1050 Bathtub Row ☎ 505/662–4493 ⊕ www.losalamoshistory.org/visit ⊠ $5.

★ Manhattan Project National Historical Park Visitor Center

HISTORIC SITE | The town of Los Alamos is a must for atomic age history buffs: the National Historical Park exploring its history is not your typical enclosed park, but rather a walking tour through the city's historic downtown that you can begin at this visitor center. Start with an orientation film on the people and events that led to the creation of the atomic bomb. Park rangers will provide you with a Historic Sites Walking Tour map. The tour will take you to the famous Fuller Lodge, where the scientists socialized and held serious talks and lectures about the bomb's progress. Another key stop on the tour is the sculpture of head scientist Dr. Robert Oppenheimer and his military counterpart General Leslie Groves. ⊠ 475 20th St. ☎ 505/661–6277 ⊕ www.nps.gov/mapr ⊠ Walking tour free; entry to some sites may require fee.

🍴 Restaurants

Blue Window Bistro

$$$ | **AMERICAN** | This brightly colored and elegant restaurant is a welcome rest along the Manhattan Project National Historical Park walking tour. The kitchen turns out a mix of New Mexican, American, and Continental dishes, from first-rate salads to traditional filet mignon to shredded-chicken blue-corn enchiladas. **Known for:** filet mignon and New York strip steaks; one of the best cocktail, wine, and beer selections in town; stop on the Manhattan Project National Historical Park walking tour. $ Average main: $25 ⊠ 1789 Central Ave. ☎ 505/662–6305 ⊕ www.labluewindowbistro.com ⊗ Closed weekends.

El Parasol Los Alamos

$ | **SOUTHWESTERN** | An unabashedly local joint, the authentic New Mexican menu here consists of all the staples: burritos, tacos,

You can reach Valles Caldera National Preserve in just over an hour driving from Santa Fe.

tamales, and more. You can also try their Frito pie, which is a legendary Southwestern beef chile dish topped with—you guessed it—Fritos brand corn chips. **Known for:** Frito pie made with delicious red chile; burritos smothered in red or green chile—or both; homemade biscochitos (traditional New Mexican cookies). ⑤ *Average main: $10* ⊠ *1903 Central Ave.* ☎ *505/661–0303* ⊕ *www. elparasol.com/los-alamos* ⊘ *No dinner.*

Valles Caldera National Preserve

20 miles northwest of Bandelier National Monument.

A high-forest drive brings you to the awe-inspiring Valles Grande, which at 14 miles in diameter is one of the world's largest calderas and which became Valles (*vah*-yes) Caldera National Preserve in 2000.

Sights

★ Valles Caldera National Preserve

NATURE PRESERVE | The caldera resulted from the eruption and collapse of a 14,000-foot peak more than 1¼ million years ago; the flow out the bottom created the Pajarito Plateau and the ash from the eruption spread as far east as Kansas. You can't imagine the volcanic crater's immensity until you spot what look like specks of dust on the lush meadow floor and realize they're elk. The Valles Caldera Trust manages this 89,000-acre multiuse preserve with the aim to "protect and preserve the scientific, scenic, geologic, watershed, fish, wildlife, historic, cultural, and recreational values of the Preserve, and to provide for multiple use and sustained yield of renewable resources within the Preserve."

The preserve is open to visitors for hiking, cross-country skiing, horseback riding, horse-drawn carriage rides, van wildlife photography tours, mountain-bike tours, bird-watching, fly-fishing, and many other outdoorsy endeavors. ⊠ *NM 4, mile marker 39.2, 10 miles west of junction with NM 501, Jemez Springs* ☎ *575/829–4100* ⊕ *www.nps.gov/vall* ☎ *$15 on foot or bicycle; $25 per vehicle, good for 7 days* ☉ *Visitor center closed Sun.*

Georgia O'Keeffe Country

It's a 20-minute drive north of Santa Fe to reach the Española Valley, where you head northwest to the striking mesas, cliffs, and valleys that so inspired the artist Georgia O'Keeffe—she lived in this area for the final 50 years of her life. Passing through the small, workaday city of Española, U.S. 84 continues to the sleepy village of Abiquiú and eventually up past Ghost Ranch, areas where O'Keeffe both lived and worked.

Abiquiú

50 miles northwest of Santa Fe.

This tiny, very traditional Hispanic village was originally home to freed *genizaros,* indigenous and mixed-blood slaves who served as house servants, shepherds, and other key roles in Spanish, Mexican, and American households well into the 1880s. Many descendants of original families still live in the area, although since the late 1980s Abiquiú and its surrounding countryside have become a nesting ground for those fleeing big-city life, among them actresses Marsha Mason and Shirley MacLaine. Abiquiú—along with parts of the nearby Española Valley—is also a hotbed of organic farming, with many of the operations here selling their goods at the Santa Fe Farmers' Market and to restaurants throughout the Rio Grande Valley.

Sights

Abiquiú Studio Tour

TOUR—SIGHT | A number of artists live in Abiquiú, and several studios showing traditional Hispanic art, as well as contemporary works and pottery, are open regularly to the public; many others open each year over Columbus Day weekend (second weekend of October) for the annual Abiquiú Studio Tour. ⊠ *Abiquiu* ☎ *505/257–0866* ⊕ *www.abiquiustudiotour.org*.

Georgia O'Keeffe Home & Studio

HOUSE | In 1945 Georgia O'Keeffe bought a large, dilapidated late-18th-century Spanish-colonial adobe compound just off the plaza in Abiquiú. Upon the 1946 death of her husband, photographer Alfred Stieglitz, she left New York City and began dividing her time permanently between this home, which figured prominently in many of her works, and the one in nearby Ghost Ranch. The patio is featured in *Black Patio Door* (1955) and *Patio with Cloud* (1956). O'Keeffe died in 1986 at the age of 98 and left provisions in her will to ensure that the property's houses would never be public monuments.

Highly engaging one-hour tours are available by advance reservation through Santa Fe's Georgia O'Keeffe Museum, which owns the house and operates the tours Tuesday–Saturday from early March through late November (call for hours); the cost is $45 for a standard tour and $65 for a more intensive behind-the-scenes tour. Both tours focus on O'Keeffe's interior decor style, with aesthetics drawing on Native American and Spanish influences to make her home distinctly modern. Tours depart by shuttle bus from the tour office, which is next to the Abiquiu Inn. Book well ahead in summer, as these tours fill up quickly. ⊠ *21120 U.S. 84* ☎ *505/946–1098* ⊕ *www.okeeffemuseum.org/tickets-and-tours* 🎫 *$45* ⊗ *Closed Sun., Mon., and late Nov.–early Mar.*

 Restaurants

Café Abiquiu at the Abiquiu Inn

$$ | ECLECTIC | This inviting, art-filled restaurant at the Abiquiú Inn (which is also the departure point for tours of the nearby Georgia O'Keeffe Home & Studio) serves tasty New Mexican and American fare. Be sure to peek inside the adjoining art gallery featuring local work, and take a stroll through the graceful gardens. **Known for:** authentic New Mexican cuisine with local fresh ingredients; great place to refresh before or after a visit to the O'Keeffe

Home; lovely artwork and beautiful gardens. $ *Average main: $19* ✉ *Abiquiú Inn, 21120 U.S. 84* ☎ *505/685–4378* ⊕ *www.abiquiuinn. com.*

Hotels

Abiquiu Inn

$$ | **B&B/INN** | Deep in the Chama Valley, this inn has a secluded vibe amid the red-rock geography that inspired Georgia O'Keeffe. **Pros:** good base for exploring O'Keeffe Country; breathtaking high-desert scenery; charming Southwestern decor. **Cons:** service is friendly but fairly hands-off; rooms at the front of the inn get noise from the road; no free breakfast. $ *Rooms from: $189* ✉ *21120 U.S. 84* ☎ *505/685–4378* ⊕ *www.abiquiuinn.com* ⇌ *25 rooms* ✝◎❙ *No meals.*

★ Ojo Caliente Mineral Springs Resort & Spa

$$ | **RESORT** | Set in a remote village in the vicinity of the red rocks and rugged mountains of Abiquiú, this fabled hot springs resort fits the tastes and budget of all sorts of travelers, from spiritually minded adventurers on a modest budget to romance-seekers wanting an upscale yet secluded spa getaway (it's a favorite of celebs filming movies in New Mexico). **Pros:** very reasonably priced (for the simplest rooms); relaxing and serene setting; unpretentious and friendly vibe. **Cons:** a little funky and New Age-y for some tastes; remote; breakfast not included. $ *Rooms from: $169* ✉ *50 Los Baños Dr., Ojo Caliente* ☎ *505/583–2233* ⊕ *ojocaliente.ojospa.com* ⇌ *49 units* ✝◎❙ *No meals.*

Ghost Ranch

15 miles north of Abiquiú.

For art historians, the name Ghost Ranch brings to mind Georgia O'Keeffe, who lived on a small parcel of this 22,000-acre dude and cattle ranch. The ranch's owner in the 1930s—conservationist and publisher of *Nature Magazine,* Arthur Pack—first invited O'Keeffe here to visit in 1934; Pack soon sold the artist the 7-acre plot on which she lived summer through fall for most of the rest of her life. In 1955 Pack donated the rest of the ranch to the Presbyterian Church, which continues to use Pack's original structures and part of the land as a conference center, but Ghost Ranch is also open to visitors for tours, hikes, workshops, and all sorts of other activities.

Georgia O'Keeffe was inspired by the stunning landscapes surrounding Ghost Ranch, her longtime summer home.

 Sights

★ Ghost Ranch

HISTORIC SITE | FAMILY | Open to the public year-round, this sprawling, stunningly situated ranch is busiest in summer, when the majority of workshops take place, and when visitors drive up having toured the O'Keeffe home in nearby Abiquiú. Now a retreat center, the ranch offers a wealth of interesting activities for day visitors, including two different guided Georgia O'Keeffe tours across the landscape she painted during the five decades that she summered here. She first visited the property when it was a dude ranch, and soon afterward the owner sold her a cabin and a 7-acre plot that she made her summer home. Her original house is not part of the tour and is closed to the public. Other guided hikes amid the property's dramatic rock formations touch on archaeology and paleontology, history, and the several movies that have been filmed here *(Cowboys and Aliens, City Slickers, Wyatt Earp,* and a few others). Visitors can tour the **Florence Hawley Ellis Museum of Anthropology,** which contains Native American tools, pottery, and other artifacts excavated from the Ghost Ranch Gallina digs, and the adjacent **Ruth Hall Museum of Paleontology.** Workshops, which touch on everything from photography and poetry to yoga and wellness, are offered throughout the year—guests camp or stay in semi-rustic cottages or casitas. And you can also sign up for guided trail rides, hikes (guided or on your own), massages, and more. When you arrive, drop by the welcome center, which also houses a trading post stocked with books, art, O'Keeffe ephemera, and a basic coffee station (there's also a dining hall serving cafeteria-style meals throughout the day). ⊠ *U.S. 84, between mile markers 224 and 225, about 13 miles north of Abiquiú village, Abiquiu* ☎ *505/685–1000, 877/804–4678* ⊕ *www. ghostranch.org.*

The High Road to Taos

The main route to Taos (NM 68, the so-called Low Road) is a quite dramatic drive if you've got limited time, but by far the most spectacular way is via what's known as the High Road. Towering peaks, lush hillsides, orchards, and meadows surround tiny, ancient Hispanic villages that are as picturesque as they are historically fascinating. The well-signed High Road follows U.S. 285/84 north to NM 503 (a right turn just past Pojoaque toward Nambé), to County Road 98 (a left toward Chimayó), to NM 76 northeast to NM 75 east, to NM 518 north. The drive takes you through the badlands of stark, weathered rock—where numerous Westerns have been filmed—quickly into rolling foothills, lush canyons, and finally into pine forests. Although most of these insular, traditional Hispanic communities offer little in the way of shopping and dining, the region has become a haven for artists.

Depending on when you make this drive, you're in for some of the state's most radiant scenery. In mid-April the orchards are in blossom; summer turns the valleys into lush green oases; and in fall the smell of piñon adds to the sensual overload of golden leaves and red-chile ristras hanging from the houses. In winter the fields are covered with quilts of snow, and the lines of homes, fences, and trees stand out like bold pen-and-ink drawings against the sky. But the roads can be icy and treacherous—if in doubt, stick with the Low Road to Taos. ■ TIP→ **If you decide to take the High Road just one way between Santa Fe and Taos, you might want to save it for the return journey—the scenery is even more stunning when traveling north to south.**

Pojoaque and Nambé Pueblos

17 miles north of Santa Fe.

Pojoaque and Nambé Pueblos are sovereign Native American nations within the United States. Each has its own government, traditions, and culture as well as some sights that are accessible to tourists.

Sights

★ High Road Art Tour

TOUR—SIGHT | From Chimayó to Peñasco, you can find mostly low-key but often high-quality art galleries, many of them run out of the owners' homes. During the final two weekends in September each year, more than three dozen artists show their work in the High Road Art Tour; for a studio map, or plenty of useful information on galleries open not just during the tour but year-round, visit the website. ⊠ *Chimayo* ⊕ *www.highroadnewmexico.com.*

Nambé Falls and Nambé Lake

BODY OF WATER | There's a shady picnic area and a large fishing lake that's open April through October at this scenic and popular hiking area along the High Road, just east of Pojoaque (the cost is $15 per carload for a day pass). The waterfalls are about a 15-minute hike in from the parking and picnic area along a rocky, clearly marked path. The water pours over a rock precipice—a loud and dramatic sight given the river's modest size. ⊠ *Poechunu Poe Rd., Off NM 503, Nambe* ☎ *505/455–2304* ⊕ *www.nambepueblo.org/nambe-falls-lake* ⊠ *$15.*

Poeh Cultural Center and Museum

LOCAL INTEREST | Situated just off U.S. 285/84 at Pojoaque Pueblo, this impressive complex of traditional adobe buildings, including the three-story Sun Tower, makes an engaging first stop as you begin a drive north of Santa Fe toward Taos. The facility comprises a museum, a cultural center, and artists' studios, all with the mission of preserving the arts and culture of Pueblo communities. The museum holds some 10,000 photographs, including many by esteemed early-20th-century photographer Edward S. Curtis, as well as more than 600 works of both traditional and contemporary pottery, jewelry, textiles, and sculpture. There's also a lovely gift shop of locally made Native American arts and crafts. ⊠ *78 Cities of Gold Rd., North Side* ☎ *505/455–5041* ⊕ *www.poehcenter.org* ⊠ *$10* ☾ *Closed Sun.*

Chimayó

28 miles north of Santa Fe, 12 miles northeast of Nambé/ Pojoaque.

From U.S. 285/84 north of Pojoaque, scenic NM 503 winds past horse paddocks and orchards in the narrow Nambé Valley, then ascends into the red-sandstone canyons with a view of Truchas Peaks to the northeast before dropping into the bucolic village of

The most iconic church found on the High Road to Taos is El Santuario de Chimayó.

Chimayó. Nestled into hillsides where gnarled piñons seem to grow from bare bedrock, Chimayó is famed for its weaving, its red chiles, and its two chapels, particularly El Santuario de Chimayó.

Sights

★ El Santuario de Chimayó

RELIGIOUS SITE | This small, frontier, adobe church has a fantastically carved and painted reredos (altar screen) and is built on the site where, believers say, a mysterious light came from the ground on Good Friday in 1810 leading to the discovery of a large wooden crucifix beneath the earth. The chapel sits above a sacred *pozito* (a small hole), the dirt from which is believed to have miraculous healing properties. Dozens of abandoned crutches and braces placed in the anteroom—along with many notes, letters, and photos—testify to this. The Santuario draws a steady stream of worshippers year-round—Chimayó is considered the Lourdes of the Southwest. During Holy Week as many as 50,000 pilgrims come here. The shrine is a National Historic Landmark. It's surrounded by small adobe shops selling every kind of religious curio imaginable and some very fine traditional Hispanic work from local artists.

The church is an active community with the Catholic Mass celebrated indoors and outside in a large open area. Please observe house of worship norms. ⊠ *15 Santuario Dr., Chimayo* ☎ *505/351–9961* ⊕ *www.holychimayo.us* ⊠ *Free.*

 Restaurants

Rancho de Chimayó

$$ | **MEXICAN** | In a century-old adobe hacienda tucked into the mountains, with whitewashed walls, hand-stripped vigas, and cozy dining rooms, the Rancho de Chimayó is still owned and operated by the family that first occupied the house. Consistently good, reasonably priced New Mexican fare is served (the carne adovada with posole is especially good), and it's hard to deny the enchanting ambience of the place. **Known for:** beautiful rancho decor and ambience; great gift shop with restaurant items and local artists; gorgeous terraced back patio. $ *Average main: $17* ⊠ *300 Juan Medina Rd., Chimayo* ☎ *505/351–4444* ⊕ *www. ranchodechimayo.com* ⊙ *Closed Mon.*

Shopping

★ Centinela Traditional Arts

TEXTILES/SEWING | The Trujillo family weaving tradition, which started in northern New Mexico more than seven generations ago, is carried out in this colorful, inviting gallery. Irvin Trujillo and his wife, Lisa, are both gifted, renowned master weavers, creating Rio Grande–style tapestry blankets and rugs, many of them with natural dyes that authentically replicate early weavings. Most designs are historically based, but the Trujillos are never shy about innovating and their original works are as breathtaking as the traditional ones. ⊠ *946 NM 76, Chimayo* ☎ *505/351–2180* ⊕ *www. chimayoweavers.com.*

Ortega's Weaving Shop

TEXTILES/SEWING | This shop in the center of town sells Rio Grande- and Chimayó-style textiles made by the family whose Spanish ancestors brought the craft to New Mexico in the 1600s. The Galeria Ortega, next door, sells traditional and contemporary arts and crafts in New Mexican and Native American styles. ⊠ *53 Plaza del Cerro, Chimayo* ☎ *505/351–4215, 877/351–4215* ⊕ *www. ortegasweaving.com.*

Oviedo Carvings & Bronze

ART GALLERIES | Long-acclaimed artist Marco Oviedo has earned a reputation for his sometimes whimsical, sometimes inspirational bronze carvings, which depict everything from Native figures to regional wildlife. Most of these are no more than a foot tall, and prices are quite reasonable. ⊠ *NM 76, 1 mile east of CR 98, Chimayo* ☎ *505/351–2280* ⊕ *www.oviedoart.us.*

Truchas

9 miles northeast of Chimayó.

Truchas (Spanish for "trout") is where Robert Redford shot the movie *The Milagro Beanfield War* (based on the novel written by Taos author John Nichols). This pastoral village is perched dramatically on the rim of a deep canyon beneath the towering Truchas Peaks, mountains high enough to be almost perpetually capped with snow. The tallest of the Truchas Peaks is 13,102 feet, the second-highest point in New Mexico. Truchas has been gaining appeal with artsy, independent-minded transplants from Santa Fe and Taos, who have come for the cheaper real estate and the breathtaking setting. There are several excellent galleries in town.

Continue 7 miles north on NM 76, toward Peñasco, and you come to the marvelous San José de Gracia Church in the village of Trampas. It dates from circa 1760.

Shopping

★ Cardona-Hine Gallery

ART GALLERIES | With highly impressive, museum-quality artwork that might have you thinking this gallery was plucked out of Manhattan, Cardona-Hine opened in a red-roofed adobe house in the historic center of Truchas back in 1988, helping to spur the community's growth as a serious gallery destination. Inside you'll find oil paintings by the talented founders, Barbara McCauley and her late husband, Alvaro Cardona-Hine, as well as works by sculptor Marcia McEachron. ⊠ *82 County Rd. 75* ☎ *505/689–2253* ⊕ *www. cardonahinegallery.com.*

Móntez Gallery

ANTIQUES/COLLECTIBLES | Set inside a historic chapel just outside the main village in Truchas, this beautiful gallery sells Hispanic works of religious art and decoration, including *retablos* (holy images painted on wood or tin), *bultos* (carved wooden statues of saints), furniture, paintings, pottery, weavings, and jewelry. You'll find works by a number of award-winning local artists here. ⊠ *132 CR 75* ☎ *505/231–8272* ⊕ *www.montezsantafe.com.*

Peñasco

15 miles north of Truchas.

Although still a modest-size community, Peñasco is one of the "larger" villages along the High Road and a good bet if you need to fill your tank with gas or pick up a snack at a convenience store. The village is also home to a growing number of fine galleries as well as one of the most celebrated small-town restaurants in northern New Mexico, Sugar Nymphs Bistro.

Sights

San José de Gracia Church
RELIGIOUS SITE | This Spanish-colonial adobe church is located just outside Peñasco in the village of Las Trampas. A designated National Historic Landmark, it was built between 1760 and 1776. The High Road speed limit slows and naturally dips down right in front of the church, conveniently guiding drivers to park in its large plaza. Visitors pop out of their cars in all seasons for either a quick snapshot or prolonged, highly artistic photo shoots of the picturesque church. While the church is not typically open for public tours, it does have an active Catholic community and may be open for religious services. Be sure to observe house of worship norms. ⊠ *NM 76, mile marker 24, Las Trampas* ☎ *505/351–4360 Santuario de Chimayó parish office.*

 Restaurants

★ Sugar Nymphs Bistro
$$ | **AMERICAN** | You can't miss the vivid murals on the building in sleepy Peñasco that houses both a vintage theater and an intimate restaurant where acclaimed chef-owners Kai Harper Leah and Ki Holste serve up tantalizing farm-to-table fare, from bountiful salads and creatively topped pizzas to triple-layer chocolate cake. This is hands down the best restaurant on the High Road. **Known for:** famous green-chile bison stew; satisfying Sunday brunch; decadent desserts. ⑤ *Average main: $18* ⊠ *15046 NM 75* ☎ *575/587–0311* ⊕ *www.sugarnymphs.com* ☉ *Reduced hrs in winter (call first).*

Shopping

Gaucho Blue Gallery

ART GALLERIES | This eclectic gallery carries a great mix of paintings and other pieces by local artists—notably Nick Beason's edgy monotypes and copper etchings and Lise Poulsen's felted kimonos and striking fiberworks. You'll find both contemporary and traditional works here. ⊠ *14148 NM 75* ☎ *575/587–1076* ⊕ *www. gauchoblue.com.*

Dixon

13 miles west of Peñasco.

The small village of Dixon is home to a number of artists as well as a couple of the wineries that are helping put the northern Rio Grande Valley on the map among oenophiles. Artistic sensitivity, as well as generations of dedicated farmers, account for the community's well-tended fields, pretty gardens, and fruit trees—a source of produce for restaurants and farmers' markets throughout the region. It's simple to find your way around; there's only one main road.

If you're driving the High Road, Dixon is a slight detour from Peñasco. You can either return the way you come and continue from Peñasco over the mountains into Taos, or from Dixon you can pick up NM 68, the Low Road, and continue north to Taos through the scenic Rio Grande Gorge.

◉ Sights

Dixon Studio Tour

ARTS VENUE | During the first full weekend in November, area artists open up their home studios to the public, drawing folks from throughout the region to one of the state's top small art towns. ⊠ *Dixon* ⊕ *www.dixonarts.org.*

La Chiripada Winery

WINERY/DISTILLERY | Nestled under mature shade trees down a dirt lane in Dixon's quaint village center, this producer of first-rate wines is the oldest vintner in the northern part of the state. La Chiripada's Viogner, Special Reserve Riesling, and Dolcetto have all earned considerable acclaim. There's also a nicely crafted New Mexico Port, which pairs well with dessert. There's a small art gallery, and the winery also has a tasting room in Taos at 103 Bent Street. ⊠ *NM 75, Road 1119* ☎ *505/579–4437* ⊕ *www.lachiripada. com.*

Vivác Winery

WINERY/DISTILLERY | "Vivác" means "high-altitude refuge," and that's a fitting name for this hip winery located right at the turnoff on NM 68 (the Low Road) to NM 75 (which leads to the High Road). Owned and run by a local family, the vineyards and charming tasting room, with an adjacent patio, are set deep in the Rio Grande gorge surrounded by sheer cliffs. It's a dramatic setting for sampling these elegant, generally dry wines, which feature a mix of grapes, including Italian Dolcetto, Spanish Tempranillo, French Cabernet Sauvignon, and German off-dry Riesling. The Tasting Room also sells artisanal chocolates, house-made cheeses, and jewelry. ⊠ *2075 NM 68* ☎ *505/579–4441* ⊕ *www.vivacwinery. com.*

Restaurants

Zuly's Cafe

$ | SOUTHWESTERN | This simple, cheerful spot serving authentic New Mexico fare in the village center is good to know about if you've built up an appetite tasting vino at the several wineries nearby. You might start your day off with a stick-to-your-ribs breakfast of chile-smothered huevos rancheros while enchiladas, burritos, and other local favorites are good bets for lunch or an early dinner. **Known for:** hearty breakfast burritos; green-chile cheeseburgers; wooden picnic tables for outdoor dining. ⑤ *Average main: $9* ⊠ *234 NM 75* ☎ *505/579–4001* ⊗ *Closed Sun. and Mon. No dinner Tues.–Thurs.*

ALBUQUERQUE

Updated by
Lynne Arany

Sights ★★★★☆ **Restaurants** ★★★★☆ **Hotels** ★★★☆☆ **Shopping** ★★☆☆☆ **Nightlife** ★★☆☆☆

WELCOME TO ALBUQUERQUE

TOP REASONS TO GO

★ **Dazzling views.** With mountains, volcanoes, and the Rio Grande in between, the city is an outdoor-lover's dream. Walking and biking trails abound, and you can paddle the Rio as well.

★ **Arts, heritage, and history.** From ancient adobes and Route 66's motor-court neon to the early railroad days, Albuquerque has galleries and museums that cover it all.

★ **Farm-fresh dining.** Savor traditional northern New Mexican specialties, vibrant growers' markets, and the contemporary cuisine of luxe B&Bs and inns.

★ **Microbreweries (for coffee, wine, and spirits, too).** You'll find award-winning brews and a pub, café, or winery for every mood.

★ **Roadways to ruins (and pueblos today).** Explore nearby Petroglyph National Monument, and, a bit farther out, the Jémez, Acoma, Laguna, and Zuni pueblos, and onward to Chaco Canyon.

★ **Hot air balloons.** Even if you're not in town for the famous yearly Hot Air Balloon Festival, there's still 360 days a year of blue sky to enjoy the views or take a ride yourself.

1 **Old Town.** A step back in time to the Spanish settlement on which ABQ was founded.

2 **Downtown and EDo.** A world-class group of art galleries and murals, with railroad-era architecture and the famous KiMo Theatre.

3 **Barelas and South Valley.** Home to the acclaimed National Hispanic Cultural Center and the emerging Rail Yard market and Wheels Museum developments.

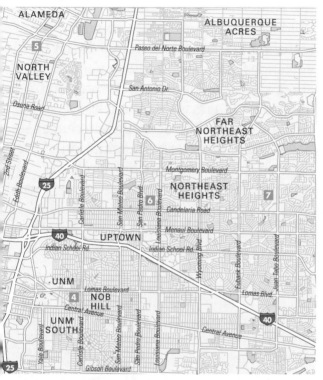

4 UNM and Nob Hill. A neighborhood rich with an extensive arts complex that stretches south of the University of New Mexico into art deco–influenced Nob Hill.

5 Los Ranchos and North Valley. Along the Rio Grande Valley, where first Pueblo peoples, then the earliest Hispanic settlers, resided, lies the city's agrarian heart.

6 Uptown and Northeast Heights. A booming residential area that begins with Uptown (the city's shopping center nexus) and rises east into the Heights, with great hiking and a breathtaking aerial tram.

7 East Side and West Side. The East Side is home to the National Museum of Nuclear Science & History, and a stretch of old Route 66 while going West will take you to the famed Petroglyph National Monument.

Perfectly set as the gateway to other New Mexico wonders like Chaco Canyon, the Four Corners area, and the Gila Wilderness, Albuquerque's own rich history and dramatic terrain—desert volcanoes, unique cottonwood bosque along the broad banks of the river that flows through its very center, and a striking confluence of mountain ranges— have long captured the imagination of folks en route from here to there.

Today's smart traveler knows something special is afoot in this wonderfully diverse and charmingly quirky historic town halved by the Rio Grande. You'll want to plan on spending at least a day or more before venturing beyond. Vibrant art galleries, growers' markets, a coffee and microbrewery scene, and world-class museums as well as superb nature trails and spectacular topography—and, of course, the seemingly endless blue sky and the joyous hot-air balloons that decorate it—make it a worthy destination of its own.

Centuries-old traces of Native American populations past and present abound throughout the Rio Grande Valley, and Albuquerque is no exception. Their trade routes are what drew the Spanish here; sections of what became their Camino Real are still intact. The little farming settlement was proclaimed "Alburquerque," after the Viceroy of New Spain—the 10th Duke of Alburquerque—in 1706. By the time Anglo traders arrived in the 1800s, that first "r" had been dropped, but that settlement, now known as Old Town, was still the heart of town. By the 1880s, with the railroad in place, the center of town moved east to meet it, in the Downtown we know today. Remnants of all linger still—and may readily be seen in the soft aging adobes in the North and South Valley, or the old Rail Yard buildings in Barelas.

In the spirit of one of the earliest local proponents of preserving the area's natural heritage, Aldo Leopold, Albuquerque is committed to protecting its exquisite bosque lands—and the waterfowl, porcupines, and other wildlife that call them home. A network of bicycle trails has been extended from there throughout the city.

A noted Public Art program, a developing innovation economy, a remarkably diverse population, and a surprisingly eclectic range of architecture further set this city apart.

A bit of quiet attention reveals Albuquerque's subtle beauty—a flock of sandhill cranes overhead; a hot-air balloon, seemingly within reach; vintage art deco buildings and motel signs along old Route 66; Pueblo Revival details on the university campus; the fabulous facade of the KiMo theater; a sudden glimpse across the western desert to a 100-mile-distant snowcapped Mt. Taylor; and the Sandia Mountains lit pink by the fading sun.

Albuquerque's terrain is diverse, too. Along the river in the North and South valleys, the elevation hovers at about 4,800 feet. East of the river, the land rises gently to the foothills of the Sandia Mountains, which climb to more than 6,000 feet; the 10,378-foot summit is a grand spot from which to view the city below. West of the Rio Grande, where Albuquerque is growing most aggressively, the terrain rises abruptly in a string of mesas topped by five volcanic cones. The changes in elevation from one part of the city to another result in corresponding changes in temperature, as much as 10°F at any time. It's not uncommon for snow or rain to fall on one part of town but for it to remain dry and sunny in another, and because temperatures can shift considerably throughout the day and evening, it's a good idea to bring along a couple of layers when exploring.

Planning

When to Go

Albuquerque is sunny year-round and each season has its own appeal, but most locals will say fall is the best time to visit. On just about any day in late August through November, big balloons sail across the sharp blue sky and the scent of freshly roasting green chiles permeates the air. Balloon Fiesta brings enormous crowds for nearly two weeks in early October (book hotels at this time as far in advance as possible). Shortly after, the weather's still great and hotel prices plummet. Albuquerque's winter days (usually 10°F warmer than those in Santa Fe) are usually mild enough for hiking, biking, and golf, or simply strolling around Old Town or Nob Hill. The occasional frigid spike in town usually thaws by morning yet Sandia Peak's ski area is hopping and barely an hour away. Spring brings winds, though plenty of sunshine, too, and hotel rates stay low until the summer crowds flock in. Hot but dry temps in mid-May through mid-July stay well below Phoenix-like extremes, but can hit the high 90s and hover there a bit, especially in June. This is followed by roughly six to eight weeks of cooler temperatures, a bit more humidity, and the spectacular late-afternoon cloud formations that herald the brief "monsoon" season.

Planning Your Time

While some of the spots on your local agenda will likely require car travel, Albuquerque does contain a handful of neighborhoods well suited to exploring on foot. In both Downtown and Old Town, you'll find plenty of parking (garages, lots, and street; but be prepared to feed street meters on weekends), and good areas to get out of the car and walk. The same is true of Nob Hill and the adjoining UNM neighborhood. For a short visit to the city, focusing your time on these two areas is amply rewarding; allow at least a half day for each. If hiking, biking, or kayaking appeal, at least another half day or so is warranted. And keep in mind the fine museums as well as the huge microbrewery and winery scenes that await—yet one more day in town can easily be filled.

Farther-afield spots require an average of 20 minutes via car to get to. A helpful strategy is to bunch together more outlying attractions that interest you, perhaps hitting Gruet Winery and the Balloon Museum the same day you go out to Petroglyph National Monument or ride the Sandia Peak Tram. Or you might combine your Tram day with a visit to the not-to-be-missed National Museum of Nuclear Science and History.

Getting Here and Around

AIR
The major gateway to New Mexico is Albuquerque International Sunport, a well-designed and attractive art-filled facility that's just 5 miles southeast of Downtown and 3 miles south of UNM/Nob Hill. The city's ABQ Ride bus service runs a shuttle from the airport to Downtown's Alvarado Transportation Center, where you can connect with local bus routes as well as the Rail Runner Express train service to Santa Fe.

CONTACTS Albuquerque International Sunport (ABQ). ✉ *2200 Sunport Blvd. SE* ☎ *505/244–7700* ⊕ *abqsunport.com.*

BIKE

With the creation of many lanes, trails, and dedicated bike paths (an impressive 400 miles worth), Albuquerque's city leaders are recognized for their bike-friendly efforts—a serious challenge given the committed car culture of its residents. The city's public works department produces the detailed Albuquerque Bicycle Map, which can be obtained free at most bike shops or viewed on their website.

Bike rental shops have clustered in the Old Town area, near the Paseo del Bosque Trail, though rentals can also be found closer to the mountains. The Paseo del Bosque Trail, which follows along the Rio Grande Valley and runs flat for most of its 16-mile run, is one of the loveliest rides (or walks) in town.

Bike share stands are scattered about Downtown and Old Town, but expansion to other neighborhoods is inevitable. A smartphone is required to charge a bike. For a 24-hour pass, there's a one-time member fee ($3), then trips under 90 minutes are free; after that it's $3/hour and up to $30 max per ride. Monthly and annual passes are available as well.

CONTACTS Albuquerque Bicycle Map. ☎ *505/768–2680* ⊕ *www. cabq.gov/bike*. **Paseo del Bosque Trail.** ⊕ *www.cabq.gov/ parksandrecreation/open-space/lands/paseo-del-bosque-trail*.

BUS

If you're not planning to explore much beyond Old Town, Downtown, and Nob Hill, the city's public bus system, ABQ Ride, is a practical option (while the bus network is extensive, it can be a slow go on other routes). Rapid Ride and the newer ART (Albuquerque Rapid Transit) lines ply Central Avenue through these neighborhoods every seven to eight minutes from early to midnight or 1 am. You can download trip-planning apps or obtain a customized trip plan at the city's public bus website, ABQ Ride.

The Alvarado Transportation Center Downtown is ABQ Ride's main hub and offers direct connections to the NM Rail Runner Express train service, as well as bus routes throughout the city. Buses accept bicycles at no additional charge, although space is limited. Service is free if you are transferring (to any route) from the Rail Runner; otherwise, the fare is $1 (bills or coins, exact change only); one-, two-, and three-day passes ($2–$6) are also available on the bus or online. ART bus tickets must be purchased before boarding (either online or from the vending machines found at each stop). Bus stops are well marked and you can get arrival statuses on your smartphone.

CONTACTS ABQ Ride. ☎ *505/243–7433* ⊕ *www.cabq.gov/transit*.

CAR

While a bus might suffice for destinations along the Route 66/Central Avenue corridor, to get a real feel for the Duke City's many treasures, a car is necessary. Getting around town is not difficult, and local roads are often quickest. The main highways through the city, north–south Interstate 25 and east–west Interstate 40, converge just northeast of Downtown and generally offer the speediest access to outlying neighborhoods and the airport. Rush-hour jams are common in the mornings and late afternoons, but they're still far less severe than in most big U.S. cities. All the major car-rental agencies are represented at Albuquerque's Sunport airport.

Because it's a driving city, most businesses and hotels have free or inexpensive off-street parking, and it's easy to find metered street parking in many neighborhoods as well as affordable garages Downtown. Problems usually arise only when there's a major event in town, such as a concert near the University of New Mexico or a festival Downtown or in Old Town, when you may want to arrive on the early side to get a space.

TAXI

Taxis are metered in Albuquerque, and service is around-the-clock. Given the considerable distances around town, cabbing it can be relatively expensive; figure about $9 from Downtown to Nob Hill, and about $20 from the airport to Downtown or EDo. There's also a $1 airport fee. The Uber/Lyft phenomenon has severely cut back taxi options in town and it is advisable to call ahead and always reconfirm taxi trips.

CONTACTS zTrip. ☎ *855/699–8747* ⊕ *www.ztrip.com.*

TRAIN

The New Mexico Rail Runner Express, a commuter-train line, provides a picturesque, hassle-free way to make a day trip to Santa Fe. These sleek bilevel trains with large windows run south for about 35 miles to the suburb of Belén (stopping in Isleta Pueblo and Los Lunas), and north about 65 miles on a scenic run right into the historic heart of Santa Fe, with stops in Bernalillo, Kewa Pueblo (Santo Domingo), and a few other spots. Albuquerque stops are Downtown (at the Alvarado Transportation Center, where the city's ABQ Ride bus hub is) and at the north end of town at Montaño and Journal Center/Los Ranchos. On weekdays, the trains run about eight or nine times per day, from about 6 am until 9 pm. Four trains usually run on Saturday and three usually run on Sunday. Fares are zone-based (one-way from $2 to $8), but day passes are just $1 more; all are discounted with an online purchase, and bicycles always ride free. Free connections to local bus service are available at most stations—keep your train ticket to get on.

CONTACTS New Mexico Rail Runner Express. ⊠ *809 Copper Ave. NW* ☎ *866/795–7245* ⊕ *www.riometro.org.*

Visitor Information

Visit Albuquerque operates tourism information kiosks at the airport (on the baggage-claim level) and at ⊠ *522 Romero Street* in Old Town. To see what's going on by date, go to ⊕ *www.abq365. com.*

CONTACTS Visit Albuquerque. ⊠ *Downtown* ☎ *505/842–9918, 800/284–2282* ⊕ *www.visitalbuquerque.org.*

Restaurants

The Duke City has long been a place for hearty home-style cooking in big portions, and to this day that remains the spirit in its many authentic New Mexican restaurants. Today Albuquerque is also firmly established as an innovative presence in farm-to-table dining, and that attitude for locally sourced ingredients influences many fine restaurants throughout the city. Of note here, too, is the city's significant Vietnamese population that has created a slew of excellent Vietnamese eateries. Indian, Japanese, Thai, Middle Eastern, and South American traditions are also spotted around town, making this New Mexico's best destination for global cuisine. Exemplary American standards—say, steak and chops or elevated old-school diner menus—are also well represented.

Whether in Nob Hill, Downtown, Old Town, the North Valley, or the Northeast Heights, the trick to dining well here is to bypass the miles of chain options, and perhaps even move beyond the ever-present "red or green" New Mexican diner's dilemma. A special meal may be had here at fancy and not-so-fancy places, and generally prices are lower than in Santa Fe or other major Southwestern cities.

Hotels

With a few notable independently owned exceptions—Hotel Albuquerque, Hotel Chaco, and Hotel Parq Central, for example—Albuquerque's lodging options fall into two categories: modern chain hotels and motels, and distinctive and typically historic inns and B&Bs.

If you are seeking charm, history, or both, Los Poblanos Inn in the North Valley is hands-down the top choice while Hotel Parq Central in EDo and Downtown's Hotel Andaluz have history and modernity, too. True Modernist fans will be happy at the Sarabande B&B; for the latest and the sleekest, Hotel Chaco is for you. And, of the chains, the Best Western Rio Grande Inn in Old Town has a solid Southwestern feel and is fairly priced to boot. Wherever you stay in Albuquerque, you can generally count on finding rates considerably lower than the national average, and much cheaper than those in Santa Fe.

Restaurant and hotel reviews have been shortened. For full information, visit Fodors.com. Restaurant prices are the average cost of a main course at dinner or, if dinner is not served, at lunch. Hotel prices are for two people in a standard double room in high season, excluding 12%–13% tax.

WHAT IT COSTS in U.S. Dollars			
$	$$	$$$	$$$$
RESTAURANTS			
under $16	$16–$23	$24–$30	over $30
HOTELS			
under $110	$110–$200	$201–$300	over $300

Shopping

Albuquerque's shopping strengths include a handful of cool retail districts, such as Nob Hill, Old Town, and along 4th Street NW above Montaño Boulevard in the North Valley. These are good neighborhoods for galleries; antiques; Native American arts; Old West finds and apparel; Mexican crafts; textiles, jewelry, pottery, glass, and other fine handicrafts by nationally acclaimed local artists; home-furnishing shops; bookstores; and offbeat gift shops. Indoor flea markets can be spotted around town, and everyone knows that museum gift shops are always worth a look-see— Albuquerque's are no exception.

Ballooning

If you've never been ballooning, you may picture a bumpy ride, where changes in altitude produce the queasy feeling you get in a tiny propeller plane, but the experience is far calmer than that. The balloons are flown by licensed pilots (don't call them operators)

Thanks to the city's favorable air patterns, Albuquerque is famous for its hot-air balloon rides.

who deftly turn propane-fueled flames on and off, climbing and descending to find winds blowing the way they want to go—though Albuquerque is known for having a favorable air pattern know as "the box." There's no real steering involved, which makes the pilots' control that much more admirable. Pilots generally land balloons where the wind dictates, so chase vehicles pick you up and return you to your departure point. Even without door-to-door service, many visitors rank a balloon ride over the Rio Grande Valley as their most memorable experience.

Several reliable companies around Albuquerque offer tours. A ride costs about $150 to $200 per person.

Rainbow Ryders
BALLOONING | One of the longest-established balloon tours is with Rainbow Ryders, an official ride concession for the Albuquerque International Balloon Fiesta. As part of the fun, you get to help inflate and pack away the balloon. In case you missed breakfast prior to your flight, a continental breakfast and glass of champagne await your return. ⊠ *5601 Eagle Rock Ave. NE, West Side* 🕾 *800/725–2477* ⊕ *www.rainbowryders.com.*

Hiking

In the foothills in Albuquerque's Northeast Heights, you'll find great hiking in Cibola National Forest (⊕ *www.fs.usda.gov/cibola*), which can be accessed from Tramway Boulevard Northeast, about

4 miles east of Interstate 25 or 2 miles north of Paseo del Norte. Just follow the road into the hillside, and you'll find several parking areas (there's a daily parking fee of $3). This is where you'll find the trailhead for the steep and challenging La Luz Trail (⊕ *www. laluztrail.com*), which rises for some 9 miles (an elevation gain of more than 3,000 feet) to the top of Sandia Crest. You can take the Sandia Peak Aerial Tram to the top and then hike down the trail, or vice versa (keep in mind that it can take up to six hours to hike up the trail, and four to five hours to hike down). Spectacular views of Albuquerque and many miles of desert and mountain beyond that are had from the trail. You can also enjoy a hike here without going the whole way—if your energy and time are limited, just hike a mile or two and back. Or enjoy one of the shorter trails that emanate from the Elena Gallegos Picnic Area (⊕ *www.cabq.gov/ openspace*), just a few miles south along Tramway. No matter how far you hike, however, pack plenty of water.

For lovely but even less rugged terrain, the Aldo Leopold Forest (along the Paseo del Bosque Trail in the North Valley) and trails at the Open Space Visitor Center on the West Side will be of interest.

Guided Tours

Abq Tours
Abq Tours offers guided history and ghost-centric walking strolls around Old Town. The standard tour lasts about 75 minutes and is offered four times daily. Longer ghost-hunting and moonlight tours are also offered on occasion—check the website for times. ⊠ *303 Romero St. NW, Plaza Don Luis N-120* ☎ *505/246–8687* ⊕ *www. abqtours.fun*.

ABQ Trolley Co.
 (AT&SF). Narrated 100-minute open-air trolley trips are the feature here—join them on a Best of ABQ City Tour (film shoot locations— including some *Breaking Bad* sites—are always included) or a brew cruise ride. There's also a 2½-hour Duke City Pedaler version and a 3½-house Hopper for those looking for a deeper look into Albuquerque's lively microbrew scene. Their Albucreepy Ghost Walk tour takes a different view of the spirit scene Downtown. Tour trollies depart year-round from Hotel Albuquerque (Old Town) while brew excursions start from Downtown (*330 Tijeras Ave. NW*). ⊠ *Hotel Albuquerque, 800 Rio Grande NW* ☎ *505/200–2642* ⊕ *www.tourabq.com*.

The city's public art program is one of the oldest in the country.

Albuquerque Historical Society

Downtown architecture—the full gamut from the railroad era to mission to modernist—is the focus of these free Saturday morning tours (10 am–11:30 am) run by the Albuquerque Historical Society; they depart from in front of Tucanos restaurant at the corner of 1st Street and Central Avenue SW. Call to confirm or arrange an alternate time. ⊕ albuqhistsoc.org.

Albuquerque Museum

With paid museum admission, the Albuquerque Museum includes free, docent-led, hour-long historical walks through Old Town, beginning at 11 am on Tuesday, Thursday, Friday, and Sunday, mid-March through November. On alternate days (Wednesday and Saturday, also at 11 am), they run tours through their magnificent Sculpture Garden. The museum also offers excellent tours of the historical collection in the late 19th-century Casa San Ysidro in Corrales (February through November; call for info). ✉ 2000 Mountain Rd. NW, Old Town ☎ 505/243–7255 museum, 505/898–3915 Casa San Ysidro ⊕ www.cabq.gov/museum.

NM Jeep Tours

Respected backcountry and local-history experts, NM Jeep Tours offers guided trips that start from Albuquerque and go as far as time and permits allow. Itineraries (ruins, ghost towns, rock formations, petroglyphs) are tailored to your interests and time frame. ☎ 505/633–0383 ⊕ nmjeeptours.com.

Every holiday season, ABQ BioPark produces an annual walk-through light show called the River of Lights.

Public Art

Albuquerque's Public Art program, started in 1978, is one of the oldest in the country, and the city is strewn with its wonders. Download a growing stock of self-guided brochures and apps for locating the 650-piece collection. ✉ *Albuquerque Convention Center, 2 Civic Plaza NW, West Lobby foyer* ☎ *505/768–3833* ⊕ *www.cabq.gov/publicart.*

Old Town

Albuquerque's social and commercial anchor since the settlement was established in 1706, Old Town and its surrounding blocks contain the wealth of the city's top cultural attractions, including several excellent museums, as well as scads of restaurants, galleries, and shops. Venturing beyond the immediate historic Old Town Plaza area—most of the museums are a short walk just north and east of the plaza—and across Mountain Road, you'll find yourself in the blooming Sawmill district. The Wells Park neighborhood (and its wealth of microbreweries and arts venues) and the Los Duranes section, where the Indian Pueblo Cultural Center commands attention, are short drives to the northeast of Old Town.

Sights

★ ABQ BioPark

ZOO | FAMILY | The city's foremost outdoor attraction and nature center, the park comprises Tingley Beach (and its trout-stocked ponds) as well as three distinct attractions: Aquarium, Botanic Garden, and Zoo. The garden and aquarium are located together (admission gets you into both facilities), just west of Old Town, off Central Avenue; the zoo is a short drive southeast, off 10th Street. You can also ride the scenic Rio Line vintage narrow-gauge railroad between the zoo and gardens and the aquarium complex; rides are free if you purchase a combination ticket to all of the park's facilities. ⊠ *903 10th St. SW, Old Town* ☎ *505/768–2000* ⊕ *www.abqbiopark.com* ☎ *Tingley Beach and grounds free; Aquarium and Botanic Garden $15; Zoo $15; Zoo train ticket $3; combination ticket for all attractions, including unlimited train tickets, $22.*

★ Albuquerque Museum

MUSEUM | FAMILY | In a modern, light-filled space, the Albuquerque Museum serves up a brilliantly curated selection of contemporary art from the museum's own Southwestern artists–centric collections and world-class touring shows; it also presents illuminating shows with regionally topical, historical, and cultural themes. "Trinity: Reflections on the Bomb," "Jim Henson: Imagination Unlimited," "Making Africa: A Continent of Contemporary Design," and Patrick Nagatani's "Excavations" are but a few that have drawn crowds. The Common Ground galleries represent an important permanent collection of primarily 20th-century paintings, all by world-renowned artists with a New Mexico connection. A changing rotation of 19th- and 20th-century photographs from the museum's extensive local archive lines the museum's walkway halls; other spaces dig even deeper into compelling aspects of Albuquerque and regional history. The Sculpture Garden contains more than 50 contemporary works by an internationally known roster of artists that includes Basia Irland, Tom Waldron, Ed Haddaway, and Fritz Scholder; Nora Naranjo-Morse's spiral land-art piece resonates deeply for a city—and a museum—that recognizes that water and land issues define Albuquerque's history and its future. Visitors may pick up a self-guided Sculpture Garden map or come for the free (with admission) docent-led tours at 11 am Wednesday and Saturday (March through November); docent-led tours of the galleries, also free, are held daily at 2 pm, year-round. The museum's innovative children's activity room always ties in to current exhibits and is an instant magnet for kids. Slate at the Museum, a casual eatery operated by Downtown's Slate Street

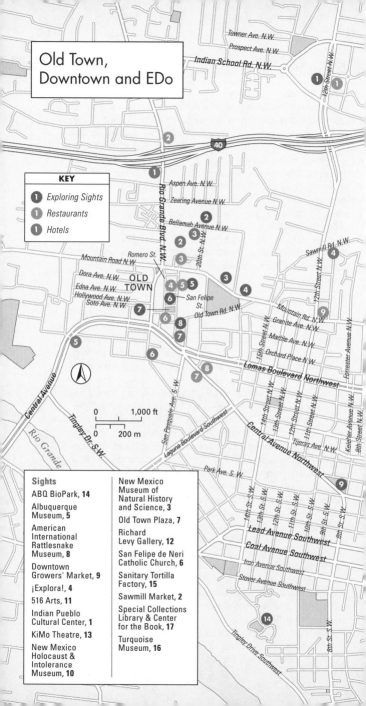

Old Town, Downtown and EDo

KEY

- ① *Exploring Sights*
- ① *Restaurants*
- ① *Hotels*

Towner Ave. N.W.

Prospect Ave. N.W.

Indian School Rd. N.W.

12th Street N.W.

Aspen Ave. N.W.

Zearing Avenue N.W.

Rio Grande Blvd. N.W.

Bellamah Avenue N.W.

20th St. N.W.

Romero St.

Mountain Road N.W.

Sawmill Rd. N.W.

12th Street N.W.

Dora Ave. N.W.

OLD TOWN

Edna Ave. N.W.

Hollywood Ave. N.W.

Soto Ave. N.W.

San Felipe St.

Old Town Rd. N.W.

Mountain Rd. N.W.

Granite Ave. N.W.

Marble Ave. N.W.

Orchard Place N.W.

15th Street N.W.

Forrester Avenue N.W.

Lomas Boulevard Northwest

Central Avenue

San Pasquale Ave. S.W.

Laguna Boulevard Southwest

Central Avenue Northwest

Tijeras Ave. N.W.

Tingley Dr. S.W.

Rio Grande

0   1,000 ft

0   200 m

Park Ave. S.W.

14th St. S.W.

13th St. S.W.

12th St. S.W.

11th St. S.W.

10th St. S.W.

9th St. S.W.

8th St. S.W.

Keleher Avenue N.W.

8th Street N.W.

Lead Avenue Southwest

Coal Avenue Southwest

Iron Avenue Southwest

Stover Avenue Southwest

Tingley Drive Southwest

Sights

ABQ BioPark, **14**

Albuquerque Museum, **5**

American International Rattlesnake Museum, **8**

Downtown Growers' Market, **9**

¡Explora!, **4**

516 Arts, **11**

Indian Pueblo Cultural Center, **1**

KiMo Theatre, **13**

New Mexico Holocaust & Intolerance Museum, **10**

New Mexico Museum of Natural History and Science, **3**

Old Town Plaza, **7**

Richard Levy Gallery, **12**

San Felipe de Neri Catholic Church, **6**

Sanitary Tortilla Factory, **15**

Sawmill Market, **2**

Special Collections Library & Center for the Book, **17**

Turquoise Museum, **16**

Restaurants

Antiquity, **6**

Artichoke Café, **13**

Church Street Café, **4**

Duran Central Pharmacy, **8**

Farina Pizzeria & Wine Bar, **14**

Golden Crown Panaderia, **9**

The Grove Café & Market, **15**

La Crêpe Michel, **5**

Range Café EDo, **12**

Range Café Old Town, **2**

Season's Rotisserie & Grill, **3**

Sixty-Six Acres, **1**

Slate Street Cafe, **10**

Villa Myriam Coffee, **11**

Vinaigrette, **7**

Hotels

Best Western Plus Rio Grande Inn, **1**

Böttger Mansion of Old Town, **7**

Casas de Sueños, **6**

El Vado Motel, **5**

Embassy Suites by Hilton Albuquerque, **10**

Hotel Albuquerque at Old Town, **2**

Hotel Andaluz/ Curio Collection by Hilton, **9**

Hotel Chaco, **3**

Hotel Parq Central, **11**

Hyatt Regency Albuquerque, **8**

Painted Lady Bed & Brew, **4**

Cafe, serves soups, salads, espresso drinks, desserts, and other tasty light fare. ⊠ *2000 Mountain Rd. NW, Old Town* 🕾 *505/243–7255 museum, 505/242–0434 shop, 505/242–5316 café* ⊕ *www.cabq.gov/museum* ⊠ *$4; free Sun. 9–1 and all day 1st Wed. each month* ⊗ *Closed Mon.*

American International Rattlesnake Museum

MUSEUM | FAMILY | Included in the largest collection of different species of living rattlers in the world are such rare and unusual specimens as an albino western diamondback and a melanistic (solid black) diamondback. From the outside the museum looks like just a plain old shop—aside from the friendly crew of tortoises who are usually there to greet you—but inside, the museum's exhibits, its engaging staff, and explanatory videos supply visitors with the lowdown on these venomous creatures. Did you know that they can't hear their own rattles and that the human death rate from rattlesnake bites is less than 1%? The mission here is to educate the public on the many positive benefits of rattlesnakes, and to contribute to their conservation. ⊠ *202 San Felipe St. NW, just off southeast corner of Plaza, Old Town* 🕾 *505/242–6569* ⊕ *www.rattlesnakes.com* ⊠ *$6.*

¡Explora!

MUSEUM | FAMILY | This imaginatively executed science museum—its driving concept is "Ideas You Can Touch"—is right across from the New Mexico Museum of Natural History and Science. ¡Explora! bills itself as an all-ages attraction (and enthralled adults abound), but there's no question that many of the innovative hands-on exhibits such as a high-wire bicycle and a kinetic sculpture display are geared to children. They offer big fun in addition to big science (and a good dose of art as well). While its colorful Bucky dome is immediately noticeable from the street, ¡Explora! also features a playground, theater, and a freestanding staircase that appears to "float" between floors. ⊠ *1701 Mountain Rd. NW, Old Town* 🕾 *505/224–8300* ⊕ *www.explora.us* ⊠ *$8.*

Indian Pueblo Cultural Center

MUSEUM | FAMILY | The multilevel semicircular layout of this museum was inspired by Pueblo Bonito, the prehistoric ruin in northwestern New Mexico. Start by visiting their permanent exhibit space "We Are of This Place: The Pueblo Story," which interprets the Pueblo people's legacy through carried-down traditions and remarkable pieces from their renowned holdings of fine Native American pottery, textiles, baskets, and other masterworks. Changing exhibits may feature close-ups of a particular artist, such as the gorgeously composed and colorful copper-plate prints of Santa Clara Pueblo painter Helen Hardin. Mural Discovery Tours are offered on Friday at 1 pm and ceremonial dances are performed year-round on weekends; there are often arts-and-crafts demonstrations as well. The museum gift shop, Shumakolowa, provides a fine overview of current Pueblo arts. Its **Pueblo Harvest** restaurant is a tasty spot for breakfast, lunch, or dinner. Note that the museum lies a bit northeast of Old Town, in the Los Duranes neighborhood—a five-minute drive away. ⊠ *2401 12th St. NW, Los Duranes* ☏ *505/843–7270, 866/855–7902* ⊕ *www.indianpueblo. org* ⬚ *$9.*

New Mexico Museum of Natural History and Science

MUSEUM | **FAMILY** | The wonders at Albuquerque's most popular museum include a simulated volcano (with a river of bubbling hot lava flowing beneath the see-through glass floor), the frigid Ice Age cave, and "Dawn of the Dinosaurs." The only Triassic exhibit in North America, this permanent hall features some of the state's own rare finds. The relatively youthful "Bisti Beast" shows off a Cretaceous-period tyrannosaur found in the Four Corners area. The Evolution Elevator (aka the Evolator) uses video, sound, and motion to whisk you through 35 million years of New Mexico's geological history. You'll also find here the LodeStar Science Center, a state-of-the-art planetarium home to the wildly popular First Friday Fractals show (tickets available online only). ⊠ *1801 Mountain Rd. NW, Old Town* ☏ *505/841–2800* ⊕ *www.nmnaturalhistory.org* ⬚ *Museum $8, DynaTheater $7, Planetarium $7; combined Museum and Planetarium $10.*

Old Town Plaza

PLAZA | **FAMILY** | Tranquil, with the lovely 1793 San Felipe de Neri Catholic Church still presiding along the north side, Old Town Plaza is a pleasant place to sit on wrought-iron benches under shade trees. Roughly 200 shops, restaurants, cafés, galleries, and several cultural sites in *placitas* (small plazas) and lanes surround the plaza. During fiestas Old Town comes alive with mariachi bands and dancing señoritas; at Christmas time it is lit with luminarias (the votive candles in paper bag lanterns known as *farolitos* up in Santa Fe). Mostly dating back to the late 1800s, styles from Queen Anne to Territorial and Pueblo Revival, and even Mediterranean, are apparent in the one- and two-story (almost all adobe) structures. ⊠ *Old Town.*

San Felipe de Neri Catholic Church

RELIGIOUS SITE | **FAMILY** | Well over two centuries after it first welcomed worshippers, this structure, erected in 1793, is still active (mass is offered daily). The building, which replaced Albuquerque's first Catholic church, has been expanded several times, but its adobe walls and other original features remain. Small gardens front and flank the church; the inside is a respite from the tourism bustle beyond its doorstep—the painting and iconography is simple, authentic, and lovely, the atmosphere hushed. Next to it is a shop and small museum that displays relics—vestments, paintings, carvings—dating from the 17th century. ■ TIP→ **There's a hidden treasure behind the church: inside the gnarled tree is a statue that some speculate depicts the Virgin Mary.** ⊠ *2005 Plaza NW, Old Town* 📷 *505/243–4628* ⊕ *www.sanfelipedeneri.org* ⊗ *Museum and gift shop closed Sun.*

★ Sawmill Market

MARKET | **FAMILY** | A former lumber-yard building located by the old AT&SF Railway line in the city's Sawmill district has been turned into a grand food hall that captures a true sense of history and place. A carefully honed collection of some two-dozen dining, shopping, and drinking vendors inhabit unique spaces from which they offer an eclectic range of high-quality wares. All embrace a definitively fresh and local ethos—some by way of Santa Fe, like Dr. Field Goods (an established spot with food-truck roots); some already Albuquerque-based (like Eldora Chocolate, Spurline, Estella Flowers, Naruto, Neko and Neko); and others talented transplants from afar (like Blue Door Patisserie and Flor Taco), but all with the same commitment to in-state growers, makers, and suppliers. Stroll around a bit and you can't help but appreciate the original architectural details (just gaze up at the fabulously restored wooden ceiling). Paxton's taproom has a seasonal rotation of New Mexico–brewed beers, as well as a steady set of the state's best craft beers on tap (wines lean local as well as international). The cool Mobile Bar is ready to serve out on their grassy patio, where any food bought inside may be enjoyed as well; more formal dine-in fare may be found at Flora, where traditional Mexican recipes are revisited with a modern twist. ⊠ *1909 Bellamah Ave. NW, Old Town* 📷 *505/563–4470* ⊕ *www.sawmillmarket.com.*

 Restaurants

Antiquity

$$$$ | **AMERICAN** | Within the thick adobe walls of this darkly lit, romantic space off the plaza in Old Town, patrons have been feasting on rich, elegantly prepared American classics for more than 50 years. This isn't the edgy, contemporary restaurant to bring an adventuresome foodie—Antiquity specializes in classics, from starters of French onion soup and Alaskan King crab cakes with a perfectly piquant remoulade sauce to main courses like Chicken Madagascar, Australian lobster tail with drawn butter, and black

Angus New York strip-loin steak with horseradish sauce. **Known for:** old-world-style service; timeless menu; congenial buzz. ⑤ *Average main: $45* ⊠ *112 Romero St. NW, Old Town* ☎ *505/247–3545* ⊕ *www.antiquityrestaurant.com* ⊗ *No lunch.*

Church Street Café

$$ | **MEXICAN** | This spacious, traditional adobe eatery features New Mexican–style family recipes, which happily feed streams of hungry tourists. Locals, too, are drawn here, especially for the alfresco dining in the lovely courtyard, amid trellises of sweet grapes and flowers, and further enhanced by the occasional accompaniment of a classical and flamenco guitarist. **Known for:** chiles rellenos stuffed with beef and cheese; historic tile and tin decorations; flower-filled courtyard seating. ⑤ *Average main: $18* ⊠ *2111 Church St. NW, Old Town* ☎ *505/247–8522* ⊕ *www.church-streetcafe.com* ⊗ *No dinner Sun.*

★ Duran Central Pharmacy

$ | **MEXICAN** | **FAMILY** | A favorite of old-timers who know their way around a blue-corn enchilada (and know that Duran's deeply authentic New Mexican red is the chile to pick for it), this welcoming spot serves fine, freshly made and warm flour tortillas, too. Duran's harkens to the days when every drugstore had a soda fountain; it's got a full kitchen now (and beer), with your choice of counter stools, cozy table, or the little shaded patio right off old Route 66. **Known for:** friendly but fast service; retro charm; old-school pharmacy still on-site since 1942. ⑤ *Average main: $11* ⊠ *1815 Central Ave. NW, Old Town* ☎ *505/247–4141* ⊕ *www.duransrx.com.*

Golden Crown Panaderia

$ | **BAKERY** | **FAMILY** | Tucked between Old Town and the Wells Park neighborhood, this aromatic, down-home-style bakery is especially well known for two things: its hearty green-chile bread and its hand-tossed (thin-crust) pizzas made with blue corn, peasant, or green-chile dough. You can also order hot cocoa, cappuccino, an award-winning local IPA or lager (or wine), some *biscochito* (the official state cookie), fruit-filled empanadas, sandwiches, and a popular coffee milkshake. **Known for:** lovely covered patio; green-chile bread; a (free) biscochito for all. ⑤ *Average main: $12* ⊠ *1103 Mountain Rd. NW, Old Town* ☎ *505/243–2424* ⊕ *www.golden-crown.biz* ⊗ *Closed Mon.*

La Crêpe Michel

$$ | **FRENCH** | When red-or-green chile overload sets in, Old Town offers an antidote: this tiny, French creperie tucked down a side alley, in what feels like a secret garden. Salads, steak frites, and a lovely dessert selection act as foils for the nicely presented crepes, both *salées* (with salmon and asparagus) and *sucrées* (with chocolate). **Known for:** peaceful setting; excellent crème caramel; great wine list. $ *Average main: $18* ⊠ *400 San Felipe St. NW, Old Town* ☎ *505/242–1251* ⊕ *www.lacrepemichel.com* ⊘ *Closed Mon.*

Range Café Old Town

$ | **AMERICAN** | **FAMILY** | A local standby for any meal, the Range Café has a high comfort quotient with hearty dishes like their Chimayó grilled-chicken sandwich with bacon and blue-cheese spread, fresh-spinach enchiladas with black beans and arroz verde, Matt's Hoosier Tenderloin Plate, and the generously plated salmon-berry salad. Chipotle barbecue beer-battered onion rings work great as a side, whether supporting burgers or standard New Mexican plates. **Known for:** exemplary New Mexican classics; colorful, funky decor; strong local roots. $ *Average main: $13* ⊠ *1050 Rio Grande Blvd. NW, Old Town* ☎ *505/508–2640* ⊕ *www. rangecafe.com.*

Seasons Rotisserie & Grill

$$$ | **AMERICAN** | Upbeat and elegant, Seasons's pleasing arches, soothing palette, and open-kitchen plan draw diners for business lunches and dinner dates; oenophiles revel in its well-chosen cellar. Wood-fueled grills and pastas dominate the seasonally changing roster of dishes with tangy sauces (Atlantic salmon has a lemon-thyme beurre blanc; vegetable and mozzarella crostada is brightened with a smoked ancho coulis; braised Iowa pork shank comes with a coal-roasted pear jus). **Known for:** wood-grilled beef and seafood; solid vegetarian options; lively rooftop scene. $ *Average main: $25* ⊠ *2031 Mountain Rd. NW, Old Town* ☎ *505/766–5100* ⊕ *seasonsabq.com* ⊘ *No lunch weekends.*

Sixty-Six Acres

$$ | **ECLECTIC** | A modern glass-framed dining spot right across from the Indian Pueblo Cultural Center, Sixty-Six Acres serves up satisfying dishes that riff freely on local and Asian traditions. Another winning inspiration from Myra Ghattas (Slate Street Café), who comes from a longtime Albuquerque restaurant family, the generous bowls, grilled sandwiches, and salads here—from Korean chicken bites to salmon and Himalayan rice—are flavorful, often gluten-free, and make vegetarian dining easy. **Known for:** green-chile burgers; casual and convivial atmosphere; pet-friendly patio with mountain views. $ *Average main: $18* ⊠ *2400 12th St. NW, Los Duranes* ☎ *505/243–2230* ⊕ *www.sixtysixacres.com.*

Vinaigrette

$$ | **AMERICAN** | Salads are the thing at Vinaigrette, just as they are at owner Erin Wade's popular original outpost in Santa Fe. Fresh,

local greens are featured, but heartier add-ons (from seared tuna and panko-crusted goat cheese to hibiscus-cured duck confit and flank steak) will satisfy the hungriest in your party. **Known for:** bright and inviting contemporary space; robust servings; patio dining in season. ⑤ *Average main: $18* ⊠ *1828 Central Ave. SW, Old Town* ☎ *505/842–5507* ⊕ *www.vinaigretteonline.com.*

Hotels

Best Western Plus Rio Grande Inn
$$ | HOTEL | FAMILY | This contemporary four-story low-rise—a short 10-minute walk from Old Town's main plaza *and* conveniently just off Interstate 40—has attractive Southwestern design and furnishings and the usual modern touches, like reliable and fast Wi-Fi. **Pros:** great value; secure, free parking; year-round pool. **Cons:** can be a hike from the rear rooms to the front desk; possible traffic noise; breakfast plan costs extra. ⑤ *Rooms from: $130* ⊠ *1015 Rio Grande Blvd. NW, Old Town* ☎ *505/843–9500, 800/959–4726 reservations only* ⊕ *www.riograndeinn.com* ⇒ *173 rooms* ⑩ *No meals.*

Böttger Mansion of Old Town
$$ | B&B/INN | A National Register property built in 1912 in the American Foursquare style, Böttger Mansion offers thoughtfully refurbished rooms incorporating fine woodwork and other period details like a claw-foot tub, a lovely mural by the original owner's grandson, or a pressed-tin ceiling. **Pros:** in the heart of Old Town, close to dining and attractions; architecturally interesting; free parking. **Cons:** stair-access only to the upper rooms; wood floors may creak; on-site cats not for everyone. ⑤ *Rooms from: $150* ⊠ *110 San Felipe St. NW, Old Town* ☎ *505/243–3639* ⊕ *www. bottger.com* ⇒ *7 rooms* ⑩ *Free Breakfast.*

Casas de Sueños
$$ | B&B/INN | This historic compound (it's a National Register property) of 1930s- and '40s-era adobe casitas is perfect if you're seeking seclusion and quiet, yet desire proximity to museums, restaurants, and shops. **Pros:** charming, quirky, and tucked away; some private patios; free parking. **Cons:** units vary in ambience and age—some are more enchanting than others; some high beds, claw baths, and tall steps—ask about accessibility; decor not for everyone. ⑤ *Rooms from: $139* ⊠ *310 Rio Grande Blvd. SW, on the south side of Central Ave., Old Town* ☎ *505/767–1000* ⊕ *www.casasdesuenos.com* ⇒ *21 casitas* ⑩ *Free Breakfast.*

El Vado Motel

$$ | HOTEL | Back in the day, El Vado was a prime Route 66 stay-over for those driving west (or back east), and now the 1937 vintage former motor court has been transformed into a desti-nation-worthy, fully modern motel, with a decor that winningly embraces midcentury modernism. **Pros:** gorgeous decor; outdoor lounging by the pool; small shops and dining spots on-site. **Cons:** limited parking, so guests may have to find spots on local streets; spillover sound travels from events on the plaza; pool on the small side. ⑤ *Rooms from: $150* ⊠ *2500 Central Ave. SW, Old Town* ☎ *505/361–1667* ⊕ *www.elvadoabq.com* ⌁ *22 rooms* ⊚*No meals.*

Hotel Albuquerque at Old Town

$$ | HOTEL | This 11-story Heritage Hotels & Resorts property over-looking Old Town has historic Territorial-style touches across its inviting facade, and attention is paid throughout its public spaces to New Mexican artisan craftwork, from Nambe Pueblo–designed metalwork to Navajo rugs. **Pros:** warmly appointed, Southwest-ern-style decor; lovely gardens and pool; mountain views avail-able. **Cons:** air-conditioning units can be loud; in-room furnishing sufficient but spare; amenity fee. ⑤ *Rooms from: $189* ⊠ *800 Rio Grande Blvd. NW, Old Town* ☎ *505/843–6300, 866/505–7829* ⊕ *www.hotelabq.com* ⌁ *188 rooms* ⊚*No meals.*

Hotel Chaco

$$$ | HOTEL | A special commitment to New Mexico shines through in this fastidious study of Chaco Canyon as an inspiration for one of Albuquerque's most popular hotels; it uses materials meant to evoke the fine stone chinking that comprise most of the 9th- to 12th-century structures found at that not-to be-missed ancient Puebloan site. **Pros:** contemplative outdoor lounge space; hip Saw-mill location; 24/7 fitness center. **Cons:** fortress-like entrance; $30 resort fee (includes parking); joint-use pool is on adjacent Hotel Albuquerque site. ⑤ *Rooms from: $259* ⊠ *2000 Bellamah Ave. NW, Old Town* ☎ *505/246–9989, 855/997–8208 reservations only* ⊕ *www.hotelchaco.com* ⌁ *118 rooms* ⊚*No meals.*

Painted Lady Bed & Brew

$$ | B&B/INN | On a quiet side street on the fringe of Albuquerque's Sawmill-Wells Park districts, a particular personality is revealed in this low-slung historic adobe: while it decidedly favors fans of the ever-growing craft brew scene, it also offers comfortably appointed suites that have been thoughtfully modernized from their original early 1900s construction. **Pros:** locally crafted metal-work and murals enhance garden areas; cool history; daily happy hour focused on local beers. **Cons:** furnishings might feel quirky and mismatched; monthly on-site beer garden events get noisy; no breakfast. $ *Rooms from: $170* ✉ *1100 Bellamah Ave. NW, Old Town* 🕾 *505/200–3999* ⊕ *www.breakfastisoverrated.com* ⤷ *2 suites* ⦿ *No meals.*

Nightlife

For the 411 on arts and nightlife, consult the freebie weekly *The Paper* (⊕ abq.news), out on Wednesday. For highlights on some of the best live music programming in town, go to AMP Concerts (⊕ ampconcerts.org). The *Albuquerque Journal*'s (⊕ www.abqjournal.com) Friday "Venue" section provides listings as well.

★ ¡Globalquerque!

MUSIC CLUBS | FAMILY | Held at the **National Hispanic Cultural Center**, ¡Globalquerque! is a dazzling two-day multistage (indoors and out) world-music festival that firmly places Albuquerque on the global music map. In addition to three evening performances, a full day is devoted to (free) kids programming. Launched in 2005 by AMP Concerts (the organization that lures acts like Lucinda Williams, Vieux Farka Toure, David Byrne, and Richard Thompson to intimate venues all around town) and Avokado Artists (known for the inspired world music line-up they present throughout the year), this festival remains a rousing success well over a decade in. ✉ *National Hispanic Cultural Center, 1701 4th St. SW at Ave. César Chavez, Barelas* 🕾 *505/724–4771* ⊕ *www.globalquerque. com.*

★ Tablao Flamenco

TAPAS BARS | Flamenco music and dance speak to something in Albuquerque's soul, and for folks new to the tradition or yearning for a taste, this venue—with tapas and vinos to match—is the perfect spot to kindle that flame. In an intimate, appropriately sultry setting, excellent small plates created by Mark Miller (of Santa Fe's Coyote Cafe fame) are served with the right cavas to complement them. Make reservations (shows are Friday through Sunday), arrive early, and be dazzled by the world-class artists performing here. ✉ *Hotel Albuquerque at Old Town, 800 Rio Grande Blvd. NW, Old Town* 🕾 *505/222–8797* ⊕ *www.tablaoflamenco.org.*

 Performing Arts

Albuquerque Little Theatre

THEATER | Albuquerque Little Theatre is a nonprofit community troupe that's been going strong since 1930. Its staff of professionals teams up with local volunteer talent to produce comedies, dramas, musicals, and mysteries that range from *Amadeus* to

Old Town has the city's largest concentration of one-of-a-kind retail shops.

The Odd Couple and *Singin' in the Rain*. The company theater, across the street from Old Town, was built in 1936, and though its facade has been redesigned in recent years, there are still many clues that the original design was by John Gaw Meem. It contains an art gallery, a large lobby, and a cocktail lounge. ⊠ *224 San Pasquale Ave. SW, Old Town* ☎ *505/242–4750* ⊕ *www.albuquerquelittletheatre.org.*

Shopping

Casa Talavera

HOUSEHOLD ITEMS/FURNITURE | Peruse a wide selection of hand-painted Mexican Talavera tiles at this Old Town stalwart that's been in business since 1970. Prices are reasonable, making the colorful geometrics, florals, mural patterns, and solids close to irresistible. Tin lighting fixtures as well as ceramic sink and cabinet knobs fill in the rest of the space in this DIY-inspiring shop (yes, they ship). ⊠ *621 Rio Grande Blvd., Old Town* ☎ *505/243–2413* ⊕ *www.casatalavera.com.*

El Vado Market

FOOD/CANDY | Just across from the BioPark, outdoor seating on El Vado Motel's plaza is surrounded by a cluster of locally committed shopkeepers and food purveyors. It's a good place for a cookie break, a fun meal inspired by Costa Rican, Mexican, or Laotian cooking traditions, or a *cerveza* from the El Vado taproom. ⊠ *2500 Central Ave. SW, Old Town* ☎ *505/361–1667* ⊕ *www.elvadoabq.com.*

★ Grey Dog Trading/Zuni Fetish Museum

ANTIQUES/COLLECTIBLES | This shop carries a very special selection of fetishes, contemporary and historic, from both Zuni and Cochiti Pueblo artisans, along with kachina dolls, baskets, and a small grouping of vintage and contemporary Native American jewelry and pottery, for the beginning and seasoned collector. Changing exhibits focus on one tradition—stone carvers, for example—and hone in on the work of one artist and perhaps that of the artist's family as well. Gorgeous hand-carved Ye'i figures by Navajo artist Sheldon Harvey are also on display, as are his paintings. Enter the **Zuni Fetish Museum** from within the gallery; an unusually fine range of Zuni-crafted fetishes awaits. The shop's owner is well respected in this field, and presents work from all 19 pueblos as well as Hopi and Navajo pieces. ⊠ *Plaza Hacienda, 1925 Old Town Rd. NW, Old Town* ☎ *505/243–0414, 877/606–0543* ⊕ *www.greydog-trading.com.*

Harwood Art Center

ART GALLERIES | On the fringe of Downtown and Old Town in the historic Sawmill/Wells Park neighborhood, Harwood Art Center is a remarkable city resource for its working-artist studios, classes, and as a gallery in its own right. Shows—predominantly of New Mexico–based artists working in nontraditional forms—take place in their historic brick school building and change monthly. ⊠ *1114 7th St. NW, off Mountain Rd., Old Town* ☎ *505/242–6367* ⊕ *www. harwoodartcenter.org.*

★ Old Town Antiques

ANTIQUES/COLLECTIBLES | Take a moment in this neat and quiet shop to appreciate the very particular eye of its owner, Connie Fulwyler, who, while not at all intrusive, will gladly fill in the backstory of any piece here. Her offerings center on 19th- and 20th-century art and history (Anglo, Mexican, and Native American), with a touch of "odd science" and politics: find a winsome piggy bank rendered in 1940s–50s Tlaquepaque glazeware, an original Harrison Begay gouache painting, vintage Taxco sombrero cufflinks, 1813 political engravings, early 20th-century Santo Domingo bowls, a Gilbert Atencio serigraph used for a menu cover, rare books and paper ephemera, and more. ⊠ *416 Romero St. NW, Old Town* ☎ *505/842–6657* ⊕ *oldtownantiquesabq.com.*

Santisima

SPECIALTY STORES | Meeting Johnny Salas, Santisima's spirited owner, is part of the fun of visiting this upper-story Old Town shop. It sells mostly artwork and objects that celebrate New Mexican santos traditions and Día de los Muertos across the globe. ⊠ *328 San Felipe St. NW, # F, Old Town* ☎ *505/246–2611.*

Spur Line Supply Co.

BOOKS/STATIONERY | A hop across the street from the Albuquerque Museum, Spur Line was at the frontline of the Sawmill District development, and it set a tone with its clever juxtaposition of vendors across a swath of New Mexico makers (it now also maintains a smaller, representative spot within the **Sawmill Market**). Check out vinyl records from Hi-Phy (there's even a modern version of a listening booth), cards and sundries from Power and Light Press (a Silver City letterpress shop), or a darn good apple fritter or chocolate ganache doughnut from the Bristol Doughnut Co. And be sure to enjoy the fall colors in the lovely hidden garden. ⊠ *800 20th St. NW, Suite B, Old Town* ☏ *505/242–6858* ⊕ *www. spurlinesupplyco.com.*

Downtown and EDo

You may visit Downtown for its anchoring arts and brews scene, events at the Pueblo Deco dazzler KiMo Theatre, or a stroll through the Downtown Growers' Market, but this neighborhood rewards those who take a closer look. Along Central Avenue and the parallel Gold Avenue, there's a prime trail of architectural detail, from the midcentury landmark Simms Building to the Venetian Gothic Revival Occidental Insurance Building along with the old federal courthouse's Spanish Mission pile. Hints of Albuquerque's 1880s railroad-era and Route 66 past abound; contemporary murals and other public art add to the appeal. The Downtown Albuquerque Arts & Cultural District website offers excellent self-guided walking tour maps (⊕ *www.downtownacd.org*). Eastern Downtown (EDo) features some great restaurants and hotels sprinkled among the residential Victorian buildings.

 Sights

Downtown Growers' Market

MARKET | **FAMILY** | Toe-tapping music and the freshest of fresh produce—and surely the delicious shade created by the towering cottonwoods here in Robinson Park—have folks gathering every Saturday morning from April through mid-November. This sweet respite on the western fringe of Downtown also hosts city crafts makers; high-quality wares range from fine block-printed linens to small-batch soaps. Get the freshest greens from the South Valley's Wholeheart Farm, an apricot scone from **Bosque Baking Co.**, or a hot brew from Java Joe's, and enjoy a stroll. ⊠ *Robinson Park, Central Ave. at 8th St. NW, Downtown* ⊕ *www.downtowngrowers.com* ☉ *Closed late Nov.–mid-Mar.*

Albuquerque's most historic theater is the Pueblo Deco masterpiece, the KiMo Theatre.

★ 516 Arts

MUSEUM | World-class contemporary art dominates the changing shows at this multilevel nonprofit that holds a special place in the New Mexico art scene. Visually compelling collaborations with an international set of museums and artists cross media boundaries, and often explore issues that are not only dear to the hearts and minds of this multicultural, environmentally diverse state, but resonate globally. The installations here are always top-notch, the works displayed are of the highest quality, the ideas—whether expressed in video, prints, sculpture, diodes, or paint—provocative. ⊠ 516 Central Ave. SW, Downtown ☎ 505/242–1445 ⊕ www.516arts.org ⊗ Closed Sun. and Mon.

★ KiMo Theatre

ARTS VENUE | Decorated with light fixtures made from buffalo skulls (the eye sockets glow amber in the dark), traditional Navajo symbols, dazzling tilework, and nine spectacular Western-theme wall murals by Carl Von Hassler, the 1927 Carl Boller–designed movie palace represents Pueblo Deco at its apex. The 660-seat KiMo (refurbished with its original balcony, hand-painted ceilings, and restored marquee) would be notable in any town, but it's a real standout for Albuquerque. Guided tours are often offered with Downtown's First Friday ARTScrawl (⊕ www.artscrawlabq. org), or you can just catch a film or a live performance here. Jazz, dance, blues, book tour readings, film—everything from traveling road shows to an inspired city-sponsored film series (Hitchcock pre-Hollywood, for example)—might turn up here. Former

Albuquerque resident Vivian Vance of *I Love Lucy* fame once performed on the stage; today you're more likely to see Dweezil Zappa, Pink Martini, Adam Ant, or a film-festival screening. ✉ *423 Central Ave. NW, at 5th St., Downtown* ☎ *505/768–3522 theater, 505/228–9857 box office* ⊕ *www.cabq.gov/kimo.*

New Mexico Holocaust & Intolerance Museum

MUSEUM | This little, but moving, 1932-vintage storefront museum packs plenty of punch with its poignant exhibits that document genocide and persecution throughout history, such as the infamous Bataan Death March, with special emphasis placed upon the Holocaust carried out by the Nazis before and during World War II. Exhibits include "The African American Experience" and others touch on child slave labor, the rescue of Bulgarian and Danish Jews, and the Nuremburg Trials. A re-created gate from a concentration camp and many artifacts related to Holocaust survivors and the Nazi party are also on display. ✉ *616 Central Ave. SW, Downtown* ☎ *505/247–0606* ⊕ *www.nmholocaustmuseum. org* ✉ *Donations accepted* ⊗ *Closed Mon.*

★ Richard Levy Gallery

MUSEUM | A stellar roster of artists with an international following (many New Mexico–based) show at this shoebox-shape gallery that would be right at home on either coast. Its clean lines are perfect for displaying pieces from photographers (Natsumi Hayashi, Hiroshi Sugimoto), multimedia artists (Mary Tsiongas, Eric Tillinghast, John Baldessari), metal-work sculptors (Emi Ozawa), and printmakers (Alex Katz, Ed Ruscha), as well as works from global initiatives like ISEA 2012: Machine Wilderness and 2009's LAND/ART New Mexico. ✉ *514 Central Ave. SW, Downtown* ☎ *505/766–9888* ⊕ *www.levygallery.com.*

Sanitary Tortilla Factory

ARTS VENUE | At a nexus of Downtown's coffee-beer-arts scene, Sanitary Tortilla is an exemplary adaptive reuse project. Now housing artist studios and gallery spaces, the eponymous onetime tortilla and chile go-to for politicos and locals of all stripes provides a cleverly curated counterpoint to the 516 Arts–Richard Levy arts nexus down on Central. Occasional outdoor installations (like Pastel FD's Botanical mural project, a collaboration with 516) complement the intriguing, often topical, shows inside. ✉ *401–403 2nd St. SW, Downtown* ☎ *505 /228–3749* ⊕ *sanitarytortillafactory. org* ⊗ *Closed Sat.–Thurs. except for events or by appointment.*

Special Collections Library & Center for the Book

LIBRARY | Designed by Arthur Rossiter in 1925 in a Spanish–Pueblo Revival style, this was the main Albuquerque library for some 50 years (renowned Santa Fe woodblock artist Gustav Baumann contributed the lovely interior embellishments). Repurposed as the Special Collections division in 1975, the old library now houses local history resources—including an exemplary collection of Albuquerque-theme historical postcards—as well as a small museum comprised of historic printing presses and related ephemera, known as the Center for the Book. Changing exhibits and public programs in the dramatic double-story, viga-lined main reading room are always well presented. ⊠ *423 Central Ave. NE, at Edith Blvd., Downtown* 🕾 *505/848–1376* ⊕ *www.abqlibrary.org/centerforthebook* 🎟 *Free* 🕙 *Closed Sun. and Mon.*

Turquoise Museum

MUSEUM | FAMILY | Now located in a former residential "castle"—replete with Victorian chandeliers—the Turquoise Museum casts fresh light on the beauty, mythology, and physical properties of turquoise, a semiprecious but adored gemstone that many people associate with the color of New Mexico's skies. Displays show how turquoise forms, the importance of individual mines, and uses of the stone by Native Americans in prehistoric times. The museum's proprietors are a multigenerational family of longtime traders with deep knowledge of the gem; if you retain nothing else, do remember that only turquoise specified as "natural" is the desirable, unadulterated stuff. A small gift shop sells historic and contemporary pieces. ⊠ *400 2nd St. SW, Downtown* 🕾 *505/433–3684* ⊕ *www.turquoisemuseum.com* 🎟 *$20* 🕙 *Closed Sun.* ☞ *Tour reservations recommended.*

 Restaurants

Artichoke Café

$$$$ | CONTEMPORARY | Locals praise this smartly contemporary EDo historic-district stalwart, and its intimate wood-lined bar area, for attentive service and French, American, and Italian dishes often prepared with organic ingredients. Specialties include steak frites; a seasonal, vegetarian house-made ravioli; and duck breast served with roasted pear and wilted arugula adorned with a plum vinaigrette. **Known for:** pleasing gallery-style decor; dynamically changing menu; high-end local favorite. 💲 *Average main: $34* ⊠ *424 Central Ave. SE, EDo* 🕾 *505/243–0200* ⊕ *www.artichokecafe.com* 🕙 *No lunch weekends.*

★ Farina Pizzeria & Wine Bar

$$ | PIZZA | A stellar spot for truly artisanal thin-crust pizza, Farina draws loyal crowds inside an old-school former EDo grocery store with hardwood floors, exposed-brick walls, a pressed-tin ceiling, and simple rows of wooden tables along with a long bar. This spirited place serves up exceptional pizzas with blistering-hot crusts and imaginative toppings; the Salsiccia, with sweet-fennel sausage, roasted onions, and mozzarella, has plenty of fans. **Known for:** award-winning pizza and Italian favorites; contemporary art-filled atmosphere; creative pizza toppings. ⑤ *Average main: $17 ✉ 510 Central Ave. SE, EDo ☎ 505/243–0130 ⊕ www. farinapizzeria.com ⊘ No lunch Sun.*

★ The Grove Café & Market

$ | **CAFÉ** | This airy, modern EDo neighborhood favorite features locally grown, seasonal specials at reasonable prices. Enjoy such fresh, quality treats as Grove Pancakes with fresh fruit, crème fraîche, local honey, and real maple syrup; a Farmers Salad with roasted golden beets, Marcona almonds, goat cheese, and lemon-basil vinaigrette; or an aged Genoa salami sandwich with olive tapenade, arugula, and provolone on an artisanal sourdough bread. **Known for:** commitment to local growers; quick-moving line to order; interesting on-site market. ⑤ *Average main: $11 ✉ 600 Central Ave. SE, EDo ☎ 505/248–9800 ⊕ www.thegrovecafemarket.com ⊘ Closed Mon. No dinner.*

Range Café EDo

$ | **AMERICAN** | **FAMILY** | Set in the heart of EDo, the former Standard Diner occupies a 1930s Texaco station with high ceilings and massive plate-glass windows and offers better-than-standard takes on diner standbys. The extensive menu offers a hybrid mix of longtime Standard faves, like bacon-wrapped meat loaf and an elevated mac n' cheese with cavatappi pasta and Gruyère, along with Range Café stalwarts like huge salads, burgers, sandwiches, and traditional entrées with surprise flourishes from both north and south of the border. **Known for:** breakfast served till 3 pm; cozy booths and patio seating; excellent beer, wine, and craft cocktails. ⑤ *Average main: $15 ✉ 320 Central Ave. SE, EDo ☎ 505/243–1440 ⊕ www.rangecafe.com.*

Slate Street Cafe

$$ | **ECLECTIC** | A high-energy, high-ceilinged dining room with a wine bar and modern lighting, this stylish restaurant sits amid pawn shops and bail-bond outposts on a quiet, unprepossessing side street Downtown. Once inside, you'll find a sophisticated, colorful space serving memorable, modern renditions of classic road fare, such as chicken fried steak, a beet-and-feta burger, and brown bag fish-and-chips alongside dishes with fancier roots, like sea scallops and capellini. **Known for:** tastings in the wine loft; excellent fish-and-chips; sleek business meeting spot. ⑤ *Average main: $20 ✉ 515 Slate St. NW, Downtown ☎ 505/243–2210 ⊕ www.slatestreetcafe.com ⊘ No dinner Sun. and Mon.*

Villa Myriam Coffee

$ | **ECLECTIC** | A visit to Villa Myriam is always satisfying, not just for the uber-fresh coffee drinks on offer and its crisply contemporary design, but for the sense of discovery—tucked away as it is in this emerging early 20th-century warehouse area not far from the train tracks. Tasty teas and sandwiches are also served. **Known for:** comfy, contemporary seating; freshly roasted beans (on-site!); flavorful spins on small-bite snacks. $ *Average main: $7* ⊠ *573 Commercial St. NE, Downtown* 🕾 *505/336–5652* ⊕ *www.vmcoffee.com* ⊘ *Closed Sun.*

 ## Hotels

Embassy Suites by Hilton Albuquerque

$$ | **HOTEL** | **FAMILY** | This all-suites high-rise with a contemporary design sits on a bluff alongside Interstate 25, affording guests fabulous views of the Downtown skyline and vast desert mesas to the west, and the Sandia Mountains to the east. **Pros:** convenient location adjacent to Interstate 25, near the Interstate 40 interchange; breakfast and nightly cocktail reception included; fitness center and indoor pool. **Cons:** suites attract families in addition to business travelers; rooms starting to show age; views limited on lower floors. $ *Rooms from: $150* ⊠ *1000 Woodward Pl. NE, Downtown* 🕾 *505/245–7100, 800/362–2779* ⊕ *www.embassysuitesalbuquerque.com* 🛏 *261 suites* ⦿ *Free Breakfast.*

Hotel Andaluz/Curio Collection by Hilton

$$ | **HOTEL** | Opened in 1939 by Conrad Hilton and now on the National Register of Historic Places, this 10-story Southwestern Territorial–style boutique hotel incorporates the Spanish-Moorish elements of the original Hilton design in its dramatic interior decor. **Pros:** historic aesthetic enhanced with tech-forward perks; nice views from the Ibiza terrace lounge; updated citrus-tone furnishings. **Cons:** fitness center access is across street; lighting may be a bit dim for some; fee for breakfast plan. $ *Rooms from: $180* ⊠ *125 2nd St. NW, Downtown* 🕾 *505/242–9090* ⊕ *www. hotelandaluz.com* 🛏 *107 rooms* ⦿ *No meals.*

★ Hotel Parq Central

$$ | **HOTEL** | A decidedly imaginative adaptation of a disused building, the landmark Parq Central occupies a striking Moravian tile–trimmed three-story former AT& SF Railroad employees' hospital that dates to 1926. **Pros:** wonderfully landscaped, historic building; smartly designed rooms with sound-blocking windows; free shuttle to airport and within 3 miles of hotel. **Cons:** desks in rooms are quite small (though hotel will provide a larger one on request); parking (free) can be sparse when Apothecary Lounge is hopping;

noise might travel to rooms nearest the Lounge. $ *Rooms from: $150* ✉ *806 Central Ave. SE, Downtown* ☎ *505/242–0040* ⊕ *www. hotelparqcentral.com* ↪ *74 rooms* ⵯ◯ⵯ *Free Breakfast.*

Hyatt Regency Albuquerque

$$ | HOTEL | In the heart of Downtown, this Hyatt high-rise comprises a pair of desert-color towers that figure prominently in the city's skyline. **Pros:** easy walk to the KiMo Theatre and Downtown art galleries/coffee shops; rooftop lap pool and 24/7 fitness center; Civic Plaza and Convention Center are adjacent. **Cons:** mazelike layout until you get your bearings; no views on lower floors; lap pool is only open seasonally. $ *Rooms from: $180* ✉ *330 Tijeras Ave. NW, Downtown* ☎ *505/842–1234* ⊕ *albuquerque.regency. hyatt.com/en/hotel/home.html* ↪ *382 rooms* ⵯ◯ⵯ *No meals.*

Nightlife

Dialogue Brewing & Art

BREWPUBS/BEER GARDENS | Beer and art mingle most successfully at this Wells Park destination great for anyone looking for a good brew and wood-fired pizza. Exuberant metal sculpture works by Ian LeBlanc rise above the outdoor patio seating. Indoors, artworks and clever design details enhance a visit to this special craft brewery, where European-style beers (and occasional art- and music-based events) are featured. ✉ *1501 1st St. NW, Downtown* ☎ *505/219–3938* ⊕ *www.dialoguebrewing.com.*

Effex Night Club

DANCE CLUBS | Albuquerque's sizable gay and lesbian community—and anyone else seeking a jumping dance scene—flocks to Effex, a vibrant, centrally located, two-level nightclub with a huge rooftop bar and an even larger downstairs dance floor. ✉ *420 Central St. SW, Downtown* ☎ *505/842–8870* ⊕ *www.effexabq.com.*

Marble Brewery

BREWPUBS/BEER GARDENS | Distinctive craft brews like hoppy Imperial Red and rich Oatmeal Stout draw fans of artisan beer to Downtown's Marble Brewery. The homey pub, with an expansive outdoor patio, contains a beautiful 40-foot bar and serves tasty apps and sandwiches. There's also live music some evenings. A growing dynasty of locations for the brewery have sprouted up around town, too. ✉ *111 Marble Ave. NW, Downtown* ☎ *505/243–2739* ⊕ *www.marblebrewery.com.*

⭐ Performing Arts

★ Chatter

CONCERTS | Holding sway at 10:30 am Sunday morning, the Chatter chamber ensemble's classical-to-modern music program draws a devoted crowd of regulars. Free cappuccino and a spoken-word performance round out the one-hour shows. Expect the best of local and guest performers—Santa Fe Opera stars often pop in during the season. Arrive early as the seating in the smartly repurposed Las Puertas (a one-time vintage door showroom in the Wells Park neighborhood, a bit north of Downtown) is open and limited; it's best to buy tickets ahead (online). You can also check online for Chatter programs at the Albuquerque Museum and elsewhere in town on other days. ⊠ *Las Puertas, 1512 1st St. NW, Downtown* ⊕ *www.chatterabq.org* ⊠ *$15.*

New Mexico Philharmonic

CONCERTS | The highly respected New Mexico Philharmonic dips deeply into the full realm of classical repertoire, including, at Christmas, Handel's *Messiah*. Most performances are at 2,000-seat **Popejoy Hall** or the **National Hispanic Cultural Center**'s superb Roy E. Disney Hall; in summer they occasionally suit up for outdoor performances at the **ABQ BioPark.** ⊠ *Albuquerque* ☎ *505/323–4343* ⊕ *www.nmso.org.*

🛍 Shopping

Bosque Baking Co.

FOOD/CANDY | Brands like Old World Rye, South Valley Sourdough, Sunflower Seed Multigrain, and Rustic Baguettes all beckon at the open-kitchen storefront location of Bosque Baking. A one-man show in an historic neighborhood on the western edge of Downtown, it's helmed by Jim Mecca, the best bread baker in town. Known to most locals by his regular presence at the Downtown Growers' Market (and the Corrales Market, too), visitors come here for great bread, empanadas (both savory and sweet), apricot scones, and perhaps a Ginger Molasses or Red Chile Chocolate Pecan cookie; in winter he's been known to whip up batches of sublime soups as well. ⊠ *922 Coal Ave. SW, Downtown* ☎ *505/234–6061* ⊕ *bosquebaking.com.*

★ The Man's Hat Shop

CLOTHING | The Man's Hat Shop has been a mainstay on Central Avenue since 1946. Anyone, man or woman, who needs just the right hat, with just the right fit, will find what they're looking for—fedora, porkpie, Cossack-style, coonskin, and of course top-of-the-line Western felt or straw. Owner Stuart Dunlap clearly loves his business and will help guide you among some 4,000 styles to a new chapeau that suits, or modify one you already have. ✉ *511 Central Ave. NW, Downtown* ☎ *505/247–9605* ⊕ *www.themanshatshop.com.*

Barelas and South Valley

The historic Barelas neighborhood, to the south of Downtown, features the must-see National Hispanic Cultural Center and the Rail Yards Market. Bounded by the Rio Grande bosque trails and the revitalizing rail district, this mostly residential neighborhood centers on 4th Street SW (a section of old Route 66) and is one of Albuquerque's oldest; it has shops and services—and earlier 20th-century architecture—that appear to have enjoyed a pause in time. Barelas gradually gives way to the broad South Valley. While perhaps somewhat rough-around-the-edges, the South Valley's deep agrarian roots may be seen in the burgeoning local farm and winery scene. Other highlights are the historic remnants found along the prefreeway byways, as well as the developing Valle de Oro National Wildlife Refuge.

◉ Sights

★ National Hispanic Cultural Center

ARTS VENUE | FAMILY | A showpiece for the city, and a showcase for Hispanic culture in Albuquerque's historic Barelas neighborhood, this beautifully designed space contains a vibrant art museum, multiple performance venues, a restaurant, a fresco-lined torreon (freestanding windowless tower) depicting the span of Hispanic (and pre-Hispanic) history, a 10,000-volume genealogical research center and library, and an education center. Its stunning and acoustically superb Roy E. Disney Center for Performing Arts and smaller Albuquerque Journal Theatre host ballet, flamenco dancing, bilingual theater, traditional Spanish and New Mexican music, the famous world music festival ¡Globalquerque!, and many other performances. Exhibits at its first-rate museum include dynamic displays of photography, paintings, sculpture, and traditional and contemporary craftwork by local artists as well as internationally known names. A vintage WPA-era school contains the library and **La Fonda del Bosque** restaurant ($, no dinner), which features Latin fusion fare indoors and out on the patio. ✉ *1701 4th St. SW, at Avenida César Chavez (Bridge Blvd.), Barelas* ☎ *505/246–2261 museum, 505/724–4771 box office, 505/800–7166 restaurant* ⊕ *www.nhccnm.org* ✍ *$6* ⊙ *Closed Mon., restaurant closed Sun. and Mon.*

At the National Hispanic Cultural Center, you can see many cultural performances including some from Ehecatl Aztec dancers.

★ Rail Yards Market

MARKET | FAMILY | The Sunday market here (May–October, 10–2) is a fine excuse to explore this wondrous, light-filled, almost cathedral-like space, said to have been the largest steam locomotive repair facility in the country in its heyday. Dating back to the early 20th century, the Atchison, Topeka & Santa Fe buildings here, built on the Atlantic & Pacific originals from the 1880s, put you at the center of how Downtown (or New Town, as it was then known)—and modern Albuquerque—came to be. The market, vibrant with growers and makers, occupies the 1917 Blacksmith Shop. Another historic railyard building nearby, the Storehouse, now houses the growing Wheels Museum, which is dedicated to interpreting local rail history with model train equipment and more (⊕ *www. wheelsmuseum.org*). A massive 1944 AT&SF Steam Locomotive (No. 2926) is under restoration in the Sawmill neighborhood and may find its home here as well (⊕ *www.nmslrhs.org*). ✉ *777 1st St. SW, Barelas* ☎ *505/600–1109* ⊕ *railyardsmarket.org* ⊘ *Closed Nov.–Apr.*

Sheehan Winery

WINERY/DISTILLERY | Sourcing his grapes from vineyards throughout the state, Sean Sheehan has triumphantly established this rural South Valley winery as a destination for those seeking the best in "old vine" wines. Lighter, brighter, and spicier components bring a special experience to tastings of the award-winning and notable favorites like a Cinsault Dry Rose and Cabernet Sauvignon Grand Reserve or the Riesling-based Cielo Dulce. A vibrant presence at festivals throughout the year, Sheehan Winery also hosts periodic "backyard" events on the winery's shaded patio; half-hour to 45-minute tastings are offered by appointment here on weekends year-round. ⊠ *1544 Cerro Vista Rd. SW, Barelas* ☎ *505/799–7912 tasting appointments, 505/280–3104 general info* ⊕ *www.sheehanwinery.com* ⊗ *Closed weekdays.*

 Restaurants

Barelas Coffee House

$ | **MEXICAN** | **FAMILY** | This eatery may look like a set in search of a script, but it's the real deal: folks come from all over the city to sup in the longtime New Mexican–style chile parlor in a historic Route 66 neighborhood south of Downtown. You may notice looks of quiet contentment on the faces of its many dedicated diners as they dive into their bowls of Barelas's potent red chile. **Known for:** local hangout with patio seating; old-fashioned hospitality; chicharrones and the huevos rancheros supreme. ⓢ *Average main: $8* ⊠ *1502 4th St. SW, Barelas* ☎ *505/843–7577* ⊗ *Closed Sun. No dinner.*

Activities

BIRD-WATCHING
Valle de Oro National Wildlife Refuge

BIRD WATCHING | **FAMILY** | This 570-acre refuge area now welcomes visitors, who can wander the developing paths as they try and spot the more than 229 species of birds that come through the diverse Rio Grande floodplain habitats—wetlands, bosque, and more—found here. ⊠ *7851 2nd St. SW, Barelas* ☎ *505/248–6667* ⊕ *www.fws.gov/refuge/valle_de_oro.*

UNM and Nob Hill

Established in 1889, the University of New Mexico (UNM) is the state's leading institution of higher education. Its outstanding galleries and museums are open to the public free of charge. The university's predominately Pueblo Revival–style architecture is noteworthy, particularly the beautifully preserved 1938 west wing of Zimmerman Library, which houses the superb Center for Southwest Research and changing topical exhibits, and the Alumni Chapel, both designed by John Gaw Meem, a Santa Fe–based architect whose mid-20th-century work became a template for new campus buildings for years to come. Newer structures, such as Antoine Predock's George Pearl Hall, may obliquely tip their hat to Meem, but are distinctive in their own right. Federico Muelas's mesmerizing 2012 "Blue Flower/Flor Azul" artwork, the 900-square-foot LED-and-sound installation on the west end of George Pearl Hall, is best seen at night. It joins the numerous contemporary sculptures that make this campus worth a stroll; Bruce Nauman's 1988 "The Center of the Universe" is a destination in itself. Stop at the campus Welcome Center (☎ 505/277–1989 ⊕ www.unm.edu) to pick up self-guided campus art and architecture tour maps.

The campus's easterly spread leads directly into the heart of Nob Hill and a quintessential assortment of Route 66 and art deco–influenced buildings. The vintage motels and gas stations with neon signage have housed a shifting landscape of galleries, microbreweries, cafés, upscale furnishing shops, and more. The circa-1947 Nob Hill Business Center sits right on old Route 66 (Central Avenue); sandwiched between Carlisle Boulevard and Amherst Drive SE, this is the heart of the neighborhood and where it first began. Anchored by fine local stalwarts Mariposa Gallery and IMEC, Amherst Drive (just the one block between Central and Silver) is a good side street to peruse; once on Silver, the nearby stretch between Bryn Mawr and Wellesley Drive SE is another notable pocket. Other noteworthy businesses—from some of the city's best restaurants, to offbeat shops, the venerable Guild indie cinema, and a mix of professional and student hangouts—run right along Central, both a few blocks east of Carlisle, and to the west, back toward UNM.

Sights

Ernie Pyle Library

LIBRARY | After several visits to New Mexico, Ernie Pyle, a Pulitzer Prize–winning news reporter, built a house in 1940 that now contains the smallest branch of the Albuquerque Public Library (it is also a National Historic Landmark). On display are photos, handwritten articles by Pyle, and news clippings about his career as a correspondent during World War II and his death from a sniper's bullet on April 18, 1945, on the Pacific island of Ie Shima. ✉ *900 Girard Blvd. SE, University of New Mexico* ☎ *505/256–2065* ⊕ *www.abqlibrary.org/erniepyle* 🎟 *Free* ⊗ *Closed Sun. and Mon.*

Maxwell Museum of Anthropology

MUSEUM | Tapping a significant collection of Southwestern artifacts and archival photos, the Maxwell's engaging shows encompass three fascinating fields: archaeology, cultural anthropology, and evolutionary anthropology. As the first public museum in Albuquerque (established in 1932), its influence has grown over

Greater Albuquerque

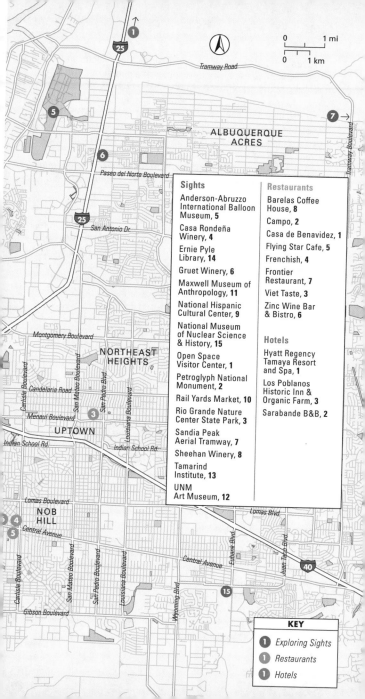

Tramway Road

ALBUQUERQUE
ACRES

Paseo del Norte Boulevard

San Antonio Dr.

Montgomery Boulevard

NORTHEAST
HEIGHTS

Carlisle Boulevard
Candelaria Road
Menaul Boulevard
UPTOWN
Indian School Rd.

San Mateo Boulevard
San Pedro Blvd.
Louisiana Boulevard
Indian School Rd.

Lomas Boulevard
NOB
HILL
Central Avenue
Gibson Boulevard

Lomas Blvd.

Central Avenue

Eubank Blvd.
Juan Tabo Blvd.
Wyoming Blvd.

Sights

Anderson-Abruzzo
International Balloon
Museum, **5**

Casa Rondeña
Winery, **4**

Ernie Pyle
Library, **14**

Gruet Winery, **6**

Maxwell Museum of
Anthropology, **11**

National Hispanic
Cultural Center, **9**

National Museum
of Nuclear Science
& History, **15**

Open Space
Visitor Center, **1**

Petroglyph National
Monument, **2**

Rail Yards Market, **10**

Rio Grande Nature
Center State Park, **3**

Sandia Peak
Aerial Tramway, **7**

Sheehan Winery, **8**

Tamarind
Institute, **13**

UNM
Art Museum, **12**

Restaurants

Barelas Coffee
House, **8**

Campo, **2**

Casa de Benavidez, **1**

Flying Star Cafe, **5**

Frenchish, **4**

Frontier
Restaurant, **7**

Viet Taste, **3**

Zinc Wine Bar
& Bistro, **6**

Hotels

Hyatt Regency
Tamaya Resort
and Spa, **1**

Los Poblanos
Historic Inn &
Organic Farm, **3**

Sarabande B&B, **2**

KEY

1 *Exploring Sights*

1 *Restaurants*

1 *Hotels*

the years, but its compact space ensures that exhibits are scaled to the essentials. A viewer—whether of a permanent exhibit on peoples of the Southwest or a temporary one—will be intrigued and informed, but not overwhelmed. Of special note is their rare and substantial collection of Mimbres pottery from AD 800–1000. The museum's gift shop is worth a look for its selection of reliably vetted Native American crafts. ⊠ *University of New Mexico, 500 University Blvd. NE, at northwest end of campus, University of New Mexico* ☎ *505/277–4405* ⊕ *maxwellmuseum.unm.edu* 🖼 *Free* ☉ *Closed Sun. and Mon.* ☞ *Parking permits available inside museum.*

Tamarind Institute

COLLEGE | This world-famous institution played a major role in reviving the fine art of lithographic printing, which involves working with plates of traditional stone and modern metal. Tamarind certification is to a printer what a degree from Juilliard is to a musician. A small gallery within the modern facility exhibits prints and lithographs by well-known masters like Jaune Quick-to-See Smith, Jim Dine, Judy Chicago, Kiki Smith, and Ed Ruscha, as well as up-and-comers in the craft. Guided tours (reservations essential) are conducted on the first Friday of each month at 1:30. ⊠ *2500 Central Ave. SE, University of New Mexico* ☎ *505/277–3901* ⊕ *tamarind.unm.edu* 🖼 *Free* ☉ *Closed Sun. and Mon.* ☞ *Parking permits available inside museum.*

★ UNM Art Museum

MUSEUM | This features magnificent 20th- and 21st-century prints, as well as photos and paintings that rival the finest collections throughout the Southwest. Changing exhibits cull from more than 30,000 archived pieces, which include groundbreaking works by modernist giants such as Bridget Riley, Richard Diebenkorn, and Elaine DeKooning. Photography—from the likes of Ansel Adams, Patrick Nagatani, and Beaumont Newhall—is a particular strength, and provocative shows have featured immense prints, complemented with video projections and a range of mixed-media installations. Transcendentalist master Raymond Jonson's work, as well as other landmark acquisitions he made, are displayed. The museum's vision for the future is to allow yet more of their impressive holdings—a Picasso print, an O'Keeffe painting—to be seen regularly. Lectures and symposia, gallery talks, and guided tours are often scheduled. ⊠ *University of New Mexico Center for the Arts, 203 Cornell Dr. NE, University of New Mexico* ☎ *505/277–4001* ⊕ *artmuseum.unm.edu* 🖼 *$5 donation suggested* ☉ *Closed Sun. and Mon.*

🍴 Restaurants

Flying Star Cafe

$ | **CAFÉ** | A staple in the city, each outpost of this locally owned order-at-the-counter-first café suits its neighborhood (some have patios and allow pets). At the original spot in Nob Hill, the university crowd crunches into a snug space to dig into a mix of creative American and New Mexican dishes (plus several types of wine and beer). **Known for:** late-night dessert; bottomless coffee and Wi-Fi; creative menu with solid basics at heart. $ *Average main: $13* ⊠ *3416 Central Ave. SE, Nob Hill* ☎ *505/255–6633* ⊕ *www. flyingstarcafe.com.*

Frenchish

$$$ | **BISTRO** | Innovative, flavorful, fun, and, indeed, French-ish, the renowned culinary team of Nelle Bauer and James Beard award semifinalist Jennifer James shines at this coolly modern spot with a refreshing bistro menu. There's the perfectly turned grilled beef rib eye, but also a winter squash–and–sautéed greens buckwheat crepe, rocket salad (with hazelnuts and pear), a french onion burger (of course), ruby trout filet, their now famous devilish egg, and a very popular carrot dog. **Known for:** twists on French classics; reservations recommended; walk-ins may sit at congenial chef's counter. $ *Average main: $27* ⊠ *3509 Central Ave. NE, Nob Hill* ☎ *505/433–5911* ⊕ *www.frenchish.co* ☉ *Closed Sun. and Mon. No lunch.*

Frontier Restaurant

$ | **CAFÉ** | **FAMILY** | This definitive student hangout—it's directly across from UNM—is open seven days from 5 am till the wee hours, and hits the spot for inexpensive diner-style American and New Mexican chow. A notch up from a fast-food joint, the chile's good (vegetarian and non), the breakfast burritos are fine (the burgers are, too), and who can resist a hot, melty oversize Frontier sweet roll? **Known for:** hours to suit both early birds and night owls; succulent cinnamon buns; roadside attraction–style decor. $ *Average main: $7* ⊠ *2400 Central Ave. SE, at Cornell Dr. SE, University of New Mexico* ☎ *505/266–0550* ⊕ *www.frontierrestaurant.com.*

Zinc Wine Bar & Bistro

$$$ | **CONTEMPORARY** | A snazzy spot in Nob Hill, Zinc captures the essence of a San Francisco neighborhood bistro with its high ceilings, hardwood floors, lovely zinc-clad bar, and table-seating replete with white tablecloths and dark-wood straight-back café chairs. Consider the starter of crispy duck-confit egg rolls with curry-chile-lime dipping sauce, or the main dish of seared

scallops with wild-rice–cranberry pilaf and a tarragon-crayfish beurre blanc—then select a matching vintage from the extensive wine list. **Known for:** seasonal, organic fare; vegan-friendly; special-event-worthy atmosphere. ⓢ *Average main: $28* ✉ *3009 Central Ave. NE, Nob Hill* ☎ *505/254–9462* ⊕ *www.zincabq.com* ☾ *No lunch weekdays.*

Nightlife

Bosque Brewing Public House

BREWPUBS/BEER GARDENS | Striking nature photographs line this hugely popular, modernly rustic pub, which offers memorable ales like Scotia (a Scotch ale) and the award-winning Bosque IPA, as well as hard seltzers and ciders year-round. There are also seasonal specialties like Last Straw, a hefeweizen, and savory repasts to accompany them. Their brewmaster has made the brewhouse a multitime National IPA Challenge Champion. ✉ *106 Girard Blvd. SE, Suite B, Nob Hill* ☎ *505/508–5967* ⊕ *www.bosquebrewing. com.*

Canteen Brewhouse

BREWPUBS/BEER GARDENS | Live music, beer, and eats (bratwurst to veggie wrap) are generously offered here. Picture casual picnic seating (indoors and out) and a sweet choice of IPAs (try the Flashback), a good red ale, a steady brown (Pecos Trail), or a briskly cold 2016 World Beer Cup–winning High Plains Pils. You should also consider the Canteen's hard ciders, wines, and seasonal selections as well. ✉ *2381 Aztec Rd. NE, University of New Mexico* ☎ *505/881–2737* ⊕ *canteenbrewhouse.com.*

★ La Cumbre Brewing Co.

BREWPUBS/BEER GARDENS | Key brews at La Cumbre include the award-winning Elevated IPA, the year-round, traditional Bavarian wheat ale A Slice of Hefen, and the lush Ryeot IPA. Food trucks await outside the convivial taproom and its outdoor-seating "corral." ✉ *3313 Girard Blvd. NE, University of New Mexico* ☎ *505/872–0225* ⊕ *www.lacumbrebrewing.com.*

O'Niell's Pub

BARS/PUBS | Serving up the Irish comfort food you'd expect, along with a touch of Cajun and Mexican for variety, O'Niell's presents an eclectic mix of local music, from jazz to jug band, western swing, and more. The expansive patio is perfect for afternoon beer and snacks. ✉ *4310 Central Ave. SE, Nob Hill* ☎ *505/255–6782* ⊕ *www.oniells.com.*

★ Outpost Performance Space

MUSIC CLUBS | This hip venue programs an inspired, eclectic slate of genres, from local *nuevo*-folk to techno, jazz, and traveling East Indian beats. Some big names—especially in the jazz world—show up at the small space, which is a key player in bringing the stellar New Mexico Jazz Festival to the state every July. ⊠ *210 Yale Blvd. SE, University of New Mexico* 🕾 *505/268–0044* ⊕ *www.outpostspace.org.*

Two Fools Tavern

BARS/PUBS | If you fancy some great fish-and-chips (and apple 'slaw) along with your crisp cold beer (local and international, draft or bottle), Two Fools is the place: convivial, fun, and lively. The food (a wide array of Irish standards plus some New Mexican ones and salads, too) is no afterthought here; it's all good, as is the impressively deep list of whiskies. Imbibe the best, with a fine selection from Scotland, Ireland, and even the United States. ⊠ *3211 Central Ave. NE, Nob Hill* 🕾 *505/265–7447* ⊕ *www.2foolstavern.com.*

Performing Arts

Popejoy Hall

ARTS CENTERS | Popejoy Hall presents blockbuster Broadway touring shows, dance performances, concerts from rock and pop to mariachi and classical, comedy acts, and lectures. **Rodey Theatre**, a smaller, 400-seat house in the same complex, stages experimental and niche works throughout the year. **Keller Hall**, also in the Center for the Arts, is a small venue with fine acoustics, a perfect home for the university's excellent chamber music program. ⊠ *University of New Mexico Center for the Arts, 203 Cornell Dr. NE, University of New Mexico* ⊹ *Enter from Central Ave. SE* 🕾 *505/925–5858 tickets, 505/277–9771 customer service* ⊕ *www. popejoypresents.com* ☞ *Free parking at remote lots includes shuttle service to venue.*

🛍 Shopping

IMEC

ART GALLERIES | A sliver of a shop that's really a gallery, IMEC (International Metalsmith Exhibition Center) carries a superb range of work by a nationally renowned group of metal- and glass-work artisans. Many are New Mexico based, like Luis Mojica, who does stunning work in sterling, resin, and mother-of-pearl, and Mary Kanda, whose intricate glass-bead pieces are richly colored. ⊠ *101 Amherst Dr. SE, Nob Hill* 🕾 *505/265–8352* ⊕ *www.shopimec.com.*

★ Kei & Molly Textiles

GIFTS/SOUVENIRS | With joyful designs composed in the spirit of traditional woodblock prints, whimsical and artful pure cotton flour-sack dish towels—and yardage, napkins, potholders, and more—roll off the silk-screen presses. View the process from their retail shop, where you will also find an irresistible selection of hand-hewn products from other local makers with keen eyes for design, like Baby Blastoff (baby and kids apparel) and Live Clay (small bowls), as well as South Valley Soaps and more. ⊠ *4400 Silver Ave. SE, Suite A, Nob Hill* ☎ *505/268–4400* ⊕ *www.keiand-molly.com.*

Mariposa Gallery

ART GALLERIES | This shop sells contemporary fine crafts, including jewelry, sculptural glass, works in mixed media and clay, and fiber arts. The changing exhibits focus on established artists (such as extraordinary metalwork by Cynthia Cook and provocative pieces by collagist Suzanne Sbarge) and worthy newcomers; its buyer's sharp eyes can result in real finds for the serious browser. ⊠ *3500 Central Ave. SE, Nob Hill* ☎ *505/268–6828* ⊕ *www.mariposa-gal-lery.com.*

Los Ranchos and North Valley

Many attractions lie north of Downtown, Old Town, and the University of New Mexico. Quite a few, including the Casa Rondeña winery and the Rio Grande Nature Center, are clustered in a contiguous stretch that comprises two of the city's longest-settled areas: the lush cottonwood-lined North Valley and Los Ranchos de Albuquerque, along the Rio Grande. Early Spanish settlers made their homes here, building on top of even earlier Pueblo homesteads. Historic adobe houses abound. The Montaño Road Bridge crosses through the area, making a sublime gateway to the West Side.

Sights

Anderson-Abruzzo International Balloon Museum

MUSEUM | FAMILY | This dramatic museum celebrates the city's legacy as the hot-air ballooning capital of the world. Albuquerque's high altitude, mild climate, and a fortuitous wind pattern known as the Albuquerque Box make it an ideal destination for ballooning. The dashing, massive facility is named for Maxie Anderson and Ben Abruzzo, who pioneered ballooning here and were part of a team of three aviators who made the first manned hot-air balloon crossing of the Atlantic Ocean in 1978. Filling the airy museum space are several fully inflated historic balloons, and both large- and small-scale replicas of gas balloons and zeppelins. You'll also see vintage balloon baskets, china and flatware from the ill-fated *Hindenburg* and an engaging display on that tragic craft, and dynamic exhibits that trace the history of the sport, dating back to the first balloon ride, in 1783. Interactive stations are set up so kids can design their own balloons. ⊠ *9201 Balloon Museum Dr. NE, off Alameda Blvd., North Valley* ☎ *505/768–6020* ⊕ *www.balloonmuseum.com* ☒ *$4, free Sun. 9–1 and 1st Fri. every month (except Oct.)* ⊗ *Closed Mon.* ☞ *No food sold on-site.*

Casa Rondeña Winery

WINERY/DISTILLERY | Perhaps the most stunning of Albuquerque's wineries, Casa Rondeña—which is technically in Los Ranchos de Albuquerque, not the city proper—was designed to resemble a Tuscan villa, with its green-tile roof and verdant grounds laced with gardens and fountains. Though a true patina of age has yet to develop (the winery was built in 1995), the vintners have made this a pleasant place for sipping. Casa Rondeña produces a very drinkable Meritage red blend as well as a respectable Viognier. You can see a vintage oak fermentation tank and a great hall with soaring ceilings, where tastings are conducted. The winery hosts chamber and jazz music events with wine receptions and dinners. ⊠ *733 Chavez Rd. NW, between Rio Grande Blvd. and 4th St. NW, Los Ranchos de Albuquerque* ☎ *505/344–5911* ⊕ *www. casarondena.com* ☒ *Free.*

★ Rio Grande Nature Center State Park

NATURE PRESERVE | **FAMILY** | Along the banks of the Rio Grande, this 270-acre refuge in an especially tranquil portion of the bosque (about midway up on the Paseo del Bosque trail) is the nation's largest cottonwood forest. There are numerous walking and biking trails that wind into the 53-acre Aldo Leopold Forest and down to the river. Bird-watchers come to view all manner of migratory waterfowl. Constructed half aboveground and half below the edge of a pond, the park's interpretive center has viewing windows and speakers that broadcast the sounds of the birds you're watching. You may see sandhill cranes, frogs, ducks, and turtles. The park has active programs for adults and children. ⊠ *2901 Candelaria Rd. NW, North Valley* ☎ *505/344–7240* ⊕ *www.rgnc.org, www. nmparks.com* ☒ *$3 per vehicle, grounds free.*

Restaurants

★ Campo

$$$ | ECLECTIC | With pink light rising on the Sandias and lavender fields aglow, dining at Los Poblanos—its menu wholly committed to finely prepared dishes made from organic and locally grown ingredients—can be a transcendent experience thanks to the pastoral setting of Albuquerque's historic North Valley. Chef Jonathan Perno's menu is a tantalizing mix of distinctive farm-to-table flavors that have been become the basis for Rio Grande Valley cuisine. **Known for:** reservations a must; inspired setting and decor with year-round views; fabulous eight-course Chef's Table menu. ⑤ *Average main: $30* ⊠ *Los Poblanos Historic Inn & Organic Farm, 4803 Rio Grande Blvd. NW, Los Ranchos de Albuquerque* ☎ *505/338–1615* ⊕ *www.lospoblanos.com* ⊗ *No dinner Mon. and Tues.*

Casa de Benavidez

$ | MEXICAN | The fajitas at this welcoming local favorite with a romantic garden patio are among the best in town (the shrimp and vegetable renditions are both generous and especially memorable), and the *carne adovada* is faultless. As always with New Mexican cuisine, all diners can choose from red and green chile; vegetarians will want to ask the kind waitstaff to serve it green. **Known for:** shaded patio seating; live Spanish guitar music; charming atmosphere in a traditional adobe house. ⑤ *Average main: $13* ⊠ *8032 4th St. NW, Los Ranchos de Albuquerque* ☎ *505/898–3311* ⊕ *www.casadebenavidez.com* ⊗ *No dinner Sun.*

🛏 Hotels

★ Hyatt Regency Tamaya Resort and Spa

$$$ | RESORT | Set spectacularly on 550 pristine acres on the Santa Ana Pueblo (just north of Albuquerque, near Bernalillo), Tamaya awaits those seeking a culturally rich and even spiritually revivifying respite. **Pros:** great amenities like outdoor heated pools, horseback riding, and free bikes; lovely backroads drive from historic Albuquerque and Corrales; convenient base for the north route to Chaco Canyon. **Cons:** pet policy limited to dogs; additional daily resort fee; breakfast not included. ⑤ *Rooms from: $219* ⊠ *1300 Tuyuna Trail, Santa Ana Pueblo* ☎ *505/867–1234* ⊕ *tamaya.regency.hyatt.com/en/hotel/home.html* ⇥ *350 rooms* ⑩ *No meals.*

★ Los Poblanos Historic Inn & Organic Farm

$$$ | B&B/INN | FAMILY | Designed in the 1930s by the renowned Pueblo Revival architect John Gaw Meem for a local political power couple, Los Poblanos stands today as a quintessential element of Albuquerque's North Valley and its pastoral soul. **Pros:** seasonal farm-to-fork dining; fine bedding and linens; visitor well-being is paramount. **Cons:** peacocks may startle (and consequently screech); some spa services are off-site; on the expensive side. ⑤ *Rooms from: $230* ✉ *4803 Rio Grande Blvd. NW, Los Ranchos de Albuquerque* ☎ *505/344–9297* ⊕ *www.lospoblanos.com* ⟿ *50 rooms* ⑩ *Free Breakfast.*

Sarabande B&B

$$ | B&B/INN | While the name of this soothing, Modernist compound is inherited from the prior owners, the current setup blends a respect for its Southwestern roots with a refreshing commitment to a high-end midcentury modern aesthetic (a rarity in these parts). **Pros:** casita-like feel; delicious breakfast; pastoral hideaway. **Cons:** five-day cancel notice required (longer at Balloon Fiesta); property manager reachable by phone/text, but not on-site 24/7; must pay half up front. ⑤ *Rooms from: $185* ✉ *5637 Rio Grande Blvd. NW, Los Ranchos de Albuquerque* ☎ *505/348–5593* ⊕ *www. sarabandebnb.com* ⟿ *5 rooms* ⑩ *Free Breakfast.*

Shopping

★ Bookworks

BOOKS/STATIONERY | This North Valley stalwart has been reviving readers' spirits for many a year in a cozy neighborhood setting. A committed independent seller, Bookworks fairly prides itself on service, and book lovers from all corners flock here for its fine stock of regional coffee-table books, a well-culled selection of modern fiction and nonfiction, architecture and design titles, well-chosen CDs, calendars, and cards, and a (small) playground's worth of kids' books. Regular signings and readings draw some very big guns to this tiny treasure. ✉ *4022 Rio Grande Blvd. NW, Los Ranchos de Albuquerque* ☎ *505/344–8139* ⊕ *www.bkwrks. com.*

Eldora Chocolate

FOOD/CANDY | Ramble north on this rural stretch of Edith Boulevard and your reward is not only a bit of Albuquerque history en route, but the unexpected wonder that is Eldora Chocolate. The actual chocolate making happens here, too, and the many shop's many awards attest to owners Steve and Andrea Prickett's attention to quality and the nuances of the chocolate bean. This is true artisanal chocolate—any aficionado is sure to learn something special about their 70% Tanzanian, say, and tastings are offered freely. ✉ *8114 Edith Blvd. NE, North Valley* ☎ *505/433–4076* ⊕ *www. eldorachocolate.com.*

★ The Farm Shop at Los Poblanos
FOOD/CANDY | FAMILY | This beautiful country inn also carries a distinctive selection of books, culinary gadgets, fine crafts from local makers (jewelry, textiles, ceramics), the same house-made lavender lotions and soaps inn guests receive, and a considerable variety of artisan jams, vinegars, and sauces. The Campo kitchen there also whips up crisply crusted breads, sandwiches, coffee, tea, and cakes for takeaway sustenance. ✉ *Los Poblanos Historic Inn & Organic Farm, 4803 Rio Grande Blvd. NW, Los Ranchos de Albuquerque* ☎ *505/938–2192 shop, 505/344–9297 inn* ⊕ *www.lospoblanos.com.*

Activities

KAYAKING
Quiet Waters Paddling Adventures
CANOEING/ROWING/SKULLING | The Rio at sunset (or in the early hours during balloon time—or just about any time) is best seen from a kayak or canoe and this reliable outfit offers rentals as well as guided and self-guided tours to help you do just that. After a 15-mile drive north from Downtown to the small historic town of Bernalillo, you are set for a serene float down the calm, cotton-wood-lined waters of the middle Rio Grande. ✉ *105D Pleasant View Dr., Bernalillo* ☎ *505/771–1234* ⊕ *www.quietwaterspaddling.com.*

Uptown and Northeast Heights

In the Northeast Heights you are approaching the foothills of the Sandia Mountains, with upscale neighborhoods that surprise with the sudden appearance of piñon and ponderosa. Trips to this area can easily be combined with more north-central venues like the Balloon Museum and local microbreweries, or the National Museum of Nuclear Science & History, which, once you've made it into the foothills, is due south. The Uptown area is closer to the center of town, and shopping and restaurants are its main attractions.

Sights

Gruet Winery
WINERY/DISTILLERY | First-time visitors may be forgiven for pausing as they approach Gruet's brick chalet-inspired building, set down as it is hard by the highway in a transitional industrial area. Inside, however, is one of the nation's most acclaimed producers of sparkling wines. Some of its vineyards—all in-state—are as close

as Santa Ana Pueblo, just north of Bernalillo, and may be seen while driving Interstate 25. Gruet (pronounced *grew*-ay) had been famous in France since the 1950s for its Champagnes. In New Mexico, the Gruet family has been producing wine since 1984, and it's earned nationwide kudos for its Methode Champenoise (employing traditional Champagne-making methods for its sparkling wine), as well as for impressive Pinot Noirs, Rosés, and Chardonnays. Most of the state's top restaurants carry Gruet vintages, as do leading wine cellars around the country. ⊠ *8400 Pan American Fwy. NE (I–25), off northbound I–25 frontage road, between Paseo del Norte and Alameda Blvd., Northeast Heights* ☎ *505/821–0055* ⊕ *www.gruetwinery.com* ⊠ *Winery free, 5-wine tasting from $12.*

★ Sandia Peak Aerial Tramway

VIEWPOINT | **FAMILY** | One of the world's longest aerial tramways, here tramway cars climb nearly three miles up the steep western face of the Sandias, giving you a dazzling close-up view (whatever the season) of the imposing rock formations and wind-blown wilderness. From the observation deck at the 10,378-foot summit you can see Santa Fe to the northeast and Los Alamos to the northwest: about 11,000 square miles of spectacular scenery. You may also see graceful hawks or eagles soaring above or mountain lions roaming the cliff sides. An exhibit room at the top surveys the wildlife and landscape of the mountain; a few steps away is **Ten 3,** where a lounge and cliffside dining await. You can also use the tram as a way to reach the Sandia Peak ski and mountain-biking area. ■TIP→ **It's much colder and windier at the summit than at the tram's base, so pack a jacket.** Tram cars leave from the base at regular intervals for the 15-minute ride to the top. Purchase tickets (all round-trip) up to 24 hours ahead online; parking fee is included. ⊠ *10 Tramway Loop NE, Far Northeast Heights* ☎ *505/856–7325, 505/856–1532, 505/764–8363 Ten 3 restaurant* ⊕ *www.sandia-peak.com* ⊠ *$25; $3 parking fee.*

🍴 Restaurants

Viet Taste

$ | **VIETNAMESE** | Excellent, authentic Vietnamese food is served up in this compact, modern, bamboo-accented restaurant (once inside, it's easy to ignore the fact that it's within one of Albuquerque's ubiquitous strip malls). Consider the popular *pho* (noodle soup) variations, order the tofu (or chicken or shrimp) spring rolls with tangy peanut sauce, dig into the spicy lemongrass with chicken, and all will be well. **Known for:** authentic Vietnamese dishes; gracious, accommodating service; well-matched beer and wine list. ⑤ *Average main: $10* ⊠ *5721 Menaul Blvd. NE, Northeast Heights* ☎ *505/888–0101* ☉ *Closed Sun.*

Shopping

Bien Mur Indian Market Center

CRAFTS | The Sandia Pueblo-run Bien Mur Indian Market Center showcases the best of regional Native American rugs, jewelry, and crafts of all kinds. It is a great place to get familiar with the distinct styles found across the 19 pueblos, and you can feel secure about the authenticity of purchases made here. The Pueblo's 107-acre American Bison Preserve is just out the door. ⊠ *100 Bien Mur Dr. NE, off Tramway Rd. NE east of I–25, Northeast Heights* ☎ *505/771–7994, 505/821–5400* ⊕ *www.sandiapueblo. nsn.us/bien-mur-indian-market.*

Page 1 Books

BOOKS/STATIONERY | One of the great independent bookstores in Albuquerque, Page 1 is a singular find for its mix of rare and used books shelved to entice the serious browser, while also offering a deep selection of literature, fiction and nonfiction, print ephemera, books for kids, gifts for the book lover, and even textbooks. Count on astute staff recommendations, as well as a regular roster of book signings, poetry readings, and children's events. ⊠ *5850 Eubank Blvd. NE, Northeast Heights* ☎ *505/294–2026* ⊕ *www. page1book.com.*

Theobroma Chocolatier

FOOD/CANDY | Out by the Sandia foothills, Theobroma Chocolatier carries beautiful, handcrafted, high-quality chocolates, truffles, and candies (most of them made on the premises). ⊠ *12611 Montgomery Blvd. NE, Northeast Heights* ☎ *505/293–6545* ⊕ *www. theobromachocolatier.com.*

Tin Can Alley

FOOD/CANDY | **FAMILY** | A stack-up of mural-painted shipping containers houses a Santa Fe Brewing outpost as well as a range of Albuquerque-based food and coffee vendors. Highlights are pizza, paletas, and Coca Flora, which offers a boutique-like setting with foods and chocolate from other places. The outdoor spaces are especially refreshing; the view over the desert west oddly enough trumps the mountain view to the east. ⊠ *6110 Alameda Blvd. NE, Northeast Heights* ☎ *505/208–0508* ⊕ *www.tincanalleyabq.com.*

Weyrich Gallery

CRAFTS | This shop carries distinctive jewelry, contemporary glass work, and hand-colored photography, as well as exquisite hand-formed ceramic Japanese tea bowls, woodblocks, and other largely Asian-inspired pieces, all at prices that are very reasonable. ⊠ *2935-D Louisiana Blvd. NE, Northeast Heights* ☎ *505/883–7410* ⊕ *www.weyrichgallery.com.*

East Side and West Side

South of Interstate 40 and the Northeast Heights, the East Side bridges the older and historic parts of Route 66 with pockets of strip-shopping centers (especially along Eubank Boulevard) and some newer development of an upscale nature. But you are at the gateway to multiple mountain chains here—the Sandias, as well as the rewarding byways of the Manzano Mountains—and before you consider heading out to them, you will want to make time for the decidedly destination-worthy National Museum of Nuclear Science & History.

Farther west, the fastest-growing part of Albuquerque lies on a broad mesa high above the Rio Grande Valley. The West Side is primarily the domain of new suburban housing developments and strip malls, some designed more attractively than others. Somewhat controversially, growth on the West Side has seemed to occur below, above, and virtually all around the archaeologically critical Petroglyph National Monument. Not far from the Monument's trails is the very special Open Space Visitor Center, a migrating sandhill crane population's winter home. The center is adjacent to another archaeological site of interest, Piedras Marcadas Pueblo, which features interpretive displays within. Allow a 20-minute drive from Old Town and the North Valley to reach either (and about the same time to travel between them).

◉ Sights

★ National Museum of Nuclear Science & History

MUSEUM | FAMILY | Previously known simply as the National Atomic Museum, this brilliant Smithsonian affiliate traces the history of the atomic age and how nuclear science has dramatically influenced the course of modern history. Exhibits include replicas of Little Boy and Fat Man (the bombs dropped on Japan at the end of World War II), a compelling display about the difficult decision to drop atomic bombs, and a look at how atomic culture has dovetailed with pop culture. There are also children's programs and an exhibit about X-ray technology. The campus also contains the 9-acre Heritage Park, which has a B-29 and other mega-airships, plus rockets, missiles, cannons, and even a nuclear sub sail. One highlight is the restored 1942 Plymouth that was used to transport the plutonium core of "the Gadget" (as that first weapon was known) down from Los Alamos to the Trinity Site for testing. ⊠ *601 Eubank Blvd. SE, a few blocks south of I–40, East Side* ☎ *505/245–2137* ⊕ *www.nuclearmuseum.org* 🎟 *$14.*

★ Open Space Visitor Center

MUSEUM | FAMILY | Sandhill cranes make their winter home here or stop for a snack en route to the Bosque del Apache, just south in Socorro. Albuquerque is right in their flyway, and the Open Space Center, which is replete with trails heading down to the shores of the Rio Grande, provides a most hospitable setting for them. The outdoor viewing station opens onto the site's expansive field, which faces out to the Sandia Mountains; the hush—aside from the occasional flock circling above—is restorative. Complementing the experience inside are changing art and photography exhibits, an interpretative display on the adjacent 14th- to 15th-century Piedras Marcadas Pueblo ruins, and well-informed guides. A native garden interspersed with mosaics and sculptures fills the patio at the center's entryway; the latter theme is introduced when you make the turn-off from busy Coors Boulevard—Robert Wilson's large-scale public art installation "Flyway" is at the northeast corner as you approach. Ongoing family activities, occasional live music, and educational and other special programming are on tap year-round. ⊠ *500 Coors Blvd. NW, West Side* ☎ *505/897–8831* ⊕ *www.cabq.gov/openspace* ☉ *Closed Sun. and Mon.*

Petroglyph National Monument

ARCHAEOLOGICAL SITE | FAMILY | Beneath the stumps of five extinct volcanoes, this park encompasses more than 25,000 ancient Native American rock drawings inscribed on the 17-mile-long West Mesa escarpment overlooking the Rio Grande Valley. For centuries, Native American hunting parties camped at the base, chipping and scribbling away. Archaeologists believe most of the petroglyphs were carved on the lava formations between 1100 and 1600, but some images at the park may date back as far as 1000 BC. A paved trail at **Boca Negra Canyon** (north of the information center on Unser Boulevard, beyond Montaño Road) leads past several dozen petroglyphs. A tad more remote is the sandy **Piedras Marcadas Canyon** trail, a few miles farther north. The trail at **Rinconada Canyon** (south of the information center on Unser) is unpaved. The rangers at the small information center will supply maps and help you determine which trail is best for the time you have. ⊠ *Visitor center, 6001 Unser Blvd. NW, at Western Trail Rd., 3 miles north of I–40 Exit 154, West Side* ☎ *505/899–0205* ⊕ *www.nps.gov/petr* 🎟 *Free; parking $1 for Boca Negra trail, free for the Piedras Marcadas and Rinconada trails.*

TAOS

Updated by
Yvonne Pesquera

◉ Sights   🍴 Restaurants   🛏 Hotels   🛍 Shopping   🍸 Nightlife

★★★☆☆   ★★★★☆   ★★★★☆   ★★★★☆   ★★★★☆

WELCOME TO TAOS

TOP REASONS TO GO

★ **Small-town sophistication:** For a tiny, remote community, Taos supports a richly urbane culinary scene, a fantastic bounty of galleries and design shops, and plenty of stylish B&Bs and inns.

★ **Indigenous and artistic roots:** The Taos Pueblo and its inhabitants have lived in this region for centuries and continue to play a vital role in the community. And few U.S. towns this size have a better crop of first-rate art museums, which document the history of one of the West's most prolific arts colonies.

★ **Desert solitude:** Few panoramas in the Southwest can compare with that of the 13,000-foot Sangre de Cristo Mountains soaring over the adobe homes of Taos, and beyond that, the endless high-desert mesa that extends for miles to the west.

★ **World-class ski slopes:** Just a 30-minute drive north of town, Taos Ski Valley has long been one of the top winter-sports resorts in the West.

1 **Historic Downtown Taos.** The heart of the city and home to the Plaza, still the community's hub of commercial and social activity more than four centuries after it was laid out.

2 **The Southside and Ranchos de Taos.** A low-key stretch of highway with some lovely eateries and hotels along with a famous ranching community.

3 **El Prado.** An unincorporated area northwest of the Plaza that features some lovely restaurants and hotels, with great views of Pueblo Peak.

4 **Taos Pueblo.** A sovereign Native American nation within the United States, the distinctive, multistory adobe buildings of the Pueblo are a one-of-a-kind historic and cultural destination.

5 **The Mesa.** The high desert area west of downtown Taos famous for its clear night sky and the Río Grande del Norte National Monument.

6 **Arroyo Seco.** A charming, historic village with funky galleries and restaurants that's also the most direct route to Taos Ski Valley.

7 **Taos Ski Valley.** New Mexico's ultimate alpine paradise.

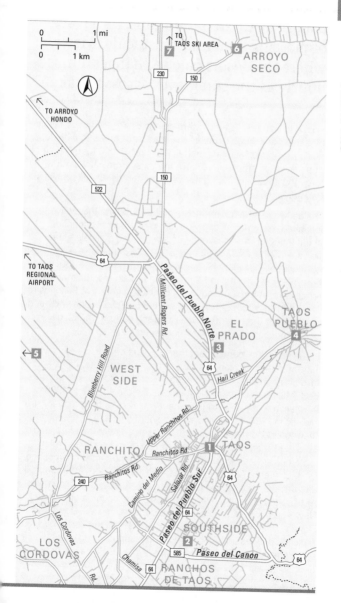

Taos casts a lingering spell. Set on an undulating mesa at the base of the Sangre de Cristo Mountains, it's a place of piercing light and spectacular views, where the desert palette changes almost hourly as the sun moves across the sky.

Adobe buildings—some of them centuries old—lie nestled amid pine trees and scrub, some in the shadow of majestic Wheeler Peak, the state's highest point, at just over 13,000 feet. The smell of piñon-wood smoke rises from the valley from early autumn through late spring; during the warmer months, the air smells of fragrant sage.

The earliest residents, members of the Taos-Tiwa tribe, have inhabited this breathtaking valley for more than a millennium; about 2,000 of their descendants still live and maintain a traditional way of life at Taos Pueblo, a 95,000-acre reserve 4 miles northeast of Taos Plaza. Spanish settlers arrived in the 1500s, bringing both farming and Catholicism to the area; their influence remains most pronounced in the diminutive village of Ranchos de Taos, 4 miles south of town, where the massive adobe walls and *camposanto* (graveyard) of San Francisco de Asís Church have been attracting photographers for generations.

In the early 20th century, another population—artists—discovered Taos and began making the pilgrimage here to write, paint, and take photographs. The early adopters of this movement, painters Bert Phillips and Ernest Blumenschein, stopped here in 1898 quite by chance to repair a wagon wheel while en route from Denver to Mexico in 1898. Enthralled with the earthy beauty of the region, they abandoned their intended plan, settled near the plaza, and in 1915 formed the Taos Society of Artists. In later years, many illustrious artists—including Georgia O'Keeffe, Ansel Adams, and D. H. Lawrence—frequented the area, helping cement a vaunted arts tradition that thrives to this day. The steadily emerging bohemian spirit has continued to attract hippies, counterculturalists, New Agers, the LGBTQ community, and free spirits. Downtown, along with some outlying villages to the south and north, such as Ranchos de Taos and Arroyo Seco, now support a rich abundance of galleries and design-driven shops. Whereas Santa Fe, Aspen, Scottsdale, and other gallery hubs in the West tend toward pricey work, much of it by artists living elsewhere, Taos remains very much an ardent hub of local arts and crafts production and sales. A half dozen excellent museums here also document the town's esteemed artistic history.

About 5,800 people live year-round within Taos town limits, but another 28,000 reside in the surrounding county, much of which is unincorporated, and quite a few others live here seasonally. This means that in summer and, to a lesser extent, during the winter ski season, the town can feel much larger and busier than you might expect, with a considerable supply of shops, restaurants, and accommodations. Still, overall, the valley and soaring mountains of Taos enjoy relative isolation, low population density, and magnificent scenery, parts of which you can access by visiting Rio Grande del Norte National Monument. These elements combine to make Taos an ideal retreat for those aiming to escape, slow down, and embrace a distinct regional blend of art, cuisine, outdoor recreation, and natural beauty.

Planning

When to Go

With more than 300 days of sunshine annually, Taos typically yields good—if sometimes chilly—weather year-round. The summer high season brings warm days (upper 80s) and cool nights (low 50s), as well as frequent afternoon thunderstorms. A packed arts and festival schedule in summer means hotels and B&Bs sometimes book well in advance, lodging rates are high, restaurants are jammed, and traffic anywhere near the plaza can slow to a standstill. Spring and fall are stunning and favor mild days and cool nights, fewer visitors, and reasonable hotel prices. In winter, especially during big years for snowfall, skiers arrive en masse but tend to stay close to the slopes and only venture into town for an occasional meal or shopping raid.

Planning Your Time

Whether you've got an afternoon or a week in the area, begin by strolling around Taos Plaza and along Bent Street, taking in the galleries, Native American crafts shops, and eclectic clothing stores, plus nearby museums, including the Harwood, Kit Carson Home, and Taos Art Museum. A few of the must-see attractions in the area are a bit farther afield, and you need at least two days and ideally three or four to take in everything. Among the top outlying attractions, it's possible to visit Taos Pueblo, the magnificent Millicent Rogers Museum, the village of Arroyo Seco, and the Rio Grande Gorge Bridge all in one day—you can connect them to make one loop to the north and west of the city. If you're headed south, stop at La Hacienda de los Martínez to gain an appreciation of early Spanish life in Taos and then to Ranchos de Taos to see the stunning San Francisco de Asís Church. If you approach Taos from the south, as most visitors do, you could also visit both these attractions on your way into town, assuming you arrive by early afternoon.

Getting Here and Around

AIR

Albuquerque International Sunport, about 130 miles away and a 2½-hour drive, is the nearest major airport to Taos. The small Santa Fe Municipal Airport, a 90-minute drive, also has daily service from Dallas, Denver, Los Angeles, and Phoenix. Alternatively, as Taos is one of the gateway towns to New Mexico if coming from Colorado, some visitors fly into Denver (five hours north) or Colorado Springs (four hours). Taos Municipal Airport, 12 miles west of town, serves public charters and private planes from Hawthorne/Los Angeles, Carlsbad/San Diego in California, Dallas, and Austin.

AIRPORTS Albuquerque International Sunport (ABQ). ⊠ *220 Sunport Blvd., Albuquerque* ☎ *505/244–7700* ⊕ *www.abqsunport.com.* **Santa Fe Regional Airport** (SAF). ⊠ *121 Aviation Dr., Santa Fe* ☎ *505/955–2900* ⊕ *www.santafenm.gov/airport.* **Taos Regional Airport** (SKX). ⊠ *24662 U.S. 64, El Prado* ☎ *575/758–4995* ⊕ *www.taosgov.com/149/Airport.*

AIRPORT TRANSFERS

From Santa Fe, your best bet is renting a car. Taos Express provides bus service between Taos and Santa Fe, including a stop at Santa Fe's train station, from which you can catch the New Mexico Rail Runner train to Albuquerque (and then a free bus to the airport). The fare is just $10 round-trip, but service is offered only on weekends (one Friday evening run, and two Saturday and Sunday runs, one in the morning, one in the evening). Twin Hearts Express has shuttle service four times daily between Taos and Albuquerque Sunport ($95 round-trip), but they don't stop in Santa Fe. Additionally, Taos Ski Valley operates a daily shuttle between the airports in Albuquerque ($85 round-trip) and Santa Fe ($65 round-trip) and the ski valley; once at the ski valley, you have to take a taxi ($35 one way) or the local Chili Line Shuttle bus ($2 round-trip) into Taos. Unless you're coming to Taos just for skiing, this is a pretty cumbersome and expensive option.

SHUTTLE CONTACTS Taos Ski Valley Airport Shuttle. ✉ *116 Sutton Pl.* ☎ *888/825–7541* ⊕ *www.skitaos.com/discover-taos/getting-here.*

BIKE

Taos-area roads are steep and hilly, and none have marked bicycle lanes, so be careful while cycling. The West Rim Trail offers a fairly flat but view-studded 9-mile ride that follows the Rio Grande Canyon's west rim from the Rio Grande Gorge Bridge to near the Taos Junction Bridge.

Gearing Up Bicycle Shop

BICYCLING | You can rent or buy bikes and equipment at this full-service bike shop. Staff can provide advice on the best routes and upcoming group rides. ✉ *616 Paseo del Pueblo Sur* ☎ *575/751–0365* ⊕ *www.gearingupbikes.com.*

CAR

A car is your most practical means both for reaching and getting around Taos. The main route from Santa Fe is via U.S. 285 north to NM 68 north, also known as the Low Road, which winds between the Rio Grande and red-rock cliffs before rising to a sweeping view of the mesa and river gorge. You can also take the spectacular and vertiginous High Road to Taos, which takes longer but offers a wonderfully scenic ride—many visitors come to Taos via the Low Road, which is more dramatic when driven south to north, and then return to Santa Fe via the High Road, which has better views as you drive south. From Denver, it's a five-hour drive south via Interstate 25, U.S. 160 west (at Walsenburg), and CO 159 to NM 522—the stretch from Walsenburg into Taos is quite scenic.

TAXI

Taxi service is virtually nonexistent in Taos. From time to time, entrepreneurial drivers will pin a business card to a bulletin board, but these ventures come and go. Uber and Lyft are both available in the city.

Visitor Information

Taos Ski Valley Chamber of Commerce. ✉ *10 Thunderbird Rd., Taos Ski Valley* ☎ *800/517–9816* ⊕ *www.taosskivalley.com.* **Taos Visitor Center.** ✉ *1139 Paseo del Pueblo Sur* ☎ *800/732–8267* ⊕ *www. taos.org.*

Restaurants

For a relatively small, remote town, Taos has a sophisticated and eclectic dining scene. It's a fine destination for authentic New Mexican fare, but you'll also find several upscale spots serving creative regional fare utilizing mostly local ingredients, a smattering of excellent Asian and Middle Eastern spots, and several very good cafés and coffeehouses are perfect for a light but bountiful breakfast or lunch.

Hotels

Taos is a well-honed tourist destination with an abundant supply of hospitality. Hotels are mostly congregated in Historic Downtown Taos, with hotels and motels along NM 68 (Paseo del Pueblo), most of them on the south side of town, that suit every need and budget; rates vary little between big-name chains and smaller establishments. Make advance reservations and expect higher rates during ski season (usually from late December to early April, and especially for lodgings on the north side of town, closer to the ski area) and in the summer. The Taos Ski Valley has a number of condo and rental units, but there's little reason to stay up here unless you're in town expressly for skiing or perhaps hiking in summer—it's too far from Taos proper to be a convenient base for exploring the rest of the area. The area's many B&Bs offer some of the best values, when you factor in typically hearty full breakfasts, personal service, and, often, roomy casitas with private entrances.

Restaurant and hotel reviews have been shortened. For full information, visit Fodors.com. Restaurant prices are the average cost of a main course at dinner or, if dinner is not served, at lunch. Hotel prices are for two people in a standard double room in high season, excluding 12%–13% tax.

WHAT IT COSTS in U.S. Dollars			
$	$$	$$$	$$$$
RESTAURANTS			
under $16	$16–$23	$24–$30	over $30
HOTELS			
under $110	$110–$200	$201–$300	over $300

River Rafting

The Taos Box, at the bottom of the steep-walled canyon far below the Rio Grande Gorge Bridge, is the granddaddy of thrilling white water in New Mexico and is best attempted by experts only—or on a guided trip—but the river also offers more placid sections such as through the Orilla Verde Recreation Area (one of the two main parcels of the Rio Grande del Norte National Monument), just south of Taos in the village of Pilar, and the Rio Grande Gorge Visitor Center, a font of information on outdoor recreation in the region. Spring runoff is the busy season, from late March through June, but rafting companies conduct tours from early March to as late as November. Shorter two-hour options usually cover the fairly tame section of the river.

CONTACTS Los Rios River Runners. ☎ 575/776–8854 ⊕ www. losriosriverrunners.com. **New Mexico River Adventures.** ☎ 800/983–7756 ⊕ www.newmexicoriveradventures.com. **Rio Grande Gorge Visitor Center.** ✉ 2873 NM 68, Pilar ☎ 575/751–4899 ⊕ www.blm. gov/visit/orilla-verde-recreation-area.

Historic Downtown Taos

The historic Taos Plaza is the central focal point of Taos. Established in 1796, the plaza began as a quadrangle for a Spanish fortlike settlement. Merchants and traders traveled from all over the West to display their wares on the plaza. Today, Taos Plaza continues to be a gathering place for the local community and visitors. Dozens of independent shops and galleries, along with several notable restaurants, hotels, and museums, thrive here. The plaza itself is a bit overrun with mediocre souvenir shops, but you only need to walk a block in any direction—especially north and east—to find better offerings.

 Sights

★ David Anthony Fine Art (DAFA)

ARTS VENUE | Showing some of the top contemporary artists—both representative and abstract—as well as beautifully designed cabinets and other furniture known for their decorative tin and steel doors, DAFA also hosts occasional musical performances in its airy gallery a short walk east of the plaza. Art highlights include contemporary glass sculptures by Jennifer Hecker and Leon Applebaum, portrait photography by William Coupon, and

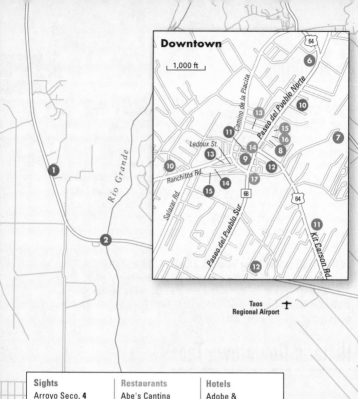

Downtown

1,000 ft

Ledoux St.

Rio Grande

Ranchitos Rd.

Salazar Rd.

Camino de la Placita

Paseo del Pueblo Norte

Paseo del Pueblo Sur

Kit Carson Rd.

Los Cordovas Rd.

Taos
Regional Airport

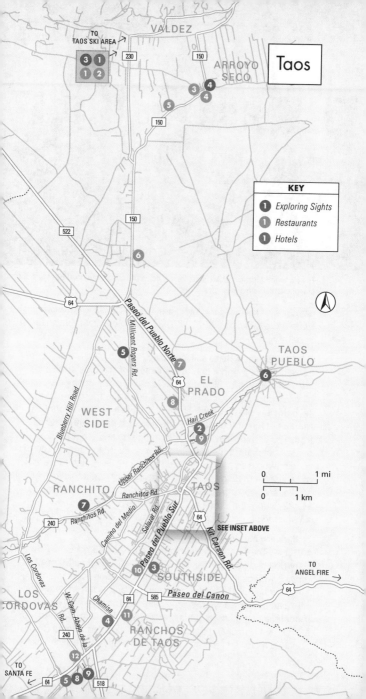

TO
TAOS SKI AREA

VALDEZ

230

150

ARROYO
SECO

Taos

WEST
SIDE

522

64

150

Paseo del Pueblo Norte

Millicent Rogers Rd.

TAOS
PUEBLO

EL
PRADO

64

Hail Creek

Blueberry Hill Road

KEY
- Exploring Sights
- Restaurants
- Hotels

RANCHITO

240

Upper Ranchitos Rd.

Ranchitos Rd.

Ranchitos Rd.

Camino del Medio

Salazar Rd.

TAOS

64

Paseo del Pueblo Sur

SEE INSET ABOVE

0   1 mi

0   1 km

TO
ANGEL FIRE

64

SOUTHSIDE

Paseo del Cañon

585

LOS
CORDOVAS

Los Cordovas

W. Gem. Abajo de la

Chamisa

64

240

RANCHOS
DE TAOS

518

TO
SANTA FE

64

The Harwood Musuem of Art is the former home of Taos painter Burt Harwood and one of the city's best museums.

paintings of kachinas by John Farnsworth. ✉ *132 Kit Carson Rd., Plaza and Vicinity* ☎ *575/770–5733* ⊕ *www.davidanthonyfineart. com.*

E. L. Blumenschein Home and Museum

HOUSE | For an introduction to the history of the Taos art scene, start with Ernest L. Blumenschein's residence, which provides a glimpse into the cosmopolitan lives led by the members of the Taos Society of Artists, of which Blumenschein was a founding member. One of the rooms in the adobe-style structure dates from 1797. On display are the art, antiques, and other personal possessions of Blumenschein and his wife, Mary Greene Blumenschein, who also painted, as did their daughter Helen. Several of Ernest Blumenschein's vivid oil paintings hang in his former studio, and works by other early Taos artists are also on display. ✉ *222 Ledoux St., Plaza and Vicinity* ☎ *575/758–0505* ⊕ *www. taoshistoricmuseums.org* ✉ *$8* ⊙ *Closed Wed. and Thurs.*

★ Harwood Museum of Art

MUSEUM | The Pueblo Revival former home of Burritt Elihu "Burt" Harwood, a dedicated painter who studied in France before moving to Taos in 1916, is adjacent to a museum dedicated to the works of local artists. Traditional Hispanic northern New Mexican artists, early art-colony painters, post–World War II modernists, and contemporary artists such as Larry Bell, Agnes Martin, Ken Price, and Earl Stroh are represented. Mabel Dodge Luhan, a major arts patron, bequeathed many of the 19th- and early-20th-century works in the Harwood's collection, including *retablos* (painted wood representations of Catholic saints) and *bultos* (three-dimensional carvings of the saints). In the Hispanic Traditions Gallery upstairs are 19th-century tinwork, furniture, and sculpture. Downstairs, among early-20th-century art-colony holdings, look for E. Martin Hennings's *Chamisa in Bloom*, which captures the Taos landscape particularly beautifully. A tour of the ground-floor galleries shows that Taos painters of the era, notably Oscar Berninghaus, Ernest Blumenschein, Victor Higgins, Walter Ufer, Marsden Hartley, and John Marin, were fascinated by the land and the people linked to it. ⊠ *238 Ledoux St., Plaza and Vicinity* ⊹ *One block south of Historic Taos Plaza* ☎ *575/758–9826* ⊕ *www.harwoodmuseum.org* ⊠ *$10* ⊘ *Closed Mon.*

★ Historic Taos Plaza

PLAZA | FAMILY | The first European explorers of the Taos Valley came here with Captain Hernando de Alvarado, a member of Francisco Vásquez de Coronado's expedition of 1540. Basque explorer Don Juan de Oñate arrived in Taos in July 1598 and established a mission and trading arrangements with residents of Taos Pueblo. The settlement developed into two plazas: the plaza at the heart of the town became a thriving business district for the early colony, and a walled residential plaza was constructed a few hundred yards behind. It remains active today, home to a throng of shlocky gift shops, plus a few more noteworthy galleries and boutiques. On any given day you can stumble upon Aztec dancers pounding traditional beats with ankle bells, flamenco dancers sharpening their performance, and buskers strumming an Americana tune. In the summer, the plaza hosts a farmers' market and a lively concert season, which turns the plaza into an open-air dance floor. On the southeastern corner is the Hotel La Fonda de Taos. Nine infamous erotic paintings by D. H. Lawrence that were naughty in his day but are quite tame by present standards can be viewed in a small gallery in the hotel. ⊠ *Plaza and Vicinity* ⊕ *www.taos.org/what-to-do/landmark-sites/taos-plaza.*

Inger Jirby Gallery

MUSEUM | This popular gallery displays Jirby's whimsical, brightly colored landscape paintings. Her work is bold and colorful, and largely dedicated to her favorite subject: the Taos landscape. She was born in Kiruna, Sweden (north of the Arctic Circle), and it was there she learned to paint, influenced by Swedish artists who had studied with Impressionists. Be sure to stroll through the lovely sculpture garden. ⊠ *207 Ledoux St., Plaza and Vicinity* ☎ *575/758–7333* ⊕ *www.jirby.com.*

Taos Art Museum at Fechin House

MUSEUM | The interior of this extraordinary adobe house, built between 1927 and 1933 by Russian émigré and artist Nicolai Fechin, is a marvel of carved Russian-style woodwork and furniture. Fechin constructed it to showcase his daringly colorful paintings, intricate wood carvings and cabinetry, and coppersmith work on fixtures. The house now contains the Taos Art Museum, which showcases a rotating collection of some 600 paintings by more than 50 Taos artists, including founders of the original Taos Society of Artists, among them Joseph Sharp, Ernest Blumenschein, Bert Phillips, E. I. Couse, and Oscar Berninghaus. ✉ *227 Paseo del Pueblo Norte, Plaza and Vicinity* ☎ *575/758–2690* ⊕ *www.taosart-museum.org* 🎟 *$10* 🕙 *Closed Mon.*

Restaurants

Doc Martin's

$$$ | **SOUTHWESTERN** | The old-world restaurant of the Historic Taos Inn takes its name from the building's original owner, a local physician who saw patients in the rooms that are now the dining areas. The creative menu hews toward innovative takes on comforting classics, with an emphasis on sustainable ingredients—a favorite is the relleno platter comprising a pair of blue corn–beer battered Anaheim chiles, green chile, pumpkin seeds, and goat cheese cream. **Known for:** authentic chiles rellenos; fresh, local ingredients; some of the best margaritas in town. $ *Average main: $25* ✉ *Historic Taos Inn, 125 Paseo del Pueblo Norte, Plaza and Vicinity* ☎ *575/758–2233* ⊕ *www.taosinn.com/doc-martins.*

Donabe Asian Kitchen

$$ | **ASIAN** | Chef-owner Marshall Thompson has long had a following in Taos, overseeing some top kitchens as well as a popular noodle cart, and Donabe is his own Asian-cuisine restaurant that serves delightful and satisfying food. The kitchen whips out an impressive array of Japanese, Korean, Chinese, Thai, and Vietnamese dishes, with various meats (including yak), fish, chicken, pork, and vegetarian options. **Known for:** unique yak dishes; impressive range of Asian continent dishes; historic building. $ *Average main: $20* ✉ *133 Paseo del Pueblo Norte, Plaza and Vicinity* ☎ *575/751–9700* ⊕ *www.donabetaos.com* 🕙 *Closed Tues.*

★ Lambert's of Taos

$$$ | **CONTEMPORARY** | Superb service, creative cuisine, and an utterly romantic setting inside a historic adobe house a short walk north of the plaza define this Taos landmark that's been a go-to for special meals since the mid-1990s (it was previously located a few blocks away). The rich fare here fuses regional and Mediterranean recipes and ingredients and includes such standouts as red-beet risotto with chèvre and watercress, and braised Colorado lamb shank with black eye pea–root veggie ragout, au jus, and turmeric raita. **Known for:** elegant dining experience; casual yet refined bar lounge upstairs; great wine list. $ *Average main: $30* ✉ *123 Bent St., Plaza and Vicinity* ☎ *575/758–1009* ⊕ *www. lambertsoftaos.com.*

★ Love Apple
$$ | **CONTEMPORARY** | It's easy to drive by the small adobe former chapel that houses this delightful farm-to-table restaurant a short drive north of Taos Plaza, but slow down—you don't want to miss the culinary magic of chef Andrea Meyer. She uses organic, mostly local ingredients in the preparation of simple yet sophisticated creations like homemade sweet-corn tamales with red-chile mole, a fried egg, and crème fraîche, and tacos (using homemade tortillas) filled with grilled antelope, potato-Gruyère gratin, and parsley gremolata. **Known for:** boldly flavored, locally sourced cuisine; romantic setting inside former chapel; cash-only policy. $ *Average main: $20* ✉ *803 Paseo del Pueblo Norte, Historic Downtown* ☎ *575/751–0050* ⊕ *www.theloveapple.net* ▭ *No credit cards* ⊘ *Closed Mon. and Tues.*

Manzanita Market
$ | **AMERICAN** | Located on the north side of the Historic Taos Plaza, Manzanita is a choice stop for an organic breakfast, lunch, or snack. This spacious and airy restaurant bills itself as a community café, in reference to its locally sourced foods from farms that use sustainable methods. **Known for:** local, organic foods; spacious and airy café environment; great coffee and smoothies. $ *Average main: $9* ✉ *103 North Plaza, Plaza and Vicinity* ☎ *575/613–4808* ⊕ *www.manzanitamarket.net* ⊘ *Closed Mon. No dinner.*

Taos Mesa Brewing Tap Room
$ | **PIZZA** | You don't have to be a craft-beer fan to enjoy this convivial taproom a five-minute walk south of the plaza, although it is a terrific place to sample a crisp Take A Knee IPA or a ruby-red Amarillo Rojo red ale. Pizza lovers also appreciate this spot, which serves delicious, generously topped pies—the inferno, with chorizo, chiles, taleggio and mozzarella cheese, and hot honey has a devoted following. **Known for:** locally brewed beers; easy, no-fuss pub pizza menu; large space with different seating areas. $ *Average main: $10* ✉ *201 Paseo del Pueblo Sur, Plaza and Vicinity* ☎ *575/758–1900* ⊕ *www.taosmesabrewing.com.*

Hotels

★ El Monte Sagrado Living Resort and Spa

$$ | RESORT | This posh, eco-minded, and decidedly quirky boutique resort—part of New Mexico's stylish Heritage Hotels & Resorts brand—has some of the swankiest rooms in town as well as a fabulous spa. **Pros:** luxurious resort experience; blend of Southwestern architecture and stunning natural landscaping; excellent spa offering restorative treatments. **Cons:** art and decor can be bold in some spots; service doesn't always measure up to premium rates; half-mile walk to the plaza includes a slight uphill. $ *Rooms from: $190* ⊠ *317 Kit Carson Rd., Plaza and Vicinity* ☎ *855/846–8267 reservations* ⊕ *www.elmontesagrado.com* ⟟ *84 rooms* ⟦◯⟧ *No meals.*

El Pueblo Lodge

$$ | HOTEL | FAMILY | Among the budget-oriented properties in town, this well-maintained adobe-style hotel with a fun retro sign out front and the vibe of an old-school Route 66 motel is a real gem. **Pros:** terrific value for its central location; short walk north of the plaza; fun decor. **Cons:** nothing fancy; located on a busy section of the main road; Southwestern retro design may feel tacky to some. $ *Rooms from: $125* ⊠ *412 Paseo del Pueblo Norte, Plaza and Vicinity* ☎ *575/758–8700, 800/433–9612* ⊕ *www.elpueblolodge. com* ⟟ *50 rooms* ⟦◯⟧ *Free Breakfast.*

★ Hacienda del Sol

$$ | B&B/INN | Art patron Mabel Dodge Luhan bought this house about a mile north of Taos Plaza in the 1920s and lived here with her husband, Tony Luhan, while building their main house. **Pros:** stunning mountain views; private retreat setting; some excellent restaurants within walking distance. **Cons:** traffic noise from the main road; some rooms are less private than others; 1-mile walk to the plaza. $ *Rooms from: $180* ⊠ *109 Mabel Dodge La., Historic Downtown* ☎ *575/758–0287, 866/333–4459* ⊕ *www.taoshaciendadelsol.com* ⟟ *12 rooms* ⟦◯⟧ *Free Breakfast.*

Historic Taos Inn

$$ | B&B/INN | A 10-minute walk north of Taos Plaza, this celebrated property is a local landmark, with some devotees having been regulars here for decades. **Pros:** legendary bar and excellent restaurant; authentic Southwestern character and rich history; unbeatable location in the heart of Historic Downtown Taos. **Cons:** highly active social scene not for everyone; some rooms are very small; noise from traffic on the main road. $ *Rooms from: $125* ⊠ *125 Paseo del Pueblo Norte, Plaza and Vicinity* ☎ *575/758–2233* ⊕ *www.taosinn.com* ⟟ *45 rooms* ⟦◯⟧ *No meals.*

Hotel La Fonda de Taos

$$ | HOTEL | This handsomely updated and elegant historic property (there's been a hotel on this location since 1820) is ideal if you wish to be in the heart of the action—it's directly on the plaza. **Pros:** great central location; fascinating history; romantic ambience. **Cons:** less than ideal if you're seeking peace and quiet; some rooms are quite small; not suitable for families. *$ Rooms from: $149 ⊠ 108 S. Plaza, Plaza and Vicinity ☎ 575/758–2211 ⊕ www.lafondataos.com ☞ 25 rooms ⓘ No meals ☞ No children under 8 allowed.*

Inn on La Loma Plaza

$$ | B&B/INN | Surrounded by thick walls, this early-1800s Pueblo Revival building—and the surrounding gardens—capture the spirit and style of Spanish-colonial Taos. **Pros:** historic ambience with modern amenities; short walk from Historic Taos Plaza; tastefully decorated rooms in the Southwestwen arts tradition. **Cons:** lots of stairs; on a busy street; one of the pricier small properties in town. *$ Rooms from: $180 ⊠ 315 Ranchitos Rd., Plaza and Vicinity ☎ 800/530–3040 ⊕ www.vacationtaos.com ☞ 12 rooms ⓘ Free Breakfast.*

★ Mabel Dodge Luhan House

$$ | B&B/INN | Quirky and offbeat—much like Taos—this National Historic Landmark was once home to the heiress who drew illustrious writers and artists—including D. H. **Pros:** historically charming and aesthetically inspiring; rural setting, yet only a 1-mile walk to the plaza; smallest rooms are reasonably priced. **Cons:** lots of stairs and uneven paths; can be noisy during summer outdoor concert season thanks to adjacent town park; located at the far end of narrow, dead-end road on which local drivers often speed. *$ Rooms from: $116 ⊠ 240 Morada La., Plaza and Vicinity ☎ 575/751–9686 ⊕ www.mabeldodgeluhan.com ☞ 21 rooms ⓘ Free Breakfast.*

Palacio de Marquesa

$$ | B&B/INN | Tile hearths, French doors, and traditional viga ceilings grace this luxury boutique hotel whose rooms stand out from the pack for their clean, uncluttered looks, posh linens, and decor inspired by female artists of local acclaim, from modernist Agnes Martin to transplanted British aristocrat Dorothy Brett. **Pros:** tranquil and secluded setting; sophisticated, contemporary rooms with lots of luxury touches; walking distance from plaza. **Cons:** a little pricey; noise from nearby main road; walk to plaza is slightly uphill. *$ Rooms from: $175 ⊠ 405 Cordoba La., Plaza and Vicinity ☎ 855/997–8230 ⊕ www.marquesataos.com ☞ 8 rooms ⓘ No meals.*

Nightlife

★ Adobe Bar

BARS/PUBS | This legendary bar, often dubbed "Taos's living room," has been the place in town for free live music nightly, epic margaritas, and a tight, packed dance floor for decades. Talented acts range from acoustic duets to stomping flamenco dancers and shouting, clapping flamenco singers. It's also a favorite spot for happy hour—there's a great menu of appetizers and cocktails, and the patio is a lovely hangout on warm evenings. ⊠ *Taos Inn, 125 Paseo del Pueblo Norte, Historic Downtown* ☎ *575/758–2233* ⊕ *www.taosinn.com/adobe-bar.*

The Alley Cantina

BARS/PUBS | Housed in the oldest structure in downtown Taos, this friendly spot has jazz, folk, and blues—as well as shuffleboard, pool, and board games for those not moved to dance. It's also one of the few places in town for a late-night bite (they close at midnight). ⊠ *121 Teresina La., Historic Downtown* ☎ *575/758–2121* ⊕ *www.alleycantina.com.*

 Performing Arts

Taos Center for the Arts

DANCE | As the cultural hub of Taos, the curtained stage at TCA hosts a variety of live performing artists of regional, national, and international acclaim throughout the year. You can expect polished productions of theater, music, dance, film, readings, and lecture presentations. The auditorium's spacious and high-ceiling lobby doubles as a gallery space for local visual artists; many of TCA's events are accompanied by opening night receptions held there. ⊠ *Taos Community Auditorium, 145 Paseo del Pueblo Norte, Historic Downtown* ☎ *575/758–2052* ⊕ *www.tcataos.org.*

Taos Chamber Music Group

CONCERTS | Since 1993, this esteemed group of musicians has performed traditional—Bach, Beethoven, Brahms—and contemporary chamber concerts. Performances are generally held in the Arthur Bell Auditorium (at the Harwood Museum of Art) and are vivid thanks to the state-of-the-art sound design. ☎ *575/770–1167* ⊕ *www.taoschambermusicgroup.org.*

Shopping

Artemisia

CLOTHING | Look to this boutique for its wide selection of one-of-a-kind wearable art by local artist Annette Randell. Many of her creations incorporate Native American designs. The store also carries jewelry, bags, and accessories by several local artists. ⊠ *117 Bent St., Plaza and Vicinity* ☎ *575/737–9800* ⊕ *www.artemisiataos.com.*

Coyote Moon

ART GALLERIES | Coyote Moon has a great selection of New Mexican, Mexican, and South American folk art, painted crosses, jewelry, and Day of the Dead figurines, some featuring American rock stars. With the spirit of magical realism, each piece is made with expert craftsmanship. ⊠ *John Dunn Shops, 120-C Bent St., Plaza and Vicinity* ☎ *575/758–4437* ⊕ *www.johndunnshops.com/project/coyote-moon.*

★ Robert L. Parsons Fine Art

ART GALLERIES | This is one of the best sources of early Taos art-colony paintings, antiques, and authentic antique Navajo blankets. Inside you'll find originals by such luminaries as Ernest Blumenschein, Bert Geer Phillips, Oscar Berninghaus, Joseph Bakos, and Nicolai Fechin. ⊠ *131 Bent St., Plaza and Vicinity* ☎ *575/751–0159* ⊕ *www.parsonsart.com.*

★ Starr Interiors

HOUSEHOLD ITEMS/FURNITURE | Here you'll find a striking collection of Zapotec Indian rugs and hangings, plus colorfully painted Oaxacan animals and masks and other folk art and furnishings. ⊠ *117 Paseo del Pueblo Norte, Plaza and Vicinity* ☎ *575/758–3065* ⊕ *www.starr-interiors.com.*

Taos Blue

HOUSEHOLD ITEMS/FURNITURE | This shop carries jewelry, pottery, and contemporary works (masks, rattles, sculpture) by dozens of talented Native Americans, as well as Spanish-colonial–style santos. ⊠ *101 Bent St., Plaza and Vicinity* ☎ *575/758–3561* ⊕ *www.taosblue.com.*

The Southside and Ranchos de Taos

The first Spanish settlers were agrarian, and many families continue to till the fertile land south of Taos, an area anchored by tine Ranchos de Taos, which is home to iconic San Francisco de Asis Church, memorialized by Georgia O'Keeffe and photographer Ansel Adams. The main approach road into Taos from the south, NM 68, is lined with gas stations, convenience stores, and chain motels, but there are a few lovely hotels and eateries too.

Ranchos de Taos is filled with atmospheric adobe buildings housing shops and galleries.

Sights

La Hacienda de los Martínez

BUILDING | Spare and fortlike, this adobe structure built between 1804 and 1827 on the bank of the Rio Pueblo served as a community refuge during Comanche and Apache raids. Its thick walls, which have few windows, surround two central courtyards. Don Antonio Severino Martínez was a farmer and trader; the hacienda was the final stop along El Camino Real (the Royal Road), the trade route the Spanish established between Mexico City and New Mexico. The restored period rooms here contain textiles, foods, and crafts of the early 19th century. There's a working blacksmith's shop, usually open to visitors on Saturday, and weavers create beautiful textiles on reconstructed period looms. ⊠ 708 Hacienda Way, off Ranchitos Rd. (NM 240), Southside ☎ 575/758–1000 ⊕ www.taoshistoricmuseums.org ☜ $8.

Ranchos de Taos

TOWN | A few minutes' drive south of the center of Taos, this village still retains some of its rural atmosphere despite the road traffic passing through. Huddled around its famous adobe church and dusty plaza are cheerful, remodeled shops and galleries standing shoulder to shoulder with crumbling adobe shells. This ranching, farming, and budding small-business community was an early home to Taos Native Americans before being settled by Spaniards in 1716. A few of the ancient adobe dwellings contain shops, galleries, and restaurants. ⊠ Southside.

★ San Francisco de Asís Church

RELIGIOUS SITE | A National Historic Landmark, this is a beloved destination among the faithful, as well as for artists, photographers, and architectural buffs. The active Catholic church regularly celebrates Mass, contains numerous Hispanic religious artifacts, and is open to the public for visiting. Be sure to show respect for house of worship norms. The building's shape is a surprise with rounded, sculpted buttresses. Construction began in 1772 and today its mud-and-straw adobe walls are replastered by hand every year in an annual event. The "Ranchos Church" has a spiritual simplicity that inspired Georgia O'Keeffe to include it in a series of paintings and Ansel Adams to photograph it many times. ⊠ *60 St. Francis Pl., Ranchos de Taos* ☎ *575/758–2754* ⊕ *www. sfranchos.org.*

Restaurants

Antonio's

$ | MEXICAN | Chef Antonio Matus has been delighting diners in the Taos area for many years with his authentic, boldly flavorful, and beautifully plated regional Mexican cuisine. In this intimate art-filled restaurant with a slate courtyard, Matus focuses more on regional Mexican than New Mexican fare. **Known for:** red-chile pork posole; chile en nogada; tres leches (three milks) cake. ⑤ *Average main: $15* ⊠ *1379 Paseo del Pueblo Sur, Southside* ☎ *575/758–2599* ⊗ *Closed weekends.*

Five Star Burgers

$ | BURGER | A standout amid the strip of mostly unmemorable fast-food restaurants along Paseo del Pueblo on the south side of town, this airy, high-ceiling contemporary space—part of a regional chain with locations in Albuquerque as well—serves stellar burgers using hormone-free Angus beef from respected Harris Ranch; turkey, veggie, Colorado lamb, bison, and salmon burgers are also available. You can also choose from an assortment of novel toppings, including fried eggs, wild mushrooms, grilled onions, and crispy jalapeños. **Known for:** green-chile cheeseburgers; various protein bowls; delicious sweet potato fries. ⑤ *Average main: $12* ⊠ *1032 Paseo del Pueblo Sur, Southside* ☎ *575/758–8484* ⊕ *www.5starburgers.com.*

Old Martina's Hall

$$ | AMERICAN | This enchanting South-meets-Southwestern-style restaurant across the road from the famed San Francisco de Asís Church is in a restored Pueblo Revival building with thick adobe walls and sturdy viga-and-latilla ceilings—it was run as a rowdy dance hall for generations by the town's iconic Martinez family (former resident and late actor Dennis Hopper used to party here). It's no less convivial today, as both an inviting spot for cocktails and happy hour snacks as for dining, in one of the beautiful salons with modern spherical chandeliers and local artwork. **Known for:** happy hour snacks and cocktails; eclectic menu with Southern influences; striking architecture and historic vibe. Ⓢ *Average main: $19* ✉ *4140 NM 68, Ranchos de Taos* ☎ *575/758–3003* ⊕ *www. oldmartinashall.com* ⊘ *Closed Mon. and Tues.*

Hotels

Adobe & Pines Inn

$$ | B&B/INN | Native American and Mexican artifacts decorate the main house of this B&B, which has expansive mountain views. **Pros:** quiet rural location; closest accommodation to historic Ranchos de Taos; beautiful gardens. **Cons:** a bit of a drive south of plaza; least expensive rooms are a bit small; noise from the main road. Ⓢ *Rooms from: $150* ✉ *4107 NM 68, Ranchos de Taos* ☎ *575/751–0947* ⊕ *www.adobepines.com* 🛏 *8 rooms* ❙⊘❙ *Free Breakfast.*

Hotel Don Fernando de Taos, Tapestry Collection by Hilton

$$ | HOTEL | Part of a portfolio of unique hotels with local person-alities, Hotel Don Fernando is backed by the reliability and value of the Hilton brand. **Pros:** local lodging backed by global brand; beautiful contemporary Southwestern art and decor; ideal venue for weddings, meetings, and social events. **Cons:** not within walk-ing distance of the plaza; noise from the main road; located near a busy intersection. Ⓢ *Rooms from: $125* ✉ *1005 Paseo del Pueblo Sur, Southside* ☎ *575/751–4444* ⊕ *www.hilton.com/en/hotels/ tsmtmup-hotel-don-fernando-de-taos* 🛏 *126 rooms* ❙⊘❙ *No meals.*

Sagebrush Inn and Suites

$$ | HOTEL | Georgia O'Keeffe once lived and painted in a third-sto-ry room of the original inn; these days it's not as upscale—or expensive—as many other lodging options in Taos, and most rooms are in a newer building, but it has a shaded patio with large trees, a serviceable restaurant, and a collection of antique Navajo rugs. **Pros:** popular bar with live music and dancing; nice grounds to wander around; charming Southwestern decor. **Cons:** not within walking distance of Taos Plaza; noise from the main road; confer-ence venue can attract large groups. Ⓢ *Rooms from: $139* ✉ *1508 Paseo del Pueblo Sur, Southside* ☎ *575/758–2254* ⊕ *www.sage-brushinn.com* 🛏 *156 rooms* ❙⊘❙ *Free Breakfast.*

🛍 Shopping

Chimayo Trading Del Norte

CRAFTS | This gallery is a treasure trove of Pueblo pottery, Navajo weavings, and fine art. Located in the plaza of San Francisco de Asís Church, its historic architecture has the feel of an old trading post. Inside, you can browse among contemporary work and traditional pieces that include jewelry, baskets, and Native American beadwork. ⊠ 1 St. Francis Church Pl., Ranchos de Taos ☎ 575/758–0504 ⊕ www.chimayotrading.com.

El Prado

As you drive north from Taos toward Arroyo Seco and points north or west, you'll first take the main thoroughfare, Paseo del Pueblo Norte (U.S. 64) through the small village of El Prado, a mostly agrarian area that's notable for having several of the area's best restaurants, bed-and-breakfasts, and shops.

👁 Sights

★ Millicent Rogers Museum

MUSEUM | More than 7,000 pieces of spectacular Native American and Hispanic art, many of them from the private collection of the late Standard Oil heiress Millicent Rogers, are on display here. Among the pieces are baskets, blankets, rugs, kachina dolls, carvings, tinwork, paintings, rare religious artifacts, and, most significantly, jewelry (Rogers, a fashion icon in her day, was one of the first Americans to appreciate the turquoise-and-silver artistry of Native American jewelers). Other important works include the pottery and ceramics of Maria Martinez and other potters from San Ildefonso Pueblo (north of Santa Fe). Docents conduct guided tours by appointment, and the museum hosts lectures, films, workshops, and demonstrations. The two-room gift shop has exceptional jewelry, rugs, books, and pottery. ⊠ 1504 Millicent Rogers Rd., off Paseo del Pueblo Norte, just south of junction with NM 150, El Prado ☎ 575/758–2462 ⊕ www.millicentrogers. org ᴣ $10 ⊗ Closed Mon. Nov.–Mar.

🍴 Restaurants

Farmhouse Café and Bakery

$ | AMERICAN | The best seats at this charming café are on the long covered patio, which is surrounded by gardens and wind sculptures and offers sweeping views of mountains. The flavorful breakfasts and lunches use ingredients sourced from more than 20 area farms and ranches, and the bakery turns out decadent made-from-scratch carrot cake, scones, cinnamon rolls, and other treats, many of them gluten-free. **Known for:** house-baked pies, cakes, and scones; huevos rancheros; veggie, local bison, and organic beef burgers. ⑤ *Average main: $10* ⊠ *1405 Paseo del Pueblo Norte, El Prado* ☎ *575/758–5683* ⊕ *www.farmhousetaos. com* ☾ *No dinner.*

★ Medley

$$ | **MODERN AMERICAN** | Set in a rustic-chic roadhouse on the scenic road between El Prado and Arroyo Seco that adjoins one of the area's best wineshops (it often hosts wine tastings), Medley strikes a happy balance between gastropub and special-night-out restaurant. You could make a meal of a few shareable small plates—tuna tartare tostadas, mac-and-cheese with roasted Hatch chiles, crispy-chicken sliders with sriracha mayo—or dive into one of the more substantial entrée offerings, such as mango-tamari-glazed salmon or a 10-ounce porterhouse steak with brussels sprouts hash and house-made apple-bacon jam. **Known for:** elaborate and satisfying small plates; terrific mountain views from courtyard; extensive wine list. ⑤ *Average main: $23* ⊠ *100 NM 150, El Prado* ☎ *575/776–5656* ⊕ *www.medleytaos.com* ☾ *Closed Sun. and Mon.*

Orlando's

$ | **MEXICAN FUSION** | This family-run, local favorite is likely to be crowded during peak hours, while guests wait patiently to devour perfectly seasoned favorites such as *carne adovada* (red chile–marinated pork), blue-corn enchiladas, and scrumptious shrimp burritos. You can eat in the cozy dining room or outside on the umbrella-shaded front patio. **Known for:** delicious tiger shrimp blue corn enchilada; avocado pie for dessert; great sangria. ⑤ *Average main: $11* ⊠ *1114 Don Juan Valdez Ln., El Prado* ☎ *575/751–1450* ☾ *Closed Sun.*

Nightlife

KTAOS Solar Bar

BARS/PUBS | A fun place to cap off a day of exploring Arroyo Seco or playing outside in Taos Ski Valley, this bar and restaurant is part of the KTAOS Solar Center, home to the world-celebrated and solar-powered KTAOS (101.9 FM) radio station. It's a first-rate live-music venue that brings in all types of great rock, blues, folk, and indie bands. You can dine and drink in the festive bar or out on a sprawling green lawn with stunning views of the Sangre de

Cristos. On Friday, family-friendly movies are shown for free on a giant screen. ⊠ *9 NM 150, El Prado* ☎ *575/758–5826* ⊕ *www. ktao.com.*

 ## Shopping

Casa Cristal Pottery

HOUSEHOLD ITEMS/FURNITURE | Located 2½ miles north of the Taos Plaza, Casa Cristal has a huge stock of stoneware, serapes, clay pots, Native American ironwood carvings, fountains, sweaters, ponchos, clay fireplaces, Mexican blankets, tiles, piñatas, and blue glassware from Guadalajara. You'll feel like you've arrived at a Mexican market, and that's because many of their crafts hail from south of the border (though there are regional New Mexican and Native American crafts to be found, too). Shipping is available for some of the more delicate or larger pieces you don't want to carry home. ⊠ *1306 Paseo del Pueblo Norte, El Prado* ☎ *575/758–1530.*

Overland Sheepskin Company

CLOTHING | This spacious store carries high-quality sheepskin coats, hats, mittens, and slippers—many with Taos beadwork. This is the original location of what has become a network of about a dozen stores, mostly in the West, and the setting—in the shadows of the Sangre de Cristo Mountains, amid a complex of several other shops and restaurants—is itself a reason for a visit. ⊠ *Overland Ranch, 1405 Paseo del Pueblo Norte, El Prado* ☎ *575/758–8820* ⊕ *www.overland.com/stores/taos-nm.*

Taos Pueblo

The Pueblo is the ancient beating heart of the entire valley, the historic and architectural basis for everything that Taos has become. A small, unmemorable casino aside, this area a short drive northeast of the plaza has been spared commercial development and remains a neighborhood of modest homes and farms. The Pueblo itself is the sole draw for visitors and worth a visit.

 ## Sights

★ Taos Pueblo

BUILDING | **FAMILY** | For nearly 1,000 years the mud-and-straw adobe walls of Taos Pueblo have sheltered Tiwa-speaking Native Americans. A United Nations World Heritage Site, this is the largest collection of multistory pueblo dwellings in the United States. The pueblo's main buildings, Hlauuma (north house)

Taos Pueblo is the largest collection of multistory pubelo dwellings in the United States.

and Hlaukwima (south house), are separated by a creek. These structures are believed to be of a similar age, probably built between 1000 and 1450. The dwellings have common walls but no connecting doorways—the Tiwas gained access only from the top, via ladders that were retrieved after entering. Small buildings and corrals are scattered about.

The pueblo today appears much as it did when the first Spanish explorers arrived in New Mexico in 1540. The adobe walls glistening with mica caused the conquistadors to believe they had discovered one of the fabled Seven Cities of Gold. The outside surfaces are continuously maintained by replastering with thin layers of mud, and the interior walls are frequently coated with thin washes of white clay. Some walls are several feet thick in places. The roofs of each of the five-story structures are supported by large timbers, or *vigas,* hauled down from the mountain forests. Pine or aspen *latillas* (smaller pieces of wood) are placed side by side between the vigas; the entire roof is then packed with dirt.

Even after 400 years of Spanish and Anglo presence in Taos, inside the pueblo the traditional Native American way of life has endured. Tribal custom allows no electricity or running water in Hlauuma and Hlaukwima, where varying numbers (roughly 150) of Taos Native Americans live full time. About 1,900 others live in conventional homes on the pueblo's 95,000 acres. The crystal-clear Rio Pueblo de Taos, originating high above in the mountains at the sacred Blue Lake, is the primary source of water for drinking and irrigating. Bread is still baked in *hornos* (outdoor domed ovens). Artisans of the Taos Pueblo produce and sell (tax-free) traditionally handcrafted wares, such as mica-flecked pottery and silver jewelry. Great hunters, the Taos Native Americans are also known for their work with animal skins and their excellent moccasins, boots, and drums.

Although the population is predominantly Catholic, the people of Taos Pueblo, like most Pueblo Native Americans, also maintain their original religious traditions. At Christmas and other sacred holidays, for instance, immediately after mass, dancers dressed in seasonal sacred garb proceed down the aisle of St. Jerome Chapel, drums beating and rattles shaking, to begin other religious rites.

The pueblo **Church of San Geronimo**, or St. Jerome, the patron saint of Taos Pueblo, was completed in 1850 to replace the one destroyed by the U.S. Army in 1847 during the Mexican War. With its smooth symmetry, stepped portal, and twin bell towers, the church is a popular subject for photographers and artists.

The public is invited to certain ceremonial dances held throughout the year (a full list of these is posted on the pueblo website's Events page): highlights include the Feast of Santa Cruz (May 3); Taos Pueblo Pow Wow (mid-July); Santiago and Santa Ana Feast Days (July 25 and 26); San Geronimo Days (September 29 and 30); Procession of the Virgin Mary (December 24); and Deer Dance or Matachines Dance (December 25). While you're at the pueblo, respect all rules and customs, which are posted prominently. There are some restrictions, which are posted, on personal photography. Guided tours are available daily and are the way to start your visit. Tours are typically led by Taos Pueblo college students, and provide insight into the history of the Pueblo and the native traditions that continue into the present day. ⊠ *120 Veterans Hwy., Taos Pueblo* ☎ *575/758–1028* ⊕ *www.taospueblo. com* 🎫 *$16.*

The Mesa

Taos is hemmed in by the Sangre de Cristo Mountains on the east, but to the west, extending from downtown clear across the precipitously deep Rio Grande Gorge (and the famous bridge that crosses it), the landscape is dominated by sweeping, high-desert scrub and wide-open spaces. The west side of the city (also called the Mesa) is mostly residential and makes for a scenic shortcut around the sometimes traffic-clogged plaza (from Ranchos de Taos, just follow NM 240 to Blueberry Hill Road to complete this bypass).

Sights

Earthship Visitor Center

BUILDING | Earthship homes are now found all over the world, but the unique off-grid design got its start in Taos. Local architect Michael Reynolds started the movement in the early 1970s, using creative license and upcycled materials such as car tires, soda cans, and beer bottles to create structures, including fully functional homes. It's a fascinating architectural experience and an inspiring environmental statement. At the Earthship Visitor Center, the informative, self-guided tour is highly recommended. Outside, on the grounds of the visitor center, you can view and photograph the exteriors of nearby private homes with their whimsical architectural flourishes. ⊠ *2 Earthship Way, West Side* ✛ *2 miles west of Rio Grande Gorge Bridge* ☎ *575/613–4409* ⊕ *www.earthship-global.com* ⊠ *$9* ⊗ *Closed Tues.*

★ Rio Grande Gorge Bridge

BRIDGE/TUNNEL | It's a dizzying experience to see the Rio Grande 650 feet underfoot, where it flows at the bottom of an immense, steep rock canyon. In summer the reddish rocks dotted with green scrub contrast brilliantly with the blue sky, where you might see a hawk lazily floating in circles. The bridge is the second-highest suspension bridge in the country. Hold on to your camera and eyeglasses when looking down. Many days just after daybreak, hot-air balloons fly above and even inside the gorge. There's a campground with picnic shelters and basic restrooms on the west side of the bridge. ⊠ *U.S. 64, 8 miles west of junction NM 522 and 150, El Prado.*

🍸 Nightlife

★ Taos Mesa Brewing

BARS/PUBS | It's worth the 15-minute drive northwest of Taos Plaza to reach this fabulously bizarre-looking pub and microbrewery near the airport, just a few miles east of the Rio Grande Gorge Bridge. In a high-ceilinged, eco-friendly building with soaring windows, sample exceptionally well-crafted Scottish Ale, Black Widow Porter, and Kolsch 45. Live music and entertainment is presented on indoor and outdoor stages—the latter has amazing mountain and mesa views. Tasty tapas and bar snacks are served, too. You can also sip the same beers and eat outstanding pizza at the Taos Mesa Brewing Tap Room, near the plaza, and there's another branch up at Taos Ski Valley. ⊠ *20 ABC Mesa Rd., Mesa* ☎ *575/758–1900* ⊕ *www.taosmesabrewing.com.*

Arroyo Seco

Set on a high mesa north of Taos, this funky, hip village and arts center is an ideal spot to browse galleries, grab a meal at one of a handful of excellent restaurants, or simply pause to admire the dramatic views before driving on to the Enchanted Circle or Taos Ski Valley.

 Sights

Arroyo Seco

TOWN | Established in 1834 by local Spanish farmers and ranchers, this charming village of about 1,700 has today become a secluded, artsy escape from the sometimes daunting summer crowds and commercialism of the Taos Plaza—famous residents include actress Julia Roberts. You reach the tiny commercial district along NM 150, about 5 miles north of the intersection with U.S. 64 and NM 522 (it's about 9 miles north of the plaza). The drive is part of the joy of visiting, as NM 150 rises steadily above the Taos Valley, offering panoramic views of the Sangre de Cristos—you pass through Arroyo Seco en route to the Taos Ski Valley.

Arroyo Seco is without any formal attractions or museums, and that's partly its charm. The main reasons for making the trip here are to behold the dramatic scenery, grab a bite at one of the handful of excellent restaurants, and browse the several galleries and boutiques, whose wares tend to be a little more idiosyncratic but no less accomplished than those sold in Taos proper. ⊠ *Arroyo Seco.*

Restaurants

Abe's Cantina y Cocina

$ | CAFÉ | Family-owned and-operated since the 1940s, no-frills Abe's is both a convenience store (nothing special, but okay for candy or chips) and a restaurant. You can have your breakfast burrito, rolled tacos, or homemade tamales at one of the small tables crowded next to the canned goods, or take it on a picnic. **Known for:** quirky small-town ambience; homemade tamales; good selection of beer. ⑤ *Average main: $9* ⊠ *489 NM 150, Arroyo Seco* 🕾 *575/776–8643* 🕙 *Closed Sun.*

Aceq

$$ | MODERN AMERICAN | Head to this cozy bistro tucked behind some galleries in Arroyo Seco's charming little business district for super, reasonably priced farm-to-table food with a decidedly global

The village of Arroyo Seco has plenty of charming shops and restaurants.

bent. There are just a few tables in the simple dining room with chunky wood tables and a small bar, plus some outdoor tables on a quiet patio. **Known for:** delicious chicken and waffles; excellent wine list; house-made pasta. $ *Average main: $19* ✉ *480 NM 150, Arroyo Seco* ☎ *575/776–0900* ⊕ *www.aceqrestaurant.com.*

★ Sabroso Restaurant and Bar

$$$ | MODERN AMERICAN | Sophisticated, innovative cuisine and outstanding wines are served in this 150-year-old adobe hacienda, where you can also relax in lounge chairs near the bar, or on a delightful patio surrounded by plum trees. The contemporary American menu changes regularly to take advantage of locally sourced meats and seasonal ingredients. **Known for:** fireplace-warmed dining room; gorgeous patio; popular happy hour. $ *Average main: $29* ✉ *470 NM 150, Arroyo Seco* ☎ *575/776–3333* ⊕ *www.sabrosotaos.com* ⊘ *Closed Tues. No lunch.*

👜 Shopping

Arroyo Seco Mercantile

ANTIQUES/COLLECTIBLES | Packed to the rafters with a varied assortment of 1930s linens, handmade quilts, candles, organic soaps, vintage cookware, hand-thrown pottery, decorated crosses, and souvenirs, this colorful shop is a highlight of shopping in the charming village of Arroyo Seco. ✉ *488 NM 150, Arroyo Seco* ☎ *575/776–8806* ⊕ *www.secomerc.com.*

★ Rottenstone Pottery

ART GALLERIES | This locally owned pottery store features handmade, wood kiln-fired pieces that are as beautiful as they are functional. From glaze-designed plates and bowls to cups and so much more, nothing here is mass-manufactured. It is a great shopping experience to find one-of-a-kind pieces. ⊠ *486 NM 150, Arroyo Seco* ☎ *575/776–1042* ⊕ *www.facebook.com/ rottenstonepottery.*

Taos Ski Valley

Skiers and snowboarders travel to this legendary ski area from all over the world for the thrill of its steep slopes. But it's not just for expert skiers; all of its services are geared toward families, helping to create a fun and light-hearted vibe. For summer visitors, Taos Ski Valley offers hiking, biking, and scenic chairlift rides. There's also an active calendar of events, including ski competitions, guest lectures, outdoor parties, and fireworks shows.

Sights

★ Taos Ski Valley

SKIING/SNOWBOARDING | **FAMILY** | With 110 runs—just under half of them for experts—and an average of more than 320 inches of annual snowfall, Taos Ski Valley ranks among the country's most respected, and challenging, resorts. The slopes, which cover a 2,600-foot vertical gain of lift-served terrain and another 700 feet of hike-in skiing, tend to be narrow and demanding (note the ridge chutes, Al's Run, Inferno), but about a quarter of them (e.g., Honeysuckle) are for intermediate skiers, and another quarter (e.g., Bambi, Porcupine) are for beginners. Taos Ski Valley is justly famous for its outstanding ski school, which is one of the best in the country. ⊠ *116 Sutton Pl., Taos Ski Valley* ☎ *888/388–8457, 800/776–1111* ⊕ *www.skitaos.com* 🎟 *Lift ticket from $90.*

 Restaurants

The Bavarian Restaurant

$$$ | **GERMAN** | The restaurant inside the romantic, magically situated alpine lodge, which also offers Taos Ski Valley's most luxurious accommodations, serves outstanding contemporary Bavarian-inspired cuisine, such as baked artichokes and Gruyère, and braised local lamb shank with mashed potatoes and red wine–roasted garlic-thyme jus. Lunch is more casual and less expensive, with burgers and salads available. **Known for:** large deck facing Kachina

Peak; authentic German dishes; imported German beers. ⑤ *Average main: $26 ⊠ 100 Kachina Rd., Taos Ski Valley ☎ 575/776–8020 ⊕ www.skitaos.com/things-to-do/bavarian.*

192 at the Blake

$$ | MODERN AMERICAN | This modern-rustic spot inside the swank Blake hotel is warmed by a roaring fireplace and draws skiers and hikers with its terrific selection of craft beers and cocktails. The extensive menu includes tasty bar snacks and a few more substantial—but still shareable—items, like a sliced-thin beef rib eye with ancho-chile demiglace and oven-roasted trout. **Known for:** delicious wild boar stew; location right at the ski lift; apres-ski cocktails. ⑤ *Average main: $20 ⊠ 116 Sutton Pl., Taos Ski Valley ☎ 575/776–5349 ⊕ www.skitaos.com/things-to-do/192.*

Hotels

The Blake

$$$$ | RESORT | This luxury boutique hotel just steps from the resort's lifts has quickly developed a reputation as the swank-iest accommodation in the Taos region. **Pros:** steps from the main lift; sizable rooms and plenty of amenities; beautiful views of the mountain. **Cons:** a 30-minute drive from Taos; feeling of remoteness if you're not outdoorsy; lobby is only modestly sized. ⑤ *Rooms from: $306 ⊠ 116 Sutton Pl., Taos Ski Valley ☎ 575/776–5335 reception, 855/208-4988 reservations ⊕ www.skitaos.com/theblake ⤴ 80 rooms* ⦿ *No meals.*

Shopping

Andean Software

CLOTHING | Begun at the ski valley in 1984 but with a second location close to the plaza, Andean Softwear carries warm, sturdy, and beautifully designed clothing and textiles from Peru, Bolivia, and Ecuador. You'll also find imports from Bali, Mexico, Turkey, and other locales with distinct arts traditions. The deliciously soft alpaca sweaters are from Peru. ⊠ *116 Sutton Pl., Taos Ski Valley ✛ Next to Blake Hotel ☎ 575/776–2508 ⊕ www.andeansoftware.com.*

Activities

HIKING
Wheeler Peak

HIKING/WALKING | Part of a designated wilderness area of Carson National Forest, this iconic mountain summit—New Mexico's highest, at 13,161 feet—can only be reached by a rigorous hike or horseback ride. Only experienced hikers should tackle this strenuous trail all the way to the top, as the 4,000-foot elevation gain is taxing, and the final mile or so to the peak is a steep scramble over loose scree. However, for a moderately challenging and still very rewarding hike, you take the trail to the halfway point, overlooking the shores of rippling Williams Lake. Numerous other rewarding hikes of varying degrees of ease and length climb up the many slopes that rise from the village of Taos Ski Valley— check with rangers or consult the Carson National Forest website for details. Dress warmly even in summer, take plenty of water and food, and pay attention to *all* warnings and instructions distributed by rangers. ⊠ *Parking area for trailhead is along Kachina Rd. by the Bavarian lodge, Taos Ski Valley* ☎ *575/758–6200* ⊕ *www. fs.usda.gov/main/carson/home.*

Williams Lake Trail

HIKING/WALKING | This is a popular trail with visitors and locals alike. Before hiking, contact the Carson National Forest Office for information on the latest trail conditions; they rank this trail as "easy to intermediate" in difficulty level. It's important to note that the Williams Lake Trail and its surrounding forest is not a park, but a federally designated wilderness area and is not staffed with rangers or facilities. Natural hazards, debris, and wildlife exist. The well-trodden hiking trail is two miles (one-way) and climbs from 10,200 feet to 11,100 feet in elevation. It leads you to a remote alpine lake that is not huge, but is quite lovely. The body of water is snow melt from the surrounding mountains so when you dip your toe in, the water is likely to be very cold even in the summer. Throughout the hike, the trail mostly follows under the shade of tree canopy and passes some large and interesting boulder fields, usually filled with the chirping of marmots. Upon arrival at the lake, you'll find people resting on the grassy slopes around its perimeter. Most hikers pack a picnic lunch while hike in with tents and plan to spend the night. Towering above Williams Lake is Wheeler Peak, the highest peak in New Mexico. Consult with the Forest Office or a local outfitter to inquire about recommended footwear, provisions, and appropriate clothing for the hike. It is advisable to stay hydrated, practice skin protection, and adjust your level of activity if necessary. ⊠ *Taos Ski Valley* ✛ *Near end of Kachina Rd. Trailhead parking lot is well-signed* ☎ *575/758–6200 Carson National Forest Office* ⊕ *www.fs.usda.gov.*

Index

Photo Credits